The
STUDY
of
TALMUD

The STUDY of TALMUD

UNDERSTANDING THE HALACHIC MIND

Abraham Hirsch Rabinowitz

JASON ARONSON INC.
Northvale, New Jersey
London

This book was set in 11 pt. Palatino by AeroType, Inc.

10 9 8 7 6 5 4 3 2 1

Library of Congress Cataloging-in-Publication Data

Rabinowitz, Abraham Hirsch.
    [Jewish mind in its halachic Talmudic expression]
    The study of Talmud : understanding the halachic mind / Abraham
Hirsch Rabinowitz.
        p. cm.
    Previously published: The Jewish mind in its halachic Talmudic expression. Jerusa-
lem : Hillel Press, ©1978.
    Includes indexes.
    ISBN 1-56821-946-6 (alk. paper)
    1. Jewish law—Philosophy. 2. Jewish law—Interpretation and
construction. 3. Tradition (Judaism) 4. Talmud—Hermeneutics.
    I. Title.
    BM520.6.R318 1996
    296.1'8—dc20   96-13496
                                                                                        CIP

Manufactured in the United States of America. Jason Aronson Inc. offers books and cassettes. For information and catalog write to Jason Aronson Inc., 230 Livingston Street, Northvale, New Jersey 07647.

To my dear wife, Channah,

"Rabbi Jose met Elijah and asked him . . . .
In what manner does woman help man?
Said he . . . she lightens his eyes
and sets him on his feet."
(Yevamoth 63a)

and mother, Rebbetzin Sarah Rabinowitz
of Birmingham, England,

For some people,
those who know the secret of life
as she does,
living and doing for others is its essence.

Contents

Foreword

The versatility and achievement of the Jewish mind is proverbial. There is hardly a field of human contemplation and endeavor in which Jews have failed to excel. Precocity and originality have usually marked the contribution of Jews to knowledge, as also a striking ability to improvise. Of the many factors that together created the Jewish mind, there can be little doubt that the contribution of the age-long preoccupation of the Jew with Talmud and halachah is formidable. The study of Talmud, undertaken at an early age and pursued assiduously, nurtured alertness, discernment, and acumen and cultured the ability to weigh situations and opinions. It encouraged debate and individual research, rewarded initiative, and lauded brilliance.

Leading to early intellectual maturity, Talmudic study admirably equipped the student for diversification, which he undertook with an intensity circumscribed only by an environment bent on his restriction. In removing the restrictions, emancipation enabled Jews to burst on the general intellectual scene and contribute grandly to the shaping of the modern mind and world.

Large segments of modern Jewry no longer study Talmud, and it seems increasingly doubtful whether under the modern conditions of general education for all, the Jewish contribution to knowledge and life will seem in retrospect to be as outstanding as it undoubtedly was in bygone years. Possibly Jews enjoy an inherited, deeper, innate desire for education and intellectual pursuits, but they no longer commence their studies better equipped than non-Jews, so that there is a more even sharing out of brilliance and achievement. Jews no longer enjoy the advantageous, intellectual start over others with which the Talmud was wont to endow them.

Quite apart from the obvious intellectual aspects of Talmud and halachah, their study inheres a distinctive mental background and approach. When studying Talmud, one does not merely embark on a voyage of intellectual involvement with the strenuous tides of two thousand years and more of Jewish mind; one embarks on a way of life. Moreover, it is a way of life that is uniquely and creatively Jewish in that it embraces and integrates Jewish history and Jewish destiny. It also binds the Jewish people together in kinship and brotherhood, real and spiritual.

When he introduced the idea of the *Daf Hayomi,* the daily study by Jews the world over of the same page of Talmud until the cycle of study is completed together by all, R. Meir Shapiro gave expression to the deep-rooted faith and spiritual concepts that underpin Talmudic study.

He said, "Aforetime, prayer was considered a personal mitzvah. So, until the saintly Ari, R. Isaac Luria, taught that before commencing to pray one should say: For the sake of God . . . in the name of all Israel. This recital succeeded in so affecting the individual that his prayer merged with that of all Israel. One prays with and for all." And he continued, "Hitherto, each individual studied a different folio of Talmud. Now, with all studying the same folio we shall succeed in welding together the entire people. For, if the Holy One, blessed be He, the Torah and Israel are one, how much more will this be so when the Holy One, blessed be He, the Torah and Israel are together in the same Tractate, the same folio on the same day!"

An inkling of what immersion in the Talmud means and has always meant for the Jew may be glimpsed from the following tale. A young scholar, after his marriage, found himself in a small village that had no *mikveh* wherein he could perform his daily ablutions. Greatly distressed, he put his problem before the author of the Responsa Avnei Nezer, the renowned Gaon of Sochatzov. On hearing the problem, the Gaon paced to and fro for some time until finally he paused and, bending over the young man, whispered to him, "My father-in-law, the saintly Rebbe of Kotzk, used to say: a page of the Talmud purifies as does a *mikveh!*"

It is hoped that the following pages, devoted to understanding some of the fundamental amalgams of the Talmudic mind and its halachic processes, will aid the reader in the quest for perception.

For, though the broad vistas of the Talmud flow outward and onward into ever-widening horizons, these horizons are only meaningfully grasped, or even intuitively perceived, when seen from the inner perspectives of the Talmud itself.

Introduction

Dynamic, Autonomous Framework

Halachah, from the Hebrew root *halach*, to walk, is the system of law and behavior by which Israel has toiled across the tortuous tides of history since the revelation at Sinai. It is not tradition nor is it convention, though indeed halachah embraces both traditions and conventions. It is a unique system of God-given law covering every aspect of religious, personal, social, national, and international behavior.

The fact of givenness, of the essence of halachah, predicates neither sterility nor attrition. On the contrary, halachah is a viable, dynamic, ever-expanding system that inheres the ability to cope with the continuously changing social, economic, and political face of humankind. That this is so is due to the particularly structured dynamics that are part of and coterminal with the essence of halachah. This infrastructure cannot be separated from the body of halachah since its composites are themselves halachoth. As such they continually urge reexamination and probing of basic principle in the light of the challenge presented from within Jewry or by the world at large.

These devices guarantee the continued probity of halachic development and expansion by setting both guidelines and limitations on the halachic response to stimulus. But they do not function only as halachic reflexes. Primarily, they are responsible for the internal processes of halachic thought per se. They determine what is authentic halachah and how authentic halachah is to be determined. In this capacity, they ensure the integrity of halachah as an independent system of law that expresses itself within the bounds of a unique, autonomous framework.

The present work is an attempt to see halachah, its norms and fundamental tenets, its modes of thought, presumptions, and premises through the eyes of halachah itself.

What are the prepositions underlying halachic decision, the categories implicit in halachic judgment and explanation, and the modes of argument whereby halachic conclusions are supported and established? How does the halachah see its origins, its sources? How does it conceive its personality, its élan vital? How does it view the individual, society, and the state of Israel? How does it come to grips with the problems of those it leads, directs, trains, and educates?

These are but some of the questions discussed, not perhaps sufficiently to satisfy but in sufficient measure to afford appreciation of the essential picture.

In order to gain perspective for our study, it is necessary to draw in bold, sharp lines a portrait of Judaism. From this portrait the indispensable, vibrant character of halachah will emerge.

Portrait of Judaism

We may look at Judaism from various vantage points. However, each vantage point is incomplete in itself and must be combined with the others in order to form the whole. Though it is important to analyze the parts of the whole, one is not to be deluded into seeing the part as the whole. All vantage points are to be grasped integrally and instantly, as one. It is as though all of history were to be grasped in a single instantaneous flash of inspiration without time span, without stages, without development, simply mankind present, past and future at this moment. Or as a great work of art is conceived in the mind of the master, without and beyond temporal and spatial irrelevancies.

When we discuss Judaism from the mystical, philosophical, halachic, or practical aspects, we are in fact analyzing parts of an integrated oneness comprised in every way and detail of all the aspects together. Thought is governed by them all, but so is deed. Understanding is achieved by differentiation, essence by the intuition and inspiration that produce the vision of unity.

It is an explosive, shattering vision and once grasped is never forgotten. Once grasped, neither man nor his world are ever the same again. Once grasped, man becomes an adherent of Totality, sensing, seeing, experiencing Totality in every minute fragment.

His horizons are both particular and universal at the same time. The particular is of cosmic significance. The universal is embraced by the segment. A single formula lies at the base of both cosmos and particle.

Religious and Scientific Constructions

The diverse approaches found in Judaism are to be understood in the sense of mathematical constructions directed towards understanding the basic formula. Thus, both mysticism and halachah present such constructions, the one in spiritual terms the other in practical terms. This, in much the same way as theoretical physics postulates mathematical constructions in order to understand the subatomic world.

The mystic, the halachist, as well as the pure scientist live in an ideal world. There is no question here of rational or irrational approaches. Given their own criteria, the structures are perfectly logical in themselves. More so, since science recognizes that it is unable to know or even to visualize the subatomic world that forms the subject of its study, it is in no way able to reject *any* such construction concerning reality. Science constructs with its tools, the spirit with tools of the spirit.

There is a deeper kinship and parallelism between the structural world of the scientist and that of the student of Judaism. For, as the scientist is unable to visualize the world reflected by his or her constructions, so the religious philosopher, the mystic, or halachist is unable to portray the reality behind his construction, for the reality is God. Judaism, which traditionally upholds two basic constructions, the mystic and the halachic, avoided antinomianism on the one hand and mechanical practice on the other. By insisting on both constructions, meditation and deed suffused one another so that the mystic was enabled to live concretely, and the halachist mystically.

Since both are constructions, both deal minutely with every aspect of Totality, human and cosmic. Judaism demands that Jews live the fusion of both so that their lives exemplify in practice the basic formula toward which they are directed. Judaism goes further and insists that since man, though endowed with soul, is human, achievement and success in his role as man lies in the practical, halachic construction, and he cannot achieve purpose or fulfillment by ignoring his role as a human being and concentrating on the spirit alone. Thus devotion to the mystical construction alone will end in failure, while devotion to the practical realization of the halachic structure ends in success because man was placed in this world to realize himself in a practical manner. True, in so far as his practicality lacks suffusion of the spirit, it is bereft of the richness, depth, and dimension that could have been achieved, but it has succeeded in the realization of basic purpose. On the other hand, the mystical construction alone fails to achieve duty for the human being qua human being in a practical world. With this general background in mind, let us attempt to outline panoramically the two structures.

The Vision of the Mystic

The mystic sees:

Worlds within worlds. Action, reaction, and chain reaction between worlds. Stages within stages. Reality within reality. Action, reaction, and chain reaction between stages within stages within worlds within worlds within realities within realities. All inexorably linked in a multitude of manifestation. All traceable ultimately to the One, the source of all that is. No item lacks significance nor is so frail or so unimportant in this vast world of worlds that its impact fails to register in all of the worlds. Tangible and intangible, thought and deed, beauty and ugliness, consciousness and instinct, light and darkness, good and evil, prophecy and dreams, man and angel are intertwined in essence. There are no fast dividing lines. Mind and matter are one but two, are two but are to become one. Heaven and earth are both reality. The latter, albeit purposeful, is, however, a condescending reality born of necessity. Uninterrupted flow, spiritual, unperceived though nonetheless real, is the essence of all earthly, cosmic, and supra-cosmic relationships. Free will of puny mighty man is the current activating universe within universe. Activating in such manner that mind as well as deed dominate matter completely. Dominate, suffuse, transform matter into spirit so that the boundary lines between matter and spirit are blurred and ultimately dissolved. Of necessity man exists. Of necessity evil exists. Man exists to manifest God. Evil exists to manifest man.

There are limits, but these are of cosmic proportions. Within these limits man is monarch of all he surveys. The appointed heavenly host but do his bidding for good or ill because action and interaction, cause and effect from the material to the spiritual to the material to the spiritual *ad infinitum* is the universal law of all that is of God, but is not He.

Matter, space, and time are both reality and delusion. Reality is God and God alone. His manifestation in creation is spiritual, and the spirituality thus manifested, though it be but the shadow of the shadow of the shadow, is permanent. For the shadow of God is His shadow. A thought in the mind of God is eternal as God. So that all is spirit though differing in form. The form is meaningless because all is spirit. It is a question of degree—of spiritual degree.

But man is real, temporal, physical, and able to remain so. He need never become aware of the fact that he is spirit, and the scene is so set that it depends on him and him alone. He may take the world as well as himself at face value and arrive at all the wrong conclusions for all the seemingly correct reasons. This is his dilemma, this his delusion. This ultimately is the starting point of Torah—for man.

The Concrete World of the Halachist

The halachist sees:

Real time, tangible place, and actual space. The need for order and discipline in both society and the individual. Justice, norms, and habitual traits as the cornerstone of personal and national life. The good of the community and its continuance. The sacred nature of life and its preservance. Man and man, man and society, man and God.

Perseverance, thrift, toil and devotion, belief in action. Scrupulous attention to detail, to duty, and toward responsibility. Balanced flights of the spirit, contained yearning, controlled joy, and perspective in all things. Critical examination and measurement against a tangible yardstick. Guidance and education the mainstay of the individual. Honesty and satisfaction with one's lot though striving to improve it. Strict personal morality, decency, integrity, and virtue. Sensitivity to the needs of others, convention and tradition, and moderation in all things. Doing good because it is good, reviling evil because it is evil, acting rightly because it is right.

His code is of God unchanging and timeless, recognizing human weakness but not lowering standards because of it. Striving to uplift, to dedicate individual and community. Self-sacrifice a necessity, lust abhorrent, the requirements of others his spiritual values. Respect for human dignity and worth, essential. Self-correction, improvement, acquiring knowledge, the challenge of life, the art of being human.

The Problem Facing Judaism

Judaism is living and experiencing the fusion of both scenarios. Taken together, they lead one to the grandeur of creation, of the human being and God, to participation in all branches of life and living with understanding, perspective, and moderation. Is this utopia? Possibly. But Judaism visualizes a threefold utopia: that of the individual, that of Israel, and that of mankind. The first is within the grasp and life span of the individual. The second, the challenge in fashioning a nation. The third, the challenge of that nation's example to all the nations of the world. By assimilation the individual loses his personal opportunity. By failure to participate in the upbuilding of his people, he minimizes his people's opportunity and delays blessing for mankind.

The seeds of enlightenment have been sown liberally throughout the world by Jewry in exile, so that at least a minimum framework of civilization exists. But civilization is shot through with barbarism and cruelty, and it is very far from the ideal as yet. The demand is for Israel to fashion itself as only it is able, thereby creating the light by means of which civilization may save itself, despite itself.

Judaism has a problem. It does not pander; it demands. It opposes self-indulgence, self-righteousness, self-abuse. It is pitted against the superficial, against self-ignorance, against lack of awareness. It decries fatalism, pessimism, insensitivity, and the extreme in any direction. It declares that man has free will, conscience, and ability. It holds that the world is not evil, neither is man, though both may easily become so. Neither is at the center of things, nor are they ends in themselves. The one is the arena in which the other can become truly man. It demands that one show responsibility toward oneself, toward society, toward nature, and toward God.

It demands that one develop a personality suffused with knowledge, understanding, sympathy, and feeling, but it is not prepared to wait for these until one becomes a philosopher. It demands containment, restraint, and moderation but has little time for saints. It demands participation in the joy and happiness of the whole, identification with sadness and bereavement regardless of personal whim and mood.

It demands essential equality while propagating spiritual degree and achievement and considers riches a greater trial for man than poverty. It demands that man live the ideal life in this world. In its practicality it demands that man act as if he loves, in order to engender love, and is not prepared to countenance the contrary though love be far away. Human worth, nobility, dignity, and character are its touchstone, ethical conduct and behavior its life blood, and the fear of God its key.

It abhors the fake because it is fake, the coarse because it is coarse, the shabby because it is shabby. It looks man in the eyes and demands that he look into himself, with, if not entirely objective eyes, at least the eyes with which he sees his fellow. It demands that he look upward to God, backward in history, and forward to redemption, and then that he look into himself for salvation.

It demands timelessness in a world of time, perspective in a hectic world, and proportion in all things, deeds rather than words and at least words when no deed is possible. It demands that one train oneself for faith, trust in God, and see oneself and one's people as instruments of Providence. It declares that in giving one receives, that one must earn not expect, and that no one, neither man nor God, owes him anything.

Of body and soul, man is immortal. The terminal points, life and death, are beyond him, but even the body is the gift of God and he may therefore cause it no harm and he must struggle with life and for life that is sacred whether he wills it or not.

He exists in order to develop understanding and appreciation of the goodness of his Creator, but such appreciation, such goodness must be attained by his own, though aided, effort. There are no absolutes in creation, the sole Absolute is God. He is endowed with the ability to realize the holy in both himself and his universe. In so far as he strives for this he becomes more man. The more man he becomes, the closer he is to God. He can come close to God but only on the Almighty's terms. He is alone and insignificant only in so far as he is estranged from Him. Blessing, warmth, love, fulfillment are dependent on him alone. They are within his grasp, but he must make them his own.

Justice, mercy, and loving kindness govern his life. He is a child of his Father but servant of his King.

No deed, no thought, no thing is so trivial or insignificant that it escapes Him. He probes all and is in all so that He may be found in all, though He is beyond, above, and other to all. He demands prayer, praise, and thanksgiving not out of need, but so that man may rise above himself. He demands deed so that man edify himself and thus pass the otherwise impenetrable barrier that exists for him between matter and spirit. He speaks to man, guides him, exhorts him, encourages and aids him to come closer to Him. This is Torah; this is Mitzvah. He demands this of the Jew, of the Jewish people, so that they in turn may show humanity the way, by example. The world appears otherwise; man seems otherwise. This is his dilemma, this his test. It is achievable, but man must choose to achieve it. For this he was created with free will, free choice to fashion himself and his world. All is open to him; he may do that which he wishes but know that for all there is a reckoning, an accounting. Man creates his own heaven, his own hell on earth and beyond. Peoples also create their heaven or their hell, and this is history. It was not Gibbon who wrote the rise and fall of the Roman Empire—it was Rome. Nor was it Spengler who wrote the decline of the West. Life is hard; man is selfish; society is corrupt. Judaism demands that man rebel, not to make life easier but to make it liveable. To replace arrogance with mercy and corruption with integrity. To endow a meaningless world with meaning, to fill void with content. To unify worlds. Judaism rejects the dichotomy between yearning and living, between the ideal and anarchy. It insists that being is becoming. Since being is living, life must be lived ideally. The ideal is never to be divorced from the concrete. In human striving both must be expressed, practically—"heavenly days on earth." Here lies the problem.

Jewish Brinkmanship

Whereas Judaism as an ideal appeals, its insistence on living the ideal is a stumbling block. It is precisely this insistence that renders Judaism on the one hand unique, on the other distant. Too much "sacrifice" is involved in practicing Judaism. A man has to be a real man to live it. He must weigh and reject, reflect and rise, translate lust into pleasure, appetite into need, practice into education, belief into action. He finds numerous arguments for his failure to come to grips with himself.

"I do not believe"—as if anyone anywhere exists without belief. "It is out of date"—as if personality traits in our modern world had so changed as to render anything edifying superfluous, anything educative needless, anything speaking to the spirit, unreal.

"It is not scientific"—as if modern science upheld a mechanistic view of the universe or as if man's spirit is governed by its canons. I have never yet met anyone who lives by science or scientifically. I have met many scientists in need of sensitive personalities, awakening of the spirit, self-control, and a good all-round education. Or as if, as implied, those who claim Judaism to be unscientific really intend to negate their spiritual essence or fulsome personalities. Do they in fact circumscribe themselves "scientifically" in anything but their refusal to be men in the fullest sense of the word?

In truth, it is the failure to face themselves that keeps them afar. The delight in laissez-faire alone condones silencing the inner self and promotes the glossy rot of society. As the Rabbis pointed out, "Israel was well aware that there was no substance to idolatry; they only worshipped it in order to permit immorality publicly." The dignified and aesthetic have little appeal to the shoddy veneer or golden glitter of modernity. Values require norms and stability, both of which it lacks in abundance.

It was Maimonides who declared that no system of law or social order can ever solve every problem for everyone. The point of law and social order is that they maintain norms and bearing for the majority. That they enable a people to progress and adapt without losing its way or its identity. Without losing its distinctive soul. In standing firm, in refusing to bend before every idle wind or "-ism," its adherents retain character, distinctiveness, originality, and a degree of channeled creativity. This is halachah.

Without the training and guidance, restriction and regimen, framework, and direction of halachah, the Jewish people are in danger of losing themselves as a people. Witness the mass assimilation rampant in those areas where Jews have ousted halachah from their lives. It is generally realized that without Judaism, the Golah is steering a dangerous course of brinkmanship and losing. What is not so generally appreciated is that similar danger faces an Israel divorced from Judaism. If the spiritual essence is lacking, there is nothing to prevent assimilation in Israel. No reason for Jews who do not wish to do so, to remain there. No distinctive challenge in building up the homeland. No particular need to strive to regenerate a people on those bases that are much more easily attainable elsewhere in the world. Further, there is no valid reason for others to come there. It is only the particular challenge of Judaism that can demand of the Jew to be in Israel, to strive for Israel, and to give up all else in order to participate in founding and building its people.

Israel cannot have it both ways. It neither can continue to live on sentiment, nor can it continue to demand the loyalty of world Jewry to a spirit that it itself rejects. Charity, sympathy, identification in times of stress or war are excellent virtues, but they are not the positive virtues required to build a nation in its restored homeland. Only the dynamism engendered by spiritual dream and challenge, both of which Judaism disburses with largesse to those who have the heart and mind to receive, can do that.

The Jew has an appointment with destiny. He can do one of two things, and the choice is his. He can opt out and assimilate, or he can strive to keep the appointment. There is no in-between, and those who sit on the fence delude themselves, fail themselves, and fail their people. We know to our cost how history deals with complacency. It is time to face reality, as men and as Jews.

Major Questions

The present work is based throughout on the primary sources of halachah and the writings of the great halachists. The liberal illustration and references are concerned for the most part with actual problems. The purpose is not to "scientifically" dissect and analyze halachah as a historic system but to enable the reader to picture halachah as the halachist sees and understands it—as a living, dynamic, contemporary system relevant to life and living. To literally see the halachah through the eyes of the halachah itself. How does the halachic mind visualize the halachah, and in what manner is the individual involved in the halachic process? What is the relationship of halachah to other systems of law, and where do they differ? What is the relationship to the secular world? How does the halachic pulse feel about the state of Israel, and what can it do about its feelings? What is the relationship of halachah to ethics? What room does it leave for the individual conscience?

Is the individual considered by halachah as creative and self-determining, playing a constructive role in life and experience, rather than passively responding, in mechanical fashion, to the promptings of halachic stimuli? How does the halachah view the Bible, and how are the two related? What part, if any, does prophecy play in law? Is the Shulchan Aruch really closed, dogmatic, and hide bound as many would have us believe? Can halachah actually cope with today? What are the essential components of Talmudic study, and how in fact is this pursued, not by the professor in the university but by the halachist and yeshivah bachur? What basic methods of exegesis and logic does the halachah employ? What sort of logical premises and legal notions guide it? What do some of its basic concepts look like? What basic mechanisms determine halachic authority, decision, transmission, and implementation?

These are some of the major questions dealt with in the work. There are, of course, many others, but one has to begin somewhere, and, though one might be unable to complete the task, one is not, as stated by the Sages, free to desist from it.

I

Through the Eyes of Halachah

1

The Independence of Jewish Law

Halachah has both a mentality and methodology distinctively its own. This book is devoted to an attempt to understand halachah and halachic thinking. It is not our intention to engage on the limited or piecemeal inquiries of the sort found in the usual discussion of halachah but on the admittedly ambitious undertaking, fraught with difficulty and pitfalls, of uncovering the bases of the halachic process as a whole. The difference between the two approaches is paralleled by the difference in the field of history between the technical historian and the philosopher of history.

Irrelevant Models

As in the field of history, many of the ideas ruminated in the comprehensive systems of the philosophers have found their way into the works of professional historiography, so in halachah we find the fundamental bases of halachic thinking absorbed by and motivating the masters of practical halachah. Hence, it is largely from their works and decisions that our tentative efforts are to be culled.

An halachic methodology exists, but whether this may be discovered by analogy with modern scientific paradigm, the seemingly obvious course to follow nowadays, is open to question. It seems altogether likely that a different kind of framework is required if halachic thinking and development are to be rendered intelligible.

A priori assumptions drawn from nonhalachic systems of law, social mores, or anthropology succeed only in misleading

regarding both the methodology and intrinsic nature of halachah. Such attempts err because on the basis of extraneous and
fundamentally irrelevant models, they falsely presuppose categories implicit in halachic judgment and explanation.

Nathan Isaacs, in his "The Influence of Judaism on Western
Law,"[1] states this argument regarding the reverse situation when
he writes cryptically, "When the juristic notions for which the
Bible has been quoted are considered, one may be tempted to
take the side of those Rabbis who opposed the teaching of the
Torah to Gentiles."[2]

It is our contention that the approach to halachah must diverge
radically from other domains of inquiry if it is to be successful.
Other domains may be employed legitimately only by way of
contrast or for throwing halachah into relief. They neither probe
nor illumine the essential halachah.

The philosopher might well be tempted to explain Ben Azzai's
principle[3] that "one who walks is as if standing still" or R. Akiba's
rule[4] to the effect that an article that moved across the street is
considered to have rested on it, in terms of Zeno's famous paradox. Superficially the resemblances are striking, especially if the
two theories are combined. Detailed analysis of the halachot
entailed shows, however, that these principles have little in common with Zeno.[5]

Social historians may be led in the direction of a "scientific"
analysis of halachah that results in the resolution of halachic
principle to the mere shades of Plebeian versus Patrician social
(non-Jewish) history. In doing so,[6] they would be relinquishing
the integrity of halachah per se and reducing many of its norms
to the level of subjective class struggle.

Agrarians who delight in equating the "resting of the land"
during the Sabbatical Year with the age-old custom of allowing
fields to lie fallow in rotation denigrate the lofty concepts of the
land resting as a "Sabbath to the Lord" and consider the institution of the sabbatical year a mere precursory insight into util-
itarian agriculture.

To identify ritual immersion with bathing is to negate the
concepts and ideals of purity and sanctification and to replace
these by hygienic considerations, so that we are led to concur in
the conclusion of the historian who wrote that Moses' major
contribution to civilization lay in his qualities as a far-sighted
sanitary engineer.

Qualitative Differences

Superficial resemblances abound since human beings and their institutions are indeed similar the world over, but in case after case careful examination shows that these resemblances break down when confronted by exact study of the content as well as the intent of the halachoth concerned.[7]

Were we even to agree with Philip Selznick[8] that we should not overlook the psychic unity of mankind and the existence of cross-cultural universals and take account of the possibility that social scientific research may yet reveal what human nature is. We would not necessarily be closer to understanding the unique theological, ethical framework of halachah.

In the words of the Jerusalem Talmud,[9] Torah may be understood only as Noah understood it. "He pondered Torah from Torah," meaning that he drew his understanding and conclusions from what God had already told him.

The Sages state this boldly in a variety of ways. On the one hand, in commenting on the verse: "He declareth His word unto Jacob, His statutes and His ordinances unto Israel. He hath not dealt so with any nation; and as for His ordinances, they have not known them."[10] The Rabbis, in describing the scene between the Emperor Hadrian and his nephew Onkelos, who became a proselyte, state even the impossibility for one uncircumcised to comprehend Torah.[11] "Why, if you indeed wished to study Torah, did you have to undergo circumcision?" he asked. "Because," Onkelos replied, "in the same way that you do not bestow pension rights upon your commanders unless they have fought for you, so a person can never learn Torah unless he is circumcised. For it is written: He declareth His words unto Jacob—unto he who is circumcised as Jacob. He hath not dealt so with any nation—because they are uncircumcised," much less to compare his way of life with that of Torah.

Halachah and Law

On the other hand, the Sages are equally insistent upon the gulf that inheres between Torah and other systems of law even when these are superficially in accord. Thus they state categorically[12] that one is forbidden to bring suit in a non-Jewish court even when, in the particular instance, the non-Jewish court would render the same decision as the Jewish court. "And these are the ordinances which thou shalt set before them."[13] Before them (i.e., Jewish courts) but not before the courts of idolators.

The spirit of justice that moves both courts to act and that underlies the decision is dissimilar in quality, so that the approach to the court and the texture of the justice dispensed is as far apart as the width of the gulf that yawns between monotheism and idolatry.[14]

The aspiration toward justice in halachah is not circumscribed by the mere settling of a dispute between the parties.[15] It is an expression of meaning and value related to a conceptually underlying pattern of thought, ideals, belief, and commitment. It is these latter that provide the relevant standards or criteria for adjudication. In forming the background structure of justice, these aspects and qualities inhere in its detailed application so that it may truly be said of the halachic court that its justice is of God.

Furthermore, it is not only that the justice of God is dispensed. It is that in its application, divine ideals are inculcated into the minds, hearts, and personalities of the litigants.

Pointedly the Torah informs the would-be litigant that he is to go up to the place that the Lord thy God shall choose,[16] for redress. In so doing, the Torah not only eschews Austin's view[17] that "the existence of law is one thing, its merit or demerit another," since the law sought and applied is specifically bound up with the place chosen by God (i.e., where His Presence is manifested), but it ensures that the seeker after justice becomes imbued by his very quest with the sense of the Presence of God. That indeed "The words of the Lord"[18] refers to the halachah[19] is indelibly imprinted on the mind of the individual.

The significance ascribed by halachah to the intent behind the law is sharply focused by the halachah when it discusses the observance by the non-Jew of the seven Noahide laws.

One who accepts the seven commandments and observes them carefully is one of the righteous of the nations of the world and has a portion in the world to come. This, provided that he acts so because the Holy One Blessed be He, enjoined them in the Torah and informed us through Moses our teacher that the sons of Noah had been previously commanded to observe them. But if he observes them in pursuance of an intellectual decision, he is not a resident proselyte and is not one of the righteous of the nations of the world, but one of the wise men.[20]

King and Judge

The distinction between halachah and law is, in fact, highlighted within the framework of the Torah commonwealth itself. As pointed out by R. Nissim of Gerona,[21] distinction exists between two of the constitutional elements embraced by Torah society. These are King and Judge.[22]

While both are heavily involved in the administration and application of law within the commonwealth, the halachah differentiates sharply between their respective functions and purpose. It must, however, be remembered that though they function in different realms, at base the two complement one another in the life of the state.

The stability of society requires both law and sanction, and in a general sense this responsibility devolves on the institute of kingship (or government) within society. This responsibility, though grounded in halachah, is secular in nature, in so far as anything grounded in Torah can be considered secular, and is largely motivated by considerations bearing on the general welfare of the population.[23] On the other hand, the function of the judge is of evident religious character and is closely bound up with the implementation of spiritual values in society. Since his task is to discharge Divine law in society, his office is directed toward and, if exemplarily carried out, results in "cleaving to godliness" and its impress on society as a whole and on its individual members.

Halachah thus recognizes, in fact, a measure of duality and its provisions and injunctions in regard to the personality, piety, behavior, functions, and limitations of authority, all of which are specifically directed toward the king, are intended to circumscribe the boundaries of the dichotomy, and prevent the spiritual imbalance that would otherwise result from untrameled secular authority.

Rabbenu Nissim discusses[24] the demand of the people for a king in Samuel's day, in this light:

[B]ut Israel tended at that time more toward the improvement of their political estate. Had they asked only for a king—"Make for us a King" — or had they sought him in order to improve their chances in war, no sin would have been impugned to them on this account. On the contrary, it would have been considered a mitzvah. Their sin lay, however, in having said: "Now make us a king *to judge us* like all the nations."[25]

That is to say that they wanted "the judgments" to be undertaken by the king and not (as hitherto) by the Torah judges.

That this is the true emphasis of the passage can be seen from what follows. "But the thing displeased Samuel, when they said: 'give us a king' to judge us."[26] It does not say, "when they said: give us a king." That alone would not have displeased him. What was hard for him [to accept] was their having said "to judge us." And because of this the Lord said to Samuel, "For they have not rejected thee, but they have rejected Me, that I should not be king over them."[27] Meaning "that they have chosen improvement of their natural [secular] lot rather than that the godly ideal devolve upon them."

We may pursue this subject a little further since it leads us into the heart of one of the principal modern problems of halachah. For clarity, it is best to conceive the relationship between king and judge in pyramid form, with Torah at the apex of the pyramid, while king and judge form the additional points of the triangle. Both king and judge draw authority and power from Torah, and both, in their separate spheres are bound by it. However, interpretation of the functions of both branches resides with the judges since they are the interpreters of Torah. Hence, while general matters affecting society legitimately fall within the province of the king, the limitations of kingship, or the constitutionality of his actions, is determined by the judges.

The constitutionality of his appointment or that of his council is not decided by the judges. This is decided in one of two ways, either by a prophet together with the sanhedrin or by popular vote.[28]

Ideally the king also sits as judge, but when he does so it is the judgment of Torah that he renders;[29] hence the rabbis always refer to David and his beth din, to Solomon and his beth din. He does not sit with the beth din to decide matters of State.

The reason for the statement in the Mishnah[30] to the affect that He (the king) may send forth the people to battle in a permissive war[31] by the decision of the court of seventy-one, is so that these pray for the success of the enterprise[32] and take care of the particular halachic problems arising in and from war.[33] But the actual power of decision to go to war resides with the king.[34] Maimonides[35] and others hold, however, that the power to wage war is vested in both king and sanhedrin.

Accepted that the present-day status of the government in Israel is that of the king[36] and the right of the government to wage war is not halachically in dispute,[37] we are nonetheless involved in a far-reaching dilemma. For if the king/government does not recognize the binding authority of Torah, and in Israel the government does not, what is the halachic position regarding the general validity of its laws and enactments?

Furthermore, we may legitimately enquire as to whether those elements that seek to "halachify" the law of the state are not groping in the dark. How can one graft religious law onto a secular base? Do we not succeed thereby in merely secularizing halachah and consequently in divesting it of its essential character and importance?

Israeli Law and Halachah

Even according to those authorities who hold that the rule *dine de'malchutha dina*—the law of the country is law—applies also to a Jewish ruler, the ruler may in no way set up a judicial system contrary to Torah. "Then Samuel told the people the *Mishpat Hameluchah*—the code of Kingship, and wrote it in a book, and laid it up before the Lord."[38] The legitimate division of authority envisaged by Rabbenu Nissim is firmly grounded in the recognition by *both* powers of Divine origin and intention. Halachah sanctions the broad powers of government to act; it does not thereby intend to abdicate its pristine position in government as well as in society.[39]

While halachah cannot sanction wholly secular government, secular government cannot, without affront, sanction halachah. It is absurd to think that one observes the sabbath, for example, because of the Knesseth enactments confirming Saturday as the official day of rest.

Statehood and Halachah

This dilemma, touched on briefly, is the result of a historical-political compromise entered into in 1947 between the then Jewish

Agency and Agudath Yisrael and since perpetuated by religious parties in the coalition governments of the Knesseth. Whether the compromise is justified or not, it is certainly responsible for much of the tension that exists between the halachah and the state. Two authorities coexist but without firm definition as to where one ends and the other begins. The result is distortion between the realms to be enjoyed by each in the life of the state.

Halachah, in welcoming the state—"separation between religion and state is absolutely forbidden"[40]—and facing the problems of statehood actually for the first time in two millenia, lacks, as pointed out by R. Jacob Emden[41] a political theory. It has always been more interested in the practice of living the inheritance of Torah than in the abstract principles of government. Hence, it is able to countenance a variety of governmental systems. It would seem, in fact, that belief in the givenness of Torah may be considered the theory behind any possible political theory and that an explicit political philosophy is superfluous. Pragmatically, halachah is able to embrace the following portrait of Jewish statehood. It is a portrait that succeeds in retaining both the independence of halachah and the legitimate aspirations of statehood.

The problem, it must be borne in mind, lies in the fact that just as halachah cannot abide totally secular statehood, totally secular statehood can brook no limitation of sovereignty, power, and authority. But statehood as envisaged by halachah is not totally secular.

In theory, halachah sees the state as both bound in outlook, tone, and perspective and limited in practice to that which does not negate Torah. This standpoint leaves a broad, legitimate, and virtually unfettered spectrum for the exercise of state's sovereign rights. It also ensures that the state does not become an end in itself, does not become estranged from the highest aspirations of human and spiritual expression, and retains character as the instrument of those it was set up to serve.

Sovereignty

By bound in outlook, tone, and perspective is meant that the state sees itself as the legitimate continuation and the present culmination of more than three and a half thousand years of Jewish history, mores, and tradition. The tone and perspectives guiding government are to be those prevailing as Jewish values and sensitivity to man, to nation, and to peoples. The enactments of government are to reflect Jewish historic sensibility and awareness. In other words, the legal and practical frameworks of the state are to leave no room for doubt that it is, in fact, a Jewish state.

Actual limitation to the power of state enactment applies only to that which is clearly contrary to halachah—for example, the recent abortion law that negates both the Jewish attitude to life and to person as well as being expressly contrary to halachah.

Within the framework, government, however elected,[42] is virtually untrammeled. The broad basic fields of government, foreign affairs and relations, internal as well as external security, defense, taxation and economics, natural resources, industrial development, the penal code, health and welfare, and the general obligations of citizenship and organization of the body politic are its exclusive domain.

Being of fundamental Jewish outlook, the state voluntarily concedes to halachah its rights as to personal status, marriage, and divorce—problems related to being Jewish—and upholds officially the institutions of Sabbath, kashruth, and religious education. Halachah accedes to the demand of the state in the areas enumerated since these are *halachically* considered the prerogatives of government in order to ensure the general welfare. It goes without saying that the state must grant authority and status to rabbinic courts administering halachic civil law for those appearing before such courts, for it is a sine qua non that Jewish law must be enabled to function in a Jewish state. Halachic-wise, this demand is perhaps the most fundamental of all its demands within the state. At worst, it is at least to parallel secular law; it can in no sense be inferior.

In this view, harmony and cooperation between the two is assured, while halachah will be enabled to solve the problems presented to the individual without undue difficulty. Halachah cannot solve these problems, and they are numerous and widespread, efficiently as long as it is basically at odds with the state—that is, as long as the state refuses to recognize its partnership with halachah in the present culmination of Jewish history.

An excellent illustration of this is to be found in the organization of Zahal. If, far be it, Zahal had failed to recognize the Sabbath or kashruth as essential basic norms, no religious Jew could in conscience serve in its ranks. With such recognition, service is not only possible but obligatory—particular problems being capable of solution by competent rabbinic authority.

The fundamental question is the willingness of the state to be Jewish, in the intention invested in the phrase, embodied in the Declaration of Independence, *Tzur Yisrael*, purposely chosen for ambiguity but that, to have any meaning or relationship with Jewish history, must be understood as "the God of Israel."

As the halachah has always realized that its basic role is within the state, though it was forced for centuries to direct its vast potentials and energies to the Galuth, so the state must understand that rebirth is not an outgrowth of nineteenth- and twentieth-century nationalism, though this formed the immediate formal background for its emergence, but the commencement of the realization of the covenant between God and Israel.

Neither Galuth, where halachah flowered, nor statehood, which has yet to prove itself, alone, have been considered the pinnacle of achievement for Jewry. Historic legitimation lies in the recognition by both, of common origin and common ends. Ultimately in the recognition that sovereignty for men as for society resides with God, so that there is no real distinction between the halachah of the individual and that of the state. This, perhaps, is the fundamental meaning of the litany: Our Father our King!

Natural Law

To revert to our main theme. We do not, therefore, approach halachah from the standpoint adopted by the student, lawyer, or judge approaching law. Neither social anthropology nor theories of natural law provide a guide to either the origins or the development of halachah. In the very nature of things, neither ethnology nor naturalism is able to illumine theo-centered halachah.

It was, in fact, the difference between the received law of the Jew and the supposed laws of nature embedded in the Bible that led, on the one hand, to the final cleavage between Judaism and Christianity and, on the other, to the development of the natural law concepts that gradually found their way into European systems of jurisprudence. The alleged discovery of the elements of natural law in the Bible and Jewish jurisprudence,[43] in fact, provided the framework for the concept of law as a means of protecting the individual against the tyranny of the state.[44] But halachah instinctively recoils from the climax of the pretensions of natural law as voiced by van Wolf (1679–1754): "Institutes of the Law of Nature and of Nations in which by an unbroken argument, all obligations and all laws are deduced from the nature of man itself."[45]

Comparative Systems

Comparative law, philosophy, social mores, or institutions fail to provide the key to halachah.

> What is more astonishing, even Roman law appears to have been of small consequence in the evolution of halachah. Despite more than a millenium of persistent scholarship and interpretation of all problems connected with Roman law, and despite the fact that the specific question of the relation between Roman and Talmudic law has engaged the attention of prominent jurists for three centuries, few indications of direct influence have been found. Jewish halachah was already well developed by the third century, the period of greatest achievement in Roman law.[46]

This is certainly true of systems later than or that themselves stem from Roman law.

Halachah can be understood only by reference to its own particular framework, emphases, and integrity as a unique and distinct authoritative system. The objection, based primarily on the exclusive nature of halachah, to the possibility of conceiving halachah as a universal religious system is of no interest to the halachah per se. The further question as to why the God of all men chose to reveal His word to a single people is a problem that cannot be entered into here. It belongs properly to the philosophy, not to the halachah, of Judaism.

Relationship with Philosophy

Confusion between halachah and other disciplines seems to have crept into certain rabbinic circles in thirteenth-century Spain, so that R. Asher b. Yehiel was led to pen the following sharp rejoinder to a colleague in Toledo regarding an issue that had been decided on other than strictly halachic grounds. The response,[47] only the relevant part of which is quoted here, deals categorically with the independence of halachah from other disciplines and shows clearly where and why Torah differed. He says:

> Regarding your words "from both [the standpoint of] logic and religion," what should I reply to this! Our Torah should not be as your idle talk, the wisdom of your logic which all the sages of religion have put aside. Shall we then bring from it an indication or proof to render guilty or innocent, to forbid or to permit. Those who hewed its foundations did not believe in Moses or in the righteous ordinances and statutes given by him in writing and by tradition. How then can those who draw its waters adduce from them proof with regard to the statutes and ordinances of Moses, peace upon him, and decide cases by virtue of the similies to which the exercise of logic has accustomed them.
>
> Is it then to be that in my day and in my place they will decide cases by means of parables. Thank God as long as I live there is yet Torah in Israel to adduce proof from the Mishnah and Talmudim, Babli and Yerushalmi, and one will not need to quote similies in order to decide things.
>
> For the wisdom of philosophy and the wisdom of the Torah and ordinances are not of one path. The wisdom of the Torah is received by Moses from Sinai, and the sage expounds it by means of the rules [middoth] given for its exposition and by comparing one thing with another. And even though the [comparison of] subjects may not be in agreement with [the tenets of] natural wisdom, we follow the tradition. But philosophy is natural [lore], and its exponents were great sages who established the natural station of all things. [However], because of their great wisdom they delved deeply, they corrupted and were required to deny the law of Moses, since all of the Torah is not [based on] natural [considerations and norms] but [is dependent] on tradition. It is of this that the verse declares: "Thou shalt be wholehearted with thy God," meaning that even if the matter goes beyond natur[al law], do not query the tradition but walk before Him wholeheartedly.

Secular Knowledge

For this reason one may not bring proof from their words to establish indications, proofs, analogues, or similarities for the righteous ordinances of God. It is of this that the wise one declared,[48] "All those who enter her will not return," meaning to say that whosoever enters first into this wisdom, will be unable to leave it so that the wisdom of Torah can enter his heart. Such a one is unable to forsake the natural wisdom to which he has become habituated. His heart is ever drawn thereafter. This being so, he will never be able to achieve the wisdom of Torah, which is paths of life. For his heart, ever drawn after natural law, will lead his spirit to compare the two wisdoms and adduce proofs from one to the other, with the result that he will pervert justice[49] since two opposites are antagonistic and cannot dwell together.

This is not to deny secular knowledge to the student of Torah.[50] Rabbenu Asher places the emphasis on the order of study, that which is first assimilated by the heart and mind dominates that which follows.

Chatham Sopher,[51] in stressing the necessity to imbue the young first with Torah and Mitzvoth and only later with the "scientific" tools required for the understanding of many parts of Torah, says:

> For one who teaches his son the life of this world first and then wishes to instruct him in the paths of the world to come—shass and possekim—. . . he is wasting his effort . . . since before the youth knows . . . he has already estranged himself by his deeds from his Father in heaven, and he will want neither God nor His Torah . . . as our eyes witness in this evil generation in several countries where the true order of study has been reversed.

R. Naphtali Zevi Yehudah Berlin[52] expresses a more lenient view, in stating that one cannot become a Gadol beTorah if at the same time one is immersed in other studies. He concludes, "All the Gedolei haTorah who were sage in secular knowledge, either studied secular subjects before immersing themselves in Torah, or after they had already waxed great in Torah. At the same time it is impossible to achieve the ultimate in Torah study."

Decision Criteria

However this may be, the actual halachah may be decided solely on halachic grounds and criteria, as stressed by Asheri. There are numerous problems, especially those involving the ingathering of the scattered tribes of Israel, that could possibly be dealt with on historical and other grounds, but halachah cannot accept such solutions. The matter was put forcibly by the late Chief Rabbi Uzziel when dealing with the problem of adopting the modern, sephardi Hebrew pronunciation in the synagogue. Decrying the efforts to solve the problem on the basis of scientific historical studies, he says,[53] "Whosoever determines the pronunciation to be used by recourse to scientific investigation, and not on the basis of the living tradition in our mouths, is mistaken, and he misleads others."[54]

In discussing the problem of halachic and state authority, the late Chief Rabbi Herzog states,[55] "But we are not engaged upon historical research,[56] nor can it avail us. From the point of view of halachah we may only take account of the reliable source material of the judgement of Torah."

A final example, from a more everyday field, may be found in the lengthy discussions of the possekim concerning determination of the date line. Chief Rabbi Uzziel, in summing up the discussion, states, "Though we must determine upon a meridian, we may not do so arbitrarily, as has been done and agreed upon by the nations, for they are not bound by the details of creation or by the mitzvoth of the Torah."[57]

Notes to Chapter One

1. In *The Legacy of Israel* (Oxford, 1927), pp. 377–406.
2. *Ibid.*, p. 382.
3. Sabb. 5b.
4. *Ibid.*, 4a.
5. See, for example, the Chiddushei HaRan on Ben Azzai, loc. cit.
6. As Finkelstein did in "The Pharisees."
7. Arnold Enker in his review essay, "Self Incrimination in Jewish Law," in *Dinei Israel*, Vol. 4 (Tel Aviv: Tel Aviv University, 1973), puts this cogently when he says, "On the basis of the analysis of Jewish Law outlined here, I would suggest that the Jewish Law treating confessions is not particularly relevant to the confessions debate, primarily because the procedural and evidentiary premises of the Jewish legal system which developed these rules are so radically different from our own that the legal issues posed are equally different" (p. cxxii).
8. Sociology and Natural Law, *Natural Law Forum*, 6 (1961), 84–104.
9. Megillah 1, 11.
10. Ps. 147, 19–20.
11. Tanhuma, Mishpatim 5.
12. Gittin, 88b.
13. Exodus, 21, 1.

14. See Maimonides, Yad, Sanhedrin 26, 7, and note 33 in Rambam Le'am ed. See also the quotation from R. Zemach Duran in *Halachah Pessukah* (Jerusalem, 1962), p. 13.
15. Cf. Birchath Shemuel to Babba Kamma, siman 2.
16. Deuteronomy 17, 8.
17. *The Province of Jurisprudence Determined*, p. 184.
18. Amos 8, 11.
19. Sabb. 138b.
20. Maim. Yad. Melachim 8, 11.
21. Derashoth Haran, No. 11.
22. This distinction is fraught with halachic consequences of the greatest moment in present-day Israel, where the standing of the Government is likened by many authorities to the standing of the king, with consequent lack of particular halachic restriction on his actions. The entire thesis of Rabbenu Nissim is discussed by the late Chief Rabbi, Isaac Herzog, in *HaTorah VeHamedina*, Vols. 7–8, pp. 13–20; and in *Mishpatim LeYisrael*, Rabbi J. Ginzberg (Jerusalem, 1956), pp. 134–137. Rabbi Herzog does not accept the possibility of such dual authority. Ginzberg, however, explains the complementary nature of the role of king/government, removing thereby Rabbi Herzog's objections. Cf. following note. Herzog does, however, accept the role of Government in regard to many aspects of the penal code. See, Yavneh, *The Jewish State and Its Problems* (1949), pp. 12–13.
23. In answering a query on this problem, the late Chief Rabbi Kook wrote, "The Mishpat Hamelech is not confined to that realm which affects the respect due to the person of the king. It is effective with regards every general matter pertaining to the people . . . it seems that when kingship does not exist, since the *mishpetei hamelech* refer to the general situation of the people, these rights revert to the people as a whole. Especially it would seem that any judge who arises in Israel has the law (i.e. status) of a king in respect to certain of the *mishpetei hameluchah*, namely those which refer to the general requirements of the people needful at the particular time, and for its position in the world." Responsa, Mishpetei Cohen, 144. See also Responsa, Chatham Sopher, *Or Hachayim*, 208, on this. Kelei Chemdah to Shofetim, 6, and others, hold that the *Mishpat Hamelech*, is effective only in regard to the Noahide laws but not the mitzvoth commanded specifically to Israel and grounded in the sanctity of Israel.
24. Derashoth *ibid.*
25. 1 Sam. 8. 5.
26. *Ibid.*, 6.
27. *Ibid.*, 7.
28. Saul Yisraeli, Resp. Amud Hayemini, (Tel Aviv, 5726), p. 59.
29. Nimmukkei Yoseph to Alfasi, Nedarim 28a. See Deut. 17, 18–19.
30. Sanh. 2, 4.
31. Halachah distinguishes between two kinds of war. A permissive war is one undertaken to expand the borders of the country. An obligatory war (*milchemeth mitzvah* or *chovah*) is one undertaken to reduce the seven nations of Canaan, to root out Amalek, or to save Israel from an enemy, Maimonides Melachim 5, 1. Nachmanides considers the conquest of the land of Israel at

all times to be a positive precept. In a unique responsum, R. Samuel b. Elkana of Altona writes two hundred years ago, Responsa Mekom Shemuel No. 8, that there is no such thing as a totally "permissive" war. All wars involve an element of mitzvah; otherwise, how is it possible to permit the wholesale endangerment of life and the desecration of the sabbath? They are only called permissive because permitted by the Sages.

32. Rashi to Ber. 3b.

33. Mahrsha to Sanh. 16.

34. Meiri to Sanhed, ed. Sopher, p. 50.

35. Commentary to Mishnah and Melachim 5, 2.

36. See supra notes 22 and 23.

37. See Mishpetei Cohen Nos. 143, 144. Responsa Chatham Sopher, Choshen Mishpat 44. Responsa Imrei Esh to Yoreh Deah No. 52. Avnei Nezer, Responsa, Yoreh Deah, 454, 54, quoted infra chap. 7. Cf. Maimonides, Melachim 4, 10. This is also of preventive war, see Rema to Orach Chayyim, 329, 6. R. Jacob Emden, in his commentary to the Haggadah of Pessach was the first in modern times to raise the issue of the conquest of Eretz Yisrael, and he resolves it positively. Elsewhere in his works, Emden derides those who think of Eretz Yisrael only in terms of a mystical or spiritual symbol. And this about two centuries before the state!

38. 1 Sam, 10, 25.

39. See Rema to Choshen Mishpat 369, 11 and Meirath Eiynaim thereon; Shach *ibid.*, 73 note 39, etc., Responsa Adereth, quoted in Beth Yoseph to Tur Choshen Mishpat, 26. So regarding the problems of the individual, certainly nationally. The problem of *Dinei De'Malchutha* is dealt with exhaustively by R. Isser Zalman Melzer, *Eben Ha'azel*, Pt. 1, chap. 8, Hal. 1, who concludes that if secular law is not, in the given instance, contrary to Torah, and the particular decision would be upheld by Torah as consonant with rectitude, or acting beyond the letter of the law (see infra chap. 4 of the present study), one must abide by it. So also Chatham Sopher, Responsa, Choshen Mishpat, No. 44. In what manner and degree this applies to Israeli law, see the discussions in the volumes of *HaTorah VeHamedina*. In particular, Rabbi E. J. Waldenberg, Hilchoth Medinah, Vol. I, Gate 3, chap. 6.

40. Ch. Rabbi Herzog, Yavneh, *loc. cit.* paragraph 11. Also Ch. R. Uzziel, *ibid.*, pp. 15–16.

41. Mitpachath Sepharim, p. 74.

42. On the problem of the religious personality of the elected member, see J. Ginsberg, Mishpatim LeIsrael (Jerusalem, 1956), pp. 67–69. In particular, the responsa of Ri Migash quoted there.

43. It is worth clearing up a misconception with respect to one of the alleged "major sources" of natural law in the halachah. This is usually found in the Seven Noahide Laws. The quotation from Maimonides, supra p. 19, suffices to dispel any serious attempt to brand these as natural law. We may note in passing that though the Talmud, Sanhedrin 57a considers infringement of the Noahide laws a capital crime, Chelkath Yoab (2d ed., sec. 14, end) explains that this was only so as long as the non-Jewish world failed to establish its own courts and procedures, fines and punishments. Once

these became established, no capital punishment was thence involved in their transgression.

44. See Isaacs, *ibid.*, pp. 383–387.
45. Quoted by Isaacs, *ibid.*, p. 385.
46. Dr. Salo Baron, *A Social and Religious History of the Jews,* Vol. 1, p. 293.
47. Responsa, Klal 55, sect. 9.
48. Proverbs 2, 19.
49. Similarly Ra'abad: "We cannot learn from the words of a non Talmudist, since such turn the halachah to their own words," quoted by Dr. Bergman, *Katuv Sham* (Jerusalem, 1957), p. 34.
50. See the Responsa of Rema, nos. 6 & 7 at length. In particular, the fulsome notes of Dr. Asher Ziv to this responsa published by Feldheim 1970. Also Rema to Yoreh Deah 246, 4.
51. Derashoth Pt. 1, p. 112.
52. Responsa Meshiv Davar, No. 44.
53. Responsa Mishpetei Uzziel, Pt. 1 (Tel Aviv, 1935), No. 1.
54. In like vein, the halachic reliability of texts reconstructed from the Geniza (see Chazon Ish, *Letters,* Pt. 1. No. 20) or texts discovered by scholars but that have not enjoyed continuous attention within the living tradition of halachah are considered unreliable for deciding halachah. Chazon Ish, Orach Chayyim, 67, 12. But see Orach Chayyim, 39, Kontress Hashiurim, sect. 6, where he says, "Afterwards I saw the responsa of the Gaon, printed in the Otzar HaGeonim to Erubin 83, and though one may not rely upon manuscripts discovered after centuries of interruption in the tradition, here it seems that these are indeed the words of the Gaon." However, see the note of R. Y. Weinberg to his Responsa, *Seridei Esh* (Jerusalem, 1962), Pt. 2, No. 12.
55. *HaTorah VeHamedinah,* Vol. 6, p. 14.
56. In this context one might add "or political theory."
57. Piskei Uzziel (Mossad Harav Kook, Jerusalem, 1977), p. 110.

2

Torah and the Secular World

Interactions

The paths then differ. To a large extent they are to be considered exclusive, but they are not entirely so. First, since many branches of halachah do not function in a state of grand isolation from the world, there is at least a one-way traffic between halachah and society at large. The general social patterns, economic organisation, cultural life, and mutual interactions of society indeed force their attention on halachah.

In doing so, they succeed in providing grist for the halachic mill. The internal canons and structure of halachah, in dealing with the problems raised by society at large, take the necessary steps to solve such problems in a manner that in effect assimilates the problem into the body of halachah, which then realizes whatever potential inheres in the problematic situation for halachic goals and purposes. These may, in fact, have little or nothing in common with the general trends of society that gave rise to the problem. On the contrary, they may, if adhered to, create new norms and fresh trends in society.[1]

Areas of Limited Assimilation

Second, there are, in fact, areas of secular knowledge and science that are assimilated within limits, by halachah. Medicine was excluded from the ban proclaimed by R. Shelomoh b. Adereth against studying philosophy and natural science when young and not yet proficient in Talmud,[2] on grounds that medical practice is permitted by the Torah,[3] but its use in deciding instances of halachah concerning *terefa* was rigidly excluded by Maimonides when its premises contradict the received tradition,[4] as by all authorities. Nonetheless, in an instance where the halachic tradition proved indecisive, R. Shelomoh Luria[5] upheld the appeal to medical and scientific evidence in order to clarify the matter, as did R. Moses Isserles,[6] who quotes Aristotle on the same problem.[7] Not infrequently, secular knowledge is employed in order to establish the relevant facts of the case, which is then decided by halachic rule. In practice, the seeking of expert scientific opinion by the halachist is now commonplace and is accepted for determining the knotty problems involving modern technology, the use of machinery and appliances on the sabbath,[8] or even to establish prima facie evidence about the problems of *Aguna*.[9]

Expert Opinion

Many halachic problems depend on receipt of expert medical opinion for their solution. These problems involve transgression of the sabbath for one who is sick or allowing him to eat on Yom Kippur or to partake of normally forbidden foods. The late Chief Rabbi Kook dealt with such problems at length in several Responsa, and he lays down a single limiting criterion:[10]

> As to the actual halachah concerning trust in doctors, we are certainly able to state, as proved from . . . , that they are believed. But this applies to an instance which has become clear to them as a result of practical experiment. And this is not only so with regards medicine, but we may say that the same applies with respect to all the sciences which are required [as aids in deciding] laws of the Torah and knowledge of which must be sought from those proficient in such branches of knowledge. Their trustworthiness is dependent upon their word that their opinion is the result of experiment and practice.[11]

The emphasis of the passage is to be understood in the light of the impossibility of deciding halachah on other than strictly halachic grounds. The scientist is called on to determine the exact material issues of the case in hand. He is not asked for his opinion concerning these facts. Hence, of such use of scientific aid, Chacham Zevi declares,[12] "This is not called proof but establishing the facts and in this matter one may adduce proof from doctors, from the senses or from science . . . for this is simply revealing the obvious."[13]

Maimonides, finding no detailed Jewish astronomical calculations to hand, in basing his calculations for the intercalation of
the calendar on Greek astronomy, says:[14]

> And the understanding of all these calculations and why we add
> this number and why we subtract, and how we know all these
> things and the proof of each detail is the science of astronomy and
> geometry upon which subjects the sages of Greece compiled
> numerous works which are presently to be found amongst schol-
> ars. But the works compiled by the sages of Israel who lived at the
> time of the prophets have not come down to us. But since all of
> these things are based upon unassailable proofs which one can-
> not question, we take no notice of the author—whether compiled
> by prophets or by the nations. For whatsoever has been fully
> understood and its truth established irrefutably, we rely upon
> whoever said it or taught it. We rely upon the established proof
> and reasoning that has been made known.[15]

In the Mishnah itself[16] we find the irrelevance of witnesses in
the face of established mathematical reckoning.[17]

General Attitude toward Scientific Study

A knowledge of the majority of the natural sciences is necessary
for the proper understanding of numerous branches of halachah,[18] and, as codified by Isserles,[19] only study of "siphrei
minim," which deny the truths of Torah, is actually eschewed.[20]
The Talmud is, in fact, replete with references to the natural
sciences, and the halachah declares[21] that one ignorant of secular
sciences is unable to sit as a member of either the Sanhedrin or of
the lower court of twenty-three.[22]

The general attitude toward such knowledge was positive,
though its position vis-à-vis Torah remained, of course, subsid-
iary, and the emphasis placed on its acquisition and use varied
from one authority to another.[23]

Maimonides, in his famous letter to the scholars of Lunel,[24]
summed up the situation in a personal declaration: "The Torah is
the hind of my love and wife of my youth in whose love I have
been engrossed since my youth. And though strange women
[other studies] have become her rival . . . God knows that these
were only taken up in the first instance . . . to be her perfumiers,
her cooks and her bakers."

Centuries later, R. Baruch of Sklov, disciple of the Gaon of Vilna, penned similar sentiments in the introduction to the translation of Euclid into Hebrew that he undertook at the Gaon's request: "For in proportion to one's lack of knowledge of the other sciences, he will lack tenfold in the wisdom of Torah. For the Torah and science are bound together."

Science in the sense of revealing the physical nature of the universe is not only tolerated in Judaism; its pursuit is elevated to the status of mitzvah.[25] The problem with such study lies in striking a balance between Torah and scientific study. Quite apart from the considerations outlined toward the end of the previous chapter, the problem refers specifically to the personality of the researcher. Immersion in scientific research is not so totally to engross the personality of the individual that this excludes either Torah study or the religious improvement of personality that results from Torah study and practice alone. This is the crux of the matter as dealt with by many thinkers and halachists.

This perspective is well brought out by noting the contrasting opinions of two famous halachists. In the lengthy discourse of Eliahu Jacob Shor,[26] the connection between Torah and general knowledge is carefully worked out, as are the drawbacks and limitations. Shor is of the opinion that without thorough grounding in the sciences, the higher reaches of Torah cannot be attained; that one fulfills a mitzvah in studying them for the sake of heaven; but that the drawbacks, religious dangers, and difficulties involved are only overcome at the expense of learning Torah, so that, in fact, one is at an impasse.[27] He concludes that the solution lies only in fostering *Yir'ath Shamayim* and attempting to achieve such knowledge by virtue of "the secret of the Lord is upon those that fear Him, and His covenant is to make them know it."[28] This is hardly a practical solution for the majority of people.

However, Rav Kook[29] comes to a different conclusion. He says:

> [A]fter one has taken care to study Torah continually and to cleanse his personal qualities, especially of anger, of pride and of nervousness, which are the source of evil qualities, and having determined upon daily study of the inner essence of Torah, each one according to his ability. It is tested and tried, that after these preparations no harm will, heaven forbid, befall him from knowledge of the sciences when they are absorbed in measure for the

sake of heaven. On the contrary, they will increase his strength in the service of God out of joy and breadth of mind.[30]

Granted the intellectual freedom and Torah encouragement to pursue scientific bent, one is ever to bear in mind the oft-quoted communication of Rav Hai Gaon to R. Samuel Hanaggid, in which Rav Hai declared that "right conduct is contingent upon the study of the Mishnah and the Talmud; he who turns his heart from these studies and busies himself with those other things [philosophy and science] will remove from himself the yoke of Torah and the fear of God. . . . Fear of heaven, dread of sin, zeal, humility, purity, and holiness are acquired only by those who are engaged in the study of the Mishnah and the Talmud."[31]

Torah does not encourage intellectual pursuit unless it is undertaken side by side with study and involvement in the problem of his duty and place in the world. In this stand, halachah unequivocally opposes the present general separation of science from ethics and the hazards for humanity that flow from such divorcement.

The Scientific Knowledge of the Sages

Third, knowledge of the world and of its affairs is of the essence of Torah, but it must not be forgotten that much of the knowledge displayed by Chazal could simply not have been learned either by experiment, in which Chazal indulged, or by recourse to the general knowledge of the times. How then did Chazal acquire their amazing scientific knowledge?

The Talmud itself states on several occasions[32] in answer to this question, "The secret of the Lord is upon those who fear Him, and His covenant is to make them know it."[33]

"Did then R. Jose[34] who renders them all susceptible to impurity know all the species of plants in the world, that he is able to consider them all as stalks? But this presents no difficulty, for, as we find generally, 'The secret of the Lord is upon those that fear Him.' "[35]

Much was known by tradition from the prophets—more, by virtue of the true knowledge of the manner in which Torah is to be studied in its other than literal senses. "Turn it over, turn it over for all is contained therein."[36] Since in essence the Torah is but the Names of the Holy One Blessed be He,[37] one who knows Their secret, knows all.

On the verse: "Observe therefore and do them; for this is your wisdom and your understanding in the sight of the peoples, that, when they hear all these statutes, shall say: "surely this great nation is a wise and understanding people.' "[38] Chatham Sopher writes:

It is true that our Sepher Torah is quantitatively small. However, it is impossible [to understand] unless one is possessed of all the other wisdoms. For how can one accept the witnesses of the new moon if one does not know all the details of the movement of the sun and moon and their courses . . . or the laws of Terefah without skill in anatomy,[39] or the song of the Levites without musical knowledge,[40] or the division of Eretz Yisrael without knowledge of surveying, topography and geography, or the laws governing the sowing of diverse kinds without knowing the manner in which they draw nourishment or how far they spread in the ground. . . . To what heights did Chazal rise in their treatment of the thirty-nine classes of forbidden work on the sabbath. Their expertise in all kinds of work is evident . . . and there is no mention of all this in the Torah and we have no books devoted to these subjects. The nations do, however, have works on all of these topics and we are [presently] forced to study their works regarding them.

Yet God said: "And thou shalt meditate therein day and night" on which Chazal comment: "and from it you shall not move." And when asked concerning the study of Greek wisdom they replied: "One should study it at a time that is neither day nor night" . . . and He has no pleasure at all when we study their works. If so, whence shall we know all that is necessary for [understanding] Torah? And the Book is small and too brief to contain it.

But, know and believe that though it be but two spans square, its measure is longer than the earth and broader than the sea and there is no science in existence, nor what is above or below, or before or aft that is not hinted at in its letters and words. Without doubt, the verse: "This month shall be unto you etc.,"[41] contains the entire science of the sanctification of the new moon, more than Maimonides copied from their books. And one who knows how to unlock the verse will find everything explained therein.

See what Nachmanides writes on the verse: "This is the book of the generations of man"[42]—that he found a work by R. Sherira Gaon in which he adduces the entire science of palmistry and facial marks from this verse. And so it is with the other sciences, for the writing is the writing of God.

So that when the nations see that we have no recourse to their books, and that we do not agree with them [in many matters] and that we have no other work but this Sepher Torah, and nonetheless everything is revealed before us in the best possible manner and exactly, they know and appreciate that we are an understanding people, able to deduce one thing from another and able to understand the indications of this holy Torah.

This is not only so with regard to knowledge of the sciences, but, as the Gaon of Vilna points out,[43] it is so of everything. He says:

The rule is that all that was, is and will be unto the end of time is included in Torah from *Bereshith* to *Le'eynei Kol Yisrael*. And not merely in a general sense but as to the details of every specie and of each one individually, and details of details of everything that happened to him from the day of his birth until his end. So also every kind of animal and beast and living thing that exists, and of herbage, of all that grows or is inert and all the fine details of every specie. . . . In general form this is contained in the first chapter, up to: "That which God created to do."

Chazal, in fact, declared, "He who occupies himself with Torah for its own sake, merits many things"[44]; not least among these is the unlocking of the secrets of the Divine manifestation in creation. For after all, the light of the days of creation was hidden away in the Torah.[45]

Notes to Chapter Two

1. See the survey of halachic literature that arose as a result of the depreciation and devaluation of currency in I. Z. Cahana, *Studies in the Responsa Literature* (Jerusalem: 1973), pp. 330–348; the vast literature on credit and interest that arose as a result of changed business conditions during the Middle Ages; the modern responsa literature on the more recent problems of artificial insemination; also the fourteen volumes of HaTorah VeHamedinah dealing with problems arising as a result of Statehood, to mention but a few of the many areas that could be quoted as examples. It is worthy of note that the bibliographical survey listing the sources alone in modern responsa literature that deal with electricity and the Sabbath published by the Institute for Science and Halachah (Jerusalem, 1975) consists of well over two hundred pages, while the literature on modern medical problems is not far behind.

2. This condition seems to have been added by Isserles, Responsa No. 7.
3. Responsa, Addereth, 418.
4. Yad, Shechit. 10,12–13. This is not so in regard to human illness; see Chazon Ish, *Hilchoth Ishuth*, 27, sect. 3.
5. Yam Shel Shelomoh, Hullin, 1, 35.
6. Responsa, 5.
7. Cf. Responsa, Addereth, 98. Chacham Zevi, 79 at length. See also the letter of Chatham Sopher to R. Eliezer Segal Horowitz, printed in R. Zevi Hirsch Chajes, *Meir Herskovitz* (Mossad Harav Kook, 1972), p. 177 – "And we should consult the experts on this in order to ascertain which action will effect." Also Noda Biyehuda, Tinyanna, 29, in regard to the kashruth of a certain fish. Noda Biyehuda says, "And I searched in the books of the naturalists." See also the interesting Responsum on the financial liabilities of the professional adviser, in Tashbatz, Pt. 2, No. 174.
8. See in particular Ma'Asseh Ugerama Behalachah, R. L. Y. Halperin, published by the Institute for Science and Halachah (Jerusalem, 1977).
9. For instance, in solving the many problems of *aguna* that resulted from the Yom Kippur war, fingerprint experts, experts in aerodynamics, impact pressures, and a host of others were liberally consulted by the Rabbinate. Cf. also Rabbi D. Feldman, *Shimusha shel Torah* (London, 1951), pp. 131–135, where the problem of identifying the presence of diverse kinds in material (*sha'atnez*) is wholly resolved by microscopic and chemical means, there being no traditional, reliable criteria available.
10. Shaar Zion, 1931, Pts. 1 and 2.
11. See the detailed survey of healing in halachic literature in *Studies in the Responsa Literature*, I. Z. Cahana, pp. 126 ff.
12. Responsa, 76.
13. See the Responsa by the late Chief Rabbi I. Herzog, Hechal Yitzchak, Even Ha'ezer, Pt. 2, No. 22, where he relies unequivocally on the medical evidence as to the age of the girl in question.
14. Yad, Kiddush Hachodesh, 17, 24.
15. Though Ra'abad criticized Maimonides' calendar calculation, his opposition was not to the use of astronomical knowledge derived from secular sources but to the fact that this knowledge was not always in keeping with halachic norms and was consequently occasionally erroneous for practical religious purposes. See Rabad of Posquieres, I. Twersky, (HUP, 1962), p. 264 ff. Twersky also quotes there the words of Rabbenu Chananel to the effect that "Although contemporary astronomers maintain contradictory views, we pay no attention to them. We are cautioned [to accept] the statements of others." Cf. the responsa of Asheri quoted at the end of the first chapter, supra.
16. Rosh Hashannah 2, 8.
17. Commentaries *loc. cit.*
18. See Kuzari, Pt. 11, paragraph 64.
19. Yoreh Deah 246,4.
20. This is also the opinion of Rivash. See Abraham M. Hershman, *Rabbi Isaac Ben Sheshet Perfet and His Times* (New York, 1943), p. 89.
21. Yad, Sanhedrin, 2, 1.

22. But see Kesseph Mishneh ad loc who quotes Remach to the effect that "I do not know from where he [Maimonides] took this, and why should Dayanim need to know medicine?" See, however, the following note.

23. "But the sages did not hand over the halachah to physics": Chazon Ish, Yoreh Deah 124, 3. Or again, "But in that case we have still not learned from Chazal until we enquire of the doctors. This is impossible. Chazal knew the science of medicine and taught us exact halachoth": Chazon Ish, Yebamoth, Likkuttim 4, 8, 9. Cf. the statement of the Sifri to Deut. 23, 2 (also Jerushalmi, Yeb. 8, 2): This is of the *Hilchoth Rofe'im*. The intention seems certainly to be *Hilchoth Refuah*. See also responsa of R. Azriel Hildersheimer, Orach Chayyim No. 74: "But what have we to do with chemistry . . . we come in the name of our sages." We do however rely on chemical analysis in determining Kashruth; see Piskei Teshuvah (Pieterkov, 5693) No. 187.

24. Responsa, 1, 12.

25. See *Olam Echad*, by the present author (Tel Aviv, 1975), in particular chap. 17.

26. Appended to Responsa, Netioth Chayim (Vilna, 1892), pp. 34b–46b.

27. *Ibid.*, 35b.

28. Psalms 25, 14. Cf. the following section in the text.

29. Iggeroth, Pt. 1, No. 43.

30. The comment of Tosaphoth Yom Tov, Derech Chamudoth to Asheri, Berachoth, chap. 5, note 43, is worth noting in this respect since he draws an halachic conclusion from it. In the name of R. Mordechai Yaffe, he explains the necessity to commence the second Berachah of the Amidah at the termination of the Sabbath with the words *Atta Chonen* though one recites "*Attah Chonantanu*" in any case, by saying that *Atta Chonen* refers to the favor bestowed on all men to know and understand the seven wisdoms, while *Attah Chonantanu* refers specifically to limmud Torah. Since the "favors" are different, they are expressed separately. To this Tos. Yom Tov rejoins, "And why should they not be expressed together? Are they not of one substance and subject . . . and furthermore it is known and obvious that such knowledge is needed for Torah. For how can one ascend to the degrees of Torah wisdom knowing neither the right nor left of even the elementary principles of general knowledge. And though the wisdom of the Torah ascends above them all, the seven wisdoms are included within it—'And all understanding thy kinswoman (Prov. 7, 4),' for, 'She hath hewn out her seven pillars' (*ibid.*, 9, 1). It is therefore unnecessary to repeat *Atta Chonen*."

31. The translation is that of Hershman, *ibid.*, p. 90. See also *ibid.*, note 4 for the alternate readings of this important passage.

32. E.g., Niddah 20b.

33. Ps. 25, 14.

34. Mishnah, Ukhtzin, 1, 4.

35. Chazon Ish, Ukh. 1. This is also true of laws not dependent on scientific knowledge. "But, in virtue of 'The secret of . . . ,' forgotten halachoth were revealed to our teachers of blessed memory, when they delved deeply into their souls, and the Holy Spirit rested upon them"—Chazon Ish, Kidd. 46, 13. Cf. Responsa Chatham Sopher, *Or Hachayim*, 208.

36. Aboth, 5, 25.

37. See Ramban, Introduction to the Torah; Or Hachayim to Ex. 31, 13, etc.

38. Deut. 4, 6.

39. Rabad encouraged the empirical study of animal anatomy by actually bringing to class parts of an animal. See Twersky, p. 34, and note 29 ad loc.

40. Kuzari, 11, 64 says, "Music was the pride of a nation which distributed their songs in such a way that they fell to the lot of the aristocracy of the people, viz., the Levites . . . who had no other occupation but music."

41. Ex. 12, 1. This is the principal biblical source for the mitzvoth regarding intercalation of the calendar and the lunar year. See commentaries ad loc.

42. Genesis 5, 1.

43. Commentary to Sepher Yetzirah, chap. 1.

44. Aboth 6, 1.

45. Zohar and Tikkunim.

3

The Ethical Bases of Halachah

Underlying Ethical Theory

In this and the following chapter we shall attempt to outline the ethical bases of halachah and discuss several of its structured ethical strata. It is necessary first to introduce in general terms the underlying ethical theory of halachah. For an ethical system, such as we conceive halachah to be, validity is grounded in a metaphysical view of the universe. Moral struggle and aspiration rest on and are determined by what is held to be the nature of the universe, and conversely the validity of ethical judgment can finally be determined only by metaphysics. An ethic grounded in a materialist view of the universe will differ profoundly from one that considers the universe indeterministic.

Harmony

Both metaphysics and ethics predicate basic postulates, and these cannot be entirely at odds with one another unless it is assumed that the human being is in a state of basic antagonism to his universe and that his role is entirely divorced from his physical environment. There must be some kind of harmony between man and his world, so that the validity of ethical standards is ultimately dependent on the constitution of the universe as a whole and man's place within it.

This approach to ethics removes the subject from subjective, relative grounds and places it in the realm of the objective and universal. Its import lies in asserting the existence of absolute standards of moral behavior that by conforming to the nature of the universe apply irrespective of changing circumstances and opinions. This is not, of course, to state that particular application of absolute standards is impervious to circumstances. Its tendency is rather to curb "ethical" behavior resulting from shifting attitudes and unbridled intuition or conscience. Irrespective of conscience and circumstance, it declares that there are certain moral norms and values that are unconditionally valid and obligatory. Further, it is only by adopting such a basic scheme of ethics that meaning may be ascribed to the moral struggle of the individual or society. For, if ethics were solely relative and subjective, there could be no such thing as moral progress or decline, no motive to uphold any moral code.

The Worlds of Torah and Science

The grand background of the creation of the universe forms the setting for Torah. The implication is clearly that Torah is part of the fundamental structure of reality. The rabbis went further than this and declared that the physical universe reflects the spiritual structure of Torah concretely.

The ethical implications of this are precisely those outlined earlier, namely that the ethical standard is absolute and that it is somehow related to or reflected in the physical composition of the universe.

We must examine this position a little more closely. It is not asserted that moral laws are to be identified with laws of nature. Moral laws represent standards to which one ought to adhere but which one may fail to live by, whereas laws of nature are statements of facts as these are found to be by scientific hypothesis. The moral laws of human nature are, however, so paralleled by laws of nature that living by them brings the individual into harmony and accord with the universe. The parallelism affirms the ultimately absolute nature of the moral standard.

Again, this is not, farbeit, to say that the moral law issues from nature. It asserts that both man and his universe were created with reference to a single standard and as such form one grand universal system. Such creation alone endows man with the possibility of moral achievement in what would otherwise prove to be an impossibly hostile setting.

There are concomitants as well as problems to be faced on this view. First, the view asserts the reality of the moral struggle. This struggle is not merely an illusion, but it is grounded in God the creator and supporter of the universe. Second, the moral struggle implies an impulse from beyond nature, and the aspiring toward the same source. And third, the moral struggle involves one in conflict of personal loyalty toward God, rather than in obedience to an impersonal convention.

The morally structured universe implies a rationalism behind moral action that ousts feelings, impulse, intuition, or simple conscience from the prime position of moral arbiters and relegates them to diminished, secondary importance. The rationalism involved is the rationalism that reigns throughout the universe—not the reasoning or sentiment that provokes one to act within the limited spheres of individual, group or society.

A universe whose physical laws parallel moral imperatives must be the kind of universe that essentially reflects the bases of ethical standards. Is this in fact so? The two essential foundations of ethics are free will and purpose. Can these be said to exist in some form in the physical universe as we know it?

It would seem that modern scientific opinion is more or less prepared to answer affirmatively. For the question really posed is, what is meant by a scientific law, and what do these laws succeed in teaching us about the basic structure of the universe? Is determinism materialist cause and effect, the stuff of the universe, or does indeterminism describe it better? Is the structure fundamentally material or, as some philosophers of science hold, mental?

Taken together, the description of scientific laws as tendencies rather than statements of what always happens, the indeterministic theory of matter and the view of the nature of the universe as mental, point to a resemblance of purposeful free will. Purposeful, since the universe is most certainly engaged in realizing, over vast spans of time and space, the countless potentials with which it is endowed. Science has been instrumental in its own fashion of conceiving the kind of universe that Torah conceived at the outset. While science grappled with matter in its search and arrived at the immaterial, Torah converted spirit into the terms of the concrete world around us.

Both, it would seem, meet and somehow coalesce on the border between. The circle is complete and the "oneness" of the universe restored.

We shall see later how this "oneness" is fostered by the exclusive emphases that underly the ethical structure of halachah.

Covenant and Consent

The basis of halachah is the covenant at Sinai and the consent of the people of Israel there expressed. The historical experiences of deliverance from Egypt, the personal manifestation of God and His summons to obey, form not only the philosophical framework of Jewish history but the living structure of the personal, ethical relationship between the Lord of the universe and the Children of Israel.

The basic elements of "covenant" presuppose free will and the idea of choice, so that the entire edifice of halachic authority rests on the assertion that man is in fact endowed with free will and has the ability to say no but did not. The Talmud,[1] recognizing the element of coercion present in the background of the events leading to Sinai, asserts that because of this background, Israel could have claimed that the initial consent of the people was tendered under duress and hence void and that the possibility of such a claim was only rendered null during the time of Mordechai and Esther when, because of the deliverance wrought on their behalf (Rashi), they reaffirmed willing acceptance of the Torah.[2] God is, as it were, powerless to bestow His injunction on man. He can only do so as the result of man's deliberate choice, and His directive enjoys authority and becomes binding only from the moment when man has so chosen. So it was with the covenant made with the patriarch Abram, which was cemented only after Abram's circumcision, so at Sinai: "We shall do and we shall hearken." Hence, the very inception of halachah is based on the ethical assumption of human worth, dignity, and personal freedom. The Sovereignty of God in the life of the people exists because it was determined on by the people, who accepted the pact and provisions proposed by God.

This determination was reiterated at the the Tent of Meeting, at Shittim,[3] by Joshua, Samuel,[4] Josiah, and Ezra so that the personal commitment and responsibility for the covenant was ever kept before the mind of the people. As a people they continually entered anew on the covenant, and, since it is a tenet of tradition that the individual is to see himself as having himself gone forth from Egypt and personally stood at the Mount, the Torah was in fact given to him and not to his forbears alone, so that he is ever involved in the renewal of his personal commitment to it.

The moral obligation toward halachah stems, then, from consent—from the agreement to become the partner of God in administering His law[5] and cause His Divine Presence to rest on Israel.[6] The jural character and actual contents of halachah have nothing to do with the obligation to observe its dictates.

God Bound by Rule of Law

The principle of covenant goes, however, much further, for a covenant is not one-sided in any of its aspects. God is Himself bound by the covenant. He is not only bound by it in a general sense, but He is also so deeply committed to it that He is, in fact, voluntarily limited by the rules of halachah and cannot interfere in its processes.

The Talmud[7] quotes a Baraitha that describes the argument between R. Eliezer and the Sages:

> He [R. Eliezer] said to them: if the halachah is in accord with my opinion, let it be proven from heaven. A heavenly voice came forth and said: what will you of R. Eliezer? The law is in accord with his opinion in every case. R. Joshua stood on his feet and said: It is not in heaven[8] for the Torah has already been given at Mt. Sinai.[9] We take no notice of the heavenly voice for You have written in the Torah: Turn after the majority.

And the Talmud continues: "R. Nathan met Elijah. He said to him: what did the Holy One Blessed be He, do at that time? He smiled, was the reply, and said: My children have overcome Me, My children have overcome Me."

The Ethical Quest of the Litigant

God, as it were, accepts on Himself the rule of law[10] that He ordained for man, so that, in fact, man partners God not only in administering the law but also in observing it. In practicing the Torah observed by God Himself, man is practically and ethically at one with the world and its Creator. The very nature of halachah is affected by this concept. For, when one examines the processes of halachah, a striking fact emerges. Exactly the same judicial logic and argumentation are employed when discussing fields of religious law such as sacrifices, tithes, sabbath, ritual purity, and so forth, as are employed when engaged on civil law, torts, or criminal charges. In the latter category, the matter under dispute is between two parties; in the former, the argumentation is, in fact, between man and God Himself. Since God is taken as the "second" party, the underlying question in the dispute is the question for man as to how he should act in a given circumstance. As will be shown later, it is this same question that underlies also civil cases, so that in halachah the major point at issue is not the rights of others but *how must I act?* It is the answer to this question that is sought by the litigant. The actual problem faced by halachah is an ethical problem, though couched in legal terminology and technicality, an approach envisaged by no other system of law.

No Fundamental Law

There is no necessity in halachah to become involved with the paradox posed by the need to validate the existence of law by presupposing the existence of basic law, which itself requires validation.[11] The basic norms, as the system itself, are suprahuman and inhere their own validity as being of God. The standard norms of halachah are recognized by covenant as obligatory, and deviation bears sanction and odium.

It is, in fact, true to say that there is no fundamental halachah, in the sense of a fundamental law, to be analyzed, because such a one does not exist or that, if it does, it exists only in the unfathomable Mind of God. Halachic thinking is in consequence directed toward the construction of a hypothetical structure in which the essential norms of halachah are those assigned to it by the investigator.

The Freedom to Expound
and Realize Revelation for Oneself

The investigator can, of course, only construct with the materials with which the halachah provides him, but the freedom to construct is of the essence of halachah. For, though the Torah was revealed in its entirety at Sinai—"And on them [the two tablets] was written according to all the words God spoke with you in the Mount"[12] – this teaches us that God showed Moses in advance all the subtle details of the biblical law and its scribal interpretation.[13] "The words" embody Holy Writ, Mishnah, Tosephoth, Haggadoth, and all that a conscientious student may develop from them in the future"[14]; the halachah bestows the fundamental right on the believer to expound Torah by the use of his intellect, reasoning, and ability to weigh opinions. "By virtue of his faith in the fact that Torah was indeed given with all its details and explanations to Moses at Sinai, the scholar expounds, promulgates new laws, offers fresh insights and novel interpretations, certain in the knowledge that he is realizing the revelation, rendering it actual and exhibiting to his generation that of which it stands in need."[15]

Halachah is not primarily directed toward teaching the Judge how to decide Divine Law. "It instructs the individual how to live."[16] In so doing, it becomes the bastion of faith in action, for without halachah, faith remains abstract, sterile, and irrelevant to life and living. Hence it obliges the individual to seek the way for himself by means of the study of Torah. In turn, the study of Torah, being the immersion by the student in pondering the thoughts of God, involves him in the realization of revelation for himself.[17]

It is for this reason that Chazal insists[18] that "one should ever study that part of Torah to which his heart inclines," for only there will his deep-seated faith come to flower and fruition, only there will the springs of his soul open the gates wide for fulfillment of spiritual yearning and personal revelation. There will he discover the particular guidelines for the conduct of his life. Study of Torah is essentially as personal and individual as Torah was when given to every member of Israel – "There were originally six hundred thousand orders of Mishnah,"[19] that is, one for each of the six hundred thousand of Israel.

As it was then bestowed on each in accord with his need, predilection, and ability:

Come and see how the Voice came forth to Israel. To each one in accord with his [individual] powers. The old heard the Voice according to their strength, the young men according to theirs. The youth according to theirs and the young according to theirs. The tots according to theirs and the babes according to theirs. The women according to theirs and even Moses according to his. For the verse says:[20] "Moses spoke, and God answered him by a voice," in a voice that Moses was able to bear. And so it says:[21] "The Voice of the Lord with power." It does not say: "with His power," but "with power," meaning, with the power that each could bear.[22] And even the women who were with child, according to their power, so that each one of them [received] according to his power [to receive].[23]

So it has remained for all generations.

Equality in Construing the Law

Arising out of this principle of voluntary involvement and immersion in halachah is a novel notion of "equality." This is not to be understood in the limited sense of "equality before the law." It is equality in making the law, in rendering its processes intelligible and relevant, in the effort to construe the law as it really is. It connotes the feeling that I, as an individual, am called on to determine for myself what the halachah is and means for me, now.

It conceives of the human being as creative and self-determining, playing a constructive role in life and experience rather than a passive, responding role. "Rejoice in your study, study out of joy and goodness of heart. Follow the ways of thy heart to understand that which is in thy heart as you see it."[24] The Yalkut, commenting on the verse "But his delight is in the law of the Lord, and in his Torah doth he meditate day and night" (Ps. 1, 2), states that at first the Torah is called "the Torah of the Lord," but after one has studied it, it is called "his" (i.e., the Torah of the individual).

Theoretical Diversity

This equality and freedom does not, however, lead to antinomianism in halachah.[25] For both the individual and the community, practice conforms to the internal rules and directives governing halachic decision, and these are binding irrespective of the interpretation or insight by which the thoughts of God are conceived by the individual in the particular situation. Diversity remains in the realm of theory, or the spirit; conformity reigns in practice.

"We are enjoined to appoint judges . . . so that the Mitzvoth of the Torah and its prohibitions be not dependent upon the will of every individual."[26]

The rebellious elder[27] is taken to task only if he delivers a practical ruling in conformity with his dissentient opinion: " 'And the man that doeth presumptuously,'[28] he is not culpable until he instructs to do"[29] – not for proposing or even teaching his nonconformist opinion to others.[30]

The Individual and Halachic Expression

Thus far as to theoretical halachah, the study of Torah. As to practice, the role of the individual is also of paramount importance. The human being is involved in a constant process of reflective and actual transformation, in the sense that he continually modifies, revises, and supplements the inheritance of skills, attitudes, and modes of experiencing the world received from his forebears.

The interplay between this constantly changing world of the individual and fixed halachic norm results in the tension whose fruit is the dynamism of halachic expansion. The individual beset by circumstance attempts to discover his particular locus within halachah. In response, halachah invests that locus with a normative halachic practice. But in order to do so, halachah has itself so expanded that it now embraces the transformation that has overtaken the individual.

Hence the individual provides impetus for movement within practical halachah. His need to know how to serve God within his particular framework of life, contingencies, and circumstance presses the halachah for answers.

Study of Torah and the Fear of God

The study of Torah may itself present problems since "at the time one is immersed in study, the love of God may well be pushed to one side"[31] and the study relegated in consequence to mere intellectual exercise. Aware of this, the rabbis, following closely on the biblical intertwining of Wisdom with the Fear of God,[32] declare,[33] "One who is possessed of Torah but has no fear of heaven, is as the treasurer who has been given the keys to the inner vaults but not the keys to the main entrance, how shall he enter! Declared R. Jannai: 'Pity one who has no courtyard but makes a gateway for his court.' Said R. Judah: 'The Holy One Blessed be He, created His world only that they should fear Him, as it is written:[34] "And God hath made it so that men should fear before Him." 'R. Shimon and R. Elazar were sitting when R. Jacob b. Acha passed by. Said one to the other: "Let us rise before him for he is a man who fears sin." Said the other: "Let us rise before him because he is a scholar." Said he, "I tell you that he fears sin and you say that he is a scholar!' "

R. Chaim of Volhozin was not slow to draw the inevitable conclusion. Thus he says, "Likewise, in the midst of studying Torah, it is permitted for one to pause a while, before the flame of the fear of God which he accepted upon himself before commencing to study, is extinguished; to ponder again for a while the fear of God."[35]

Ethics is not, of course, solely a mental exercise, or an exercise in spiritual being, so that, quite apart from the intellectual aspects of halachah, of which many are perhaps incapable, living the halachah in practice is itself the expression of ethical involvement and achievement.

Even living the halachah in practice is insufficient, thus his grandson, in the introduction to Responsa Chut Hameshulash,[36] explains the otherwise difficult passage in the Talmud[37] to the effect that David established the mitzvoth on eleven (principles); Isaiah on six, Micah on three, and so forth, to refer to the ethical principles that form the basis for fulfillment of Mitzvoth, as Hillel explained to the potential proselyte,[38] "Do not do unto others that which is hateful unto yourself—this is the entire Torah, the rest is commentary, go and study."

Thinking thoughts of Torah, even performing its Mitzvoth but lacking fear of God or the ethical milieu of Torah, are ultimately both barren and sterile. Such practice leads to a robotlike religiosity void of true spiritual meaning or fruit.

Doing

In spite of the emphasis placed on rationality by halachah, it is essential to grasp that the importance of "doing" never lost its pristine place in Judaism. Judaism was never turned into a rationale at the expense of its being a living faith. On the contrary, it ever upheld as its banner the declaration of the sages to the effect

that "he whose deeds exceed his wisdom, his wisdom shall
endure. But he whose wisdom exceeds his deeds, his wisdom
will not endure."[39] Grounded in reality, Judaism never allowed
the Torah or its ideals to become so heavenly that they were no
earthly use![40] The stress and emphasis always lay on living in
the manner compatible with its ideals so that "heavenly days
on earth" would be possible. Doing is not merely a casual consequence of antecedent events. It is an expression or vehicle
of meaning conceptually tied to an underlying pattern of thought
or intention. Whether this pattern is fully comprehended or
not, the act of doing both presupposes and actualizes the background structure.

Doing the right thing takes precedence over study of Torah,[41]
because to do anything is a voluntary exercise of will and an
expression of the personality of a living soul. Doing brings about
a change in the existing order and enables one to make his mark
on all that is around him. While involvement in the thoughts of
halachah can be accomplished within one's own shell, doing
involves going beyond the enclosure of self and affects directly or
indirectly those around him. So that although not everyone
might be able to know, or to believe, or to be, the conscious act of
doing that which is God's will, of which *all* are capable, generates
ethics in practice.

Integrity and Trustworthiness

Closely allied with "doing" is the integrity and trust with which
the halachah endows the doer. Thus the Baraitha[42] teaches, "The
laws governing the sanctification of goods or property, separation
of the heave offering and tithes, are of the body of Torah, and they
were handed over to the am ha'aretz."[43] The assumption that each
individual enjoys a *Chezkath Kashruth*[44] — that is, that he is trustworthy — though not actually stated in the Talmud, underlies many
halachoth, and we do not suspect one of transgression.[45] Even
when doubt is raised concerning this, we declare him to have
acted in error, and he does not lose his trustworthiness.[46]

This trustworthiness extends to realms such as infidelity,[47] the
fitness of forbidden foods,[48] testimony,[49] and others. The Talmud[50]
bases the elegant truism that the word of a Jew is his bond on the
verse "The remnant of Israel shall not do iniquity, nor speak lies,
neither shall a deceitful tongue be found in their mouth."[51]

Purity of Heart

Purity of heart is of the essence of the deed demanded by halachah, and intention—*kavannah*—is so important that the Talmud
declares[52] that "thoughts of transgression are even worse than
transgression itself." Even though one failed to transgress, the
intention to do so requires atonement. Hence, "if one intended to
eat the flesh of swine but it chanced that he took the flesh of a
lamb, he requires atonement and forgiveness."[53] And, "on thinking to serve idolatry one becomes a *rasha* since the verse states:[54]
lest your heart be deceived, and:[55] that I may take the house of
Israel through their heart.[56]"

On the other hand, though it is not generally the case, there
are instances when intention alone serves as deed. Thus, if one
thought to perform a mitzvah and was forcibly prevented from
doing one, the verse considers him to have performed it.[57] In the
reverse instance, that of performing a deed with evil thought, the
thought is not joined to the deed[58] and is discounted.

In the case of many mitzvoth, intention alone endows the deed
with quality, and its lack nullifies performance. Can prayer be
said to exist if the intention of the heart is lacking? While in others
such as sacrifices, the thoughts of the priest attending on the altar
determine whether the sacrifice is truly a sacrifice or whether it is
an abomination (*piggul*). Concerning all, the Torah says, "If thou
shalt hearken to the voice of the Lord thy God, to keep His
commandments and His statutes which are written in this book
of the law; if thou turn unto the Lord thy God with all thy heart,
and with all thy soul."[59]

Thus, though we learn to do what is right by habit and by
practice, whether we fully understand the ethical principles or
not—"we shall do" and then, "and we shall understand"—the
halachah recoils from mechanical deed divorced from motive
and intention, from heart and mind.

In taking cognizance of no less than five aspects and degrees of
intention involved in performing a mitzvah—the sense of being
in the presence of God; the intention to perform His will; understanding the significance of the act involved;[60] being of sound,
responsible mind; and being totally free to act[61]—halachah ensures that both the character of the "doer" and the ultimate aim
of life are involved in the deed. "And thou shalt love the Lord thy
God with all thy soul" is taken by Maimonides[62] to mean "with all

the parts of your soul, so that you weld the purpose of each part of your soul into a single whole."

Intellectual Pursuit and Civilized Behavior

Immersion in Torah study coupled with living in the fullest sense by the Word of God ensure spiritual vision and awareness for the individual, as for the group. One is able to approach God only as He has Himself provided—by thinking His thought and conforming to His ways. One may well aspire to and achieve intellectual or spiritual height without Torah and without halachah, and many have done so—but it was not God that they found.

The modern view of untrammeled intellectual pursuit, divorced from or indifferent to a way of life in keeping with the soaring of the mind, has not only succeeded in lessening moral and ethical awareness but has also lowered the standards of civilized behavior to the level of the primitive and is in serious danger of undermining society. Secularism, responsible for a general enlargement of man's horizons during the past two centuries, has succeeded in re-creating on a vast scale the barbarism and boorishness of the Dark Ages it was meant to displace. It is only by combining mind with deed as halachah demands that spiritual enlargement may hope to stem social havoc and moral anarchy. The secularist must finally come to realize that despite success in his search after knowledge of the universe, society, and the individual, he has proven a total failure to man, whom he allegedly set out to free and serve. The present widespread occupation with Jewish mysticism and philosophy, divorced almost totally from halachic practice, can result only in similar, barren failure.

Notes to Chapter Three

1. Sabb. 88a.
2. In view of the historical reiterations of the covenant (infra) it would seem that the Talmud is stressing the covenantal aspect of receiving Torah but not the actual possibility of voiding it. Chiddushei HaRan, ad loc., holds that the problem arose only because Israel was exiled from the land, i.e., a default by God the proposer of the covenant, regarding one of the major elements of the covenant, viz., possession of the land, and it is to this that the Talmud answers that Israel waived the condition when in exile during the time of Mordechai and Esther. Cf. also the statement in Yalkut Shimoni

Echa, ed. Buber, p. 104: "Israel said to Him: Master of the universe, since you exiled me among the peoples I ought not in fact be obliged to observe Your commandments, and yet I observed them."

3. See Mishneh LeMelech, *Parashath Derachim* (Constantinople, 1728), pp. 49ff.
4. With the Cuthim, 2 Kings, chap. 17.
5. Sabb. 10a.
6. Sanh. 7a.
7. B.M. 59b.
8. Deut. 30, 12.
9. I.e., it has been given completely and nothing is left of it in heaven; Deuteronomy Rabbah, 8, 6. For this reason, no prophet may claim that God communicated to him the necessity of adding to the Mitzvoth of the Torah or changing duty in it; see Maim. Yesodei HaTorah, chap. 9 and infra in the present study, chap. 6.
10. Cf. Yoma 36b, "I might have thought that the law is in accord with R. Meir [against the majority opinion] since the verse of Moses supports his opinion. Hence the need to confirm that the law is in accord with the majority, who oppose him"; Makk. 23b. "The human court decided three things and the heavenly court agreed with them"; Sot. 16a. "In three instances the halachah sets the biblical text at nought." See Addereth Eliahu to Ex. 21, 6. Sabb. 87a. "Three things Moses did on his own accord and the Holy One, blessed be He, agreed with him." Also Tanchuma to Tzav, on the war of Moses against Sichon.
11. This paradox is one of the major problems raised in criticism of Kelsen's work, *The Pure Theory of Law* (Los Angeles: University of California Press, 1967), as well as of other theories of law.
12. Deut. 9, 10.
13. Meg. 19b.
14. Midrash Kohelleth, chap. 1. This teaching of the Rabbis is axiomatic and lies at the very core of traditional Jewish thought. It is based on the fact that that which was spoken by God must in the very nature of things be all-embracing, perfect, and complete. That which God spoke requires but to be understood; it does not require addition, so that "between the separate commandments [of the Decalogue] were noted down all the precepts of the Torah in all their particulars, Jer. Shekalim, chap. 6; Shir. Rabb. sect. 5." See also Bamidbar Rabbah, chap. 13, Annaf Yoseph, note 15, where it is explained that, according to the opinion in Shir. Rabb., chap. 1, to the effect that only the first two statements of the Decalogue were said by God to the people, the 613 mitzvoth are embraced by these two alone. This fundamental concept lay behind the controversy with the Minim, who held that only the Decalogue (or at best the Written Law) is Divine Law; see Ber. 12a and Rashi thereon; Jer. Ber. 1, 5 etc. It also lies at the base of the numerous attempts to classify Torah under the ten general headings of the Decalogue; see TaRYag, by the present author, p. 41ff.
15. M. Silberg, *Principia Talmudica* (Jerusalem: Hebrew University Student's Press, 1961), p. 52.

16. E. E. Urbach, "The Religious Significance of Halachah," in *The Values of Judaism,* Machbroth Lesiphruth (Tel Aviv, 1953), pp. 24–31.
17. This, of course, portrays only briefly the basic tenet of involvement for the individual. For the community, as for the individual, other factors, which will be discussed later, come into play.
18. A.Z. 19a.
19. Quoted from early sources in the Introduction to Pitchei Olam, Orach Chayyim (London, 1964).
20. Ex. 19, 19.
21. Ps. 29, 4.
22. It is instructive that the halachah understood the words "an important person is different" employed many times by the Talmud, invariably to refer to the extra demands made on him and the additional responsibility that he bears as a result of his station, never to "privileges" resulting from it. As an important person, he is able to bear more and he is expected to act in accord. Ab initio he received more Torah; hence the additional dimension of responsibility.
23. Tanhuma, Ex. Shemoth No. 25.
24. Rashi to Sabb. 63b. s.q. Ad Kan letorah. Cf. also Iglei Tal, Introduction, on the legitimate delight experienced when studying Torah. The delight and joy are considered an integral factor in the study of *Torah Lishma,* for its own sake.
25. On the permissibility of interpreting Mishnah differently from the interpretation of the Talmud when no practical difference results, see, Responsa, Kol Mevasser, Pt. 2, Section, Simchath Yom Tov, No. 5, at length, and the section at the end of the volume, pp. 128–129, titled "Teshuvah LeHassagah."
26. Sepher Hamitzvoth, No. 176. Translation according to Kaphach.
27. Deut. chap. 17.
28. Deut. 17, 12.
29. San. 86b; Yad, Mamrim, 3, 5.
30. Maimonides, *ibid.,* 6.
31. Mahral, Tiffereth Yisrael, Introduction.
32. "The fear of the Lord is the beginning of Knowledge (Prov. 1,7)."
33. Sabb. 31a, bott. and folio b.
34. Ecclesiastes 3,14.
35. Nephesh Hachayim, Shaar 4.
36. Vilna 1881, pp. vii ff.
37. Makk. 23b–24a.
38. Sabb. 31a.
39. Aboth 3, 12.
40. It is worthy of note that the great practical halachists have always been listed among the philosophers, visionaries, and mystics of Judaism, a fact that irrefutably illustrates the point made in the text.
41. Yad, Talmud Torah, 3, 4.
42. Sabb. 32a and b.
43. I.e., they were not given over to the Beth Din to appoint guardians in the matter, but the Torah believed each individual (Rashi). This, though eating

untithed produce bears the severe punishment of death at the hand of heaven.

44. Tosaphoth to Hullin 11b, term this presumption: Chezkath Tzidkuth—a presumption of righteousness.
45. Rabad to Gerushin, 10, 9; Ridbaz to Eduth 11, 3; Ribash, Responsa 446.
46. Rema, Choshen Mishpat, 34, 4.
47. Tosaphoth to Gittin, 17a. s.q. Mishum.
48. Tur, Yoreh de'ah, 119.
49. Maimonides, Yad, Yesodei Hatorah 7, 7: "For so we are enjoined to decide a matter on the testimony of two witnesses and though it is possible that they are testifying falsely, since to our knowledge they are worthy, we accept their worthiness." Hence, a witness is not sworn in a halachic court. The very need to swear him to tell the truth would render him untrustworthy. See Resp. Rivash, No. 170. Resp. Chatham Sopher, Choshen Mishpat, No. 162. See, however, Choshen Mishpat, 28, 2, and Rema and Commentaries on it, for modern practice in this regard.
50. Pesachim 91a.
51. Zeph. 3, 1.
52. Yoma, 29a.
53. Nazir 23a.
54. Deut. 11, 16.
55. Ezekiel 14, 5.
56. Maim. Yad, Ishuth, 8.5.
57. Ber. 6a.
58. Kidd. 39b.
59. Deut. 30, 10.
60. Regarding those mitzvoth for which the reason is stated in the Torah, it is necessary to ponder the reason stated when performing the mitzvah; Bach to Orach Chayyim 8 and 625, and many authorities.
61. See Rashi to Zeb. 108b top; Sifri to Deut. 13, 6 etc.
62. Eight chapters, chap. 5.

4

The Ethical Structure of the Legal System

Law and Equity

Let us now turn our attention to the ethical structure of halachah. The duality occasioned by the conflict between law and the sense of justice, or the natural feeling for what is right, that has dogged secular systems of law is nonexistent in halachah. In origin, principle, and in application, the halachah, its morality, and its ethical bases are in harmony. "And what great nation is there, that hath statutes and ordinances so righteous as all this law, which I set before you this day?"[1] "Hearken unto Me, ye that know righteousness, the people in whose heart is My law."[2] A halachah divorced from morality or from equity is inconceivable, and no justificatory problem presents itself in halachah.

Misguided Morality

Both the morality and equity of halachah are grounded in the Divine source of halachah. Since these are of suprahuman origin, they do not always or necessarily coincide with what is deemed moral in human eyes. Hence the ethical problem posed, for example, by the law to root out Amalek, which cannot be understood absolutely by the limited vision of the humanitarian or the narrow horizons of human sight. The long perspectives of history have certainly succeeded in throwing much light on the Divine wisdom, but for man the problem is probably insoluble. It is not unreasonable to assume that here, as with certain other problems, it is the finite nature of man's mind that is at fault rather than the canons of Divine morality.

The rabbis highlighted this "conflict" when, with keen insight, they discussed the hesitations of King Saul in fulfilling the command to root out Amalek. They say,[3] When the Holy One, Blessed be He, said to Saul: "go smite Amalek," he (Saul) said (to himself), "if for a single soul in Israel the Torah said,[4] 'Bring a calf and break its neck,' how much more so of all these souls!

"If humans sinned what have the animals done! If grown ups sinned what have the children done!" A heavenly voice came forth and said to him, "Be not righteous overmuch."[5] And when he (Saul) said to Doeg, "Turn, and slay the priests of the Lord,"[6] a heavenly voice came forth and said to him, "Be not overmuch wicked."[7]

The rabbis do not mean to portray only the fickle nature of Saul's moral misgivings.[8] Their remarks embrace the canvas of history, which is replete with examples and the tragic consequences of misguided morality in the guise of generosity of the human spirit.[9]

It is important to appreciate that not only are the general, overriding principles governed by morality but that these same principles affect its detailed application, so that halachah and ethics are coextensive and there is no distinction between what the law is and what it ought to be. This, to the extent that "one who leaves the court, having had his cloak taken from him, goes with a song,"[10] because of his awareness that right as well as justice has been done (Rashi). Grounded in the religious obligation of the individual to seek and to do right in the eyes of God, following the directive of halachah in any instance automatically involves one in doing that which is ethical and righteous.[11]

Silberg[12] brings this point out well when he says that the judge who decides between the parties, informs each one of his duty. "And thou shalt make known to them [i.e., to both of them] the way in which they shall walk and the deed which they must do."[13] He informs the one as to his duty to pay and the other of the amount he is permitted to receive, so that neither transgress "thou shalt not steal" or "thou shalt not rob."

From this perspective of the function of the judge, we may well appreciate why, though the judge enjoys ample discretion in administering halachah, he has no power of clemency and is unable to mitigate sentence when passed. "The court below [i.e., the human court] cannot forgive them,"[14] for "The capital punishment inflicted by the court is independent of our will. The Torah puts him to death."[15]

It also enables us to understand the seeming vacillations of the halachic penal code, characterized by the mingling of divine punishment with punishment inflicted by the courts, or by the coexistence of civil liability "at the hand of heaven," with suit in human courts. It is not the punishment that acts as the deterrent, but the ethical imperative motivating the adherent of halachah. For him, the religious sanction is no wit less than corporal or monetary punishment.

The Quality of Deeds

On the other hand, ethical criteria are so structured into halachah that they are themselves halachoth. A few examples will suffice.

The general duties of showing good manners, kindness, consideration, sympathy, understanding, pity, love, and selflessness toward others are left largely undefined by halachah. These are duties "committed to the heart"[16] and form the bases and background, the depth and quality, of every action involving another individual or society at large. They are, in fact, taken for granted, are by their very nature entirely individual and neither require nor bear hard-and-fast rules. They are the product of a personality reared on and shaped by Torah.

Of such a nature is the general injunction to do "that which is right and good in the sight of the Lord,"[17] which, as explained by Nachmanides,[18] refers literally to observing "the mitzvoth of God and His testimonies, and statutes with the sole intention of doing that which is good and right in His eyes."

Nachmanides continues: "The verse concludes with a promise "so that it will be well with thee," since, when one does that which is good in His eyes, He does well with him because God does well with those who are good and upright in their hearts."

He follows this with an ethical statement with bearing on a broad spectrum of human relations and quotes

> a beautiful exposition of our Sages. They said: "this [viz., doing right and good] refers to compromise and to acting beyond the letter of the law." They mean to teach that first He charged them to observe the statutes and testimonies that He had ordained, whilst

now He refers in addition, to that which was not [expressly] commanded, [saying]: "set your mind upon doing the good and the right in His eyes, for He loves the good and the right." This is of great import because it is impossible to mention in the Torah all the dealings of men with their neighbours and friends, and all one's business contacts and [all matters vital to] improving society and states.[19] But having mentioned many of them, such as, "Thou shalt not go up and down as a talebearer";[20] "Thou shalt not take vengeance, nor bear any grudge";[21] "Neither shalt thou stand idly by the blood of thy neighbour";[22] "Thou shalt not curse the deaf";[23] "Thou shalt rise up before the hoary head"[24] and the like, He reiterates in general form that one is to do the good and the right in *every* instance, so that "compromise" and "acting beyond the letter of the law" fall naturally into this [framework], as for example do the halachoth concerned with neighbours' boundaries.[25] This even includes requirements such as being of unblemished repute[26] and speaking pleasantly with people[27] so that in everything one should be considered wholehearted and upright.

General Ethical Structures

The severity attached to these ethical strictures may be gauged from the declaration of the Talmud:[28] "Jerusalem was only destroyed because they based their judgements upon the [strict] law of the Torah, and did not act beyond the letter of the law." In fact, some Possekim hold that in regard to Mitzvoth between man and his fellow, acting beyond the letter of the law is the law.[29]

"Compromise" and "acting beyond the letter of the law"[30] by no means exhaust the built-in ethical directives of halachah. In fact, when the individual seeks "the way in which he should walk" before God even in purely "religious" matters, the "discussion" between him and the halachah also takes place on the basis of structured ethical considerations, as it does when he is adjudicating with his fellow. Let us turn our attention briefly to some of these.

The Ways of Pleasantness

Based on Proverbs 3, 17, *darchei no'am*, the ways of pleasantness, asserts that the laws of the Torah and the enactments of the Sages were not stated in such fashion that they would oppose the ways of pleasantness and peace. The principle affects such diverse halachoth as the four species of *lulab*[31] and problems of levirate marriage, decisively.[32]

In the Interests of Peace and Goodwill

Darchei shalom, institutions by the Sages in the interests of peace and goodwill, affects the respect due to persons, casting aspersion on others, fiscal matters, and disputes between neighbors and friends as well as with non-Jews.[33]

Adjusting Human Relations

Under the broad heading of *Tikkun ha'olam*, enactments instituted with the object of adjusting human relations, the halachah deals with social, domestic, personal, and business relations, as well as particular religious matters such as the decision to cast lots among the priests in order to determine the rotas for the altar service,[34] forms of prayer,[35] matters pertaining to divorce, theft, property, the hired worker etc. Such institutions are, however, bound by particular rules.[36]

The very function of the courts themselves in a broad spectrum of cases is due, since the cessation of traditional ordination, to the operation of this principle.[37]

Community Enactments

In fiscal and business matters, the Sages introduced many ordinances based on the way the majority of people act and deal with one another.[38] It is on this basis that custom in such areas of activity enjoys the force of law as *hilchoth medinah*.[39] Such market custom is recognized whether instituted by a court, an individual sage, or on the initiative of the residents of a particular area.[40] According to some authorities,[41] such custom becomes effective as law only after achieving recognition by competent halachic authority. The Gaon R. Yechezkel Abramsky sums up this attitude to fiscal and business matters as follows:

> The laws pertaining to fiscal matters in the judgements of Israel were not grounded in classical, social, political or economic outlooks. All the laws codified in the Choshen Mishpat concerning

matters decided and agreed upon between parties of their own free will, are directed only towards examining the intention and will of the parties on the basis of the discussion between them when the matter was concluded. And the law is based upon the recognition of the desire of the parties at the time of agreement.[42]

In regard to the ramified problems of taxation, Rashba[43] emphasizes the fact that "in these matters we do not act in accord with the laws of the Torah but according to the established enactment in each place,"[44] and "the taxation laws vary from place to place according to the circumstances, and we decide in each case in accord with the custom of the place." This position is reiterated successively over the centuries,[45] the custom being considered the halachah.[46] The "custom" referred to is the established usage,[47] and the underlying principles for the acceptance of such usage as law by halachah are, first, the validity of a stipulation in fiscal matters even though it be contrary to Torah[48] and, second, recognition of the fundamental right of a community to regulate its own affairs by decree[49] provided their enactments do not offend basic right or rights.[50] These considerations are, of course, of no avail regarding other than purely fiscal matters and affairs.[51]

Rabbinic Enactment in Modern Israel

The power of halachic enactment in various fields of halachah has assumed distinct importance in modern Israel. The Rabbinate has followed the words of the late Rabbi Kook during the conferences preceding the founding of the Israeli Chief Rabbinate in 1921:

The process of law involves two bases, law and enactment. In the form of law we are unable to change ought . . . but as enactments there is freedom to invent and enact that which the *Batei Din*, with the accord of the majority, acting for the sake of heaven, find to be for the general good. The Sages of every generation enacted many great things. . . .[52] Within the framework of our renewed national life in Eretz Yisrael there will certainly arise at times urgent need to promulgate important enactments, which, so long as they are agreed upon by the majority of the expert Sages of Israel, and later accepted by the community, will have the force of the law of the Torah.[53]

The Rabbinate has enacted a number of such *Takkanoth*.[54] These affect the establishment of a Rabbinic Court of Appeals, adoption, child marriage, maintenance, and other spheres.

There are numerous problems in the way of such enactments, and the power is neither lightly granted nor easily used. In the words of the late Chief Rabbi Isaac Herzog:[55]

> Powers are granted to the Beth Din of every generation, certainly to a kingdom of Israel, to fine and to punish, even on the basis of strong presumption alone, so to shatter the arm of wickedness and close the door before those who do wrong, and to establish that which is written: the king establishes the realm with justice . . . thus acted all the *Batei Din* in Israel, according to the situation of their generation. . . . But the institution of enactments is handed over to the ordained Sages of the Torah, *Gedolei HaTorah* and *Pessak*, who know how to preserve the limits and conditions, and who will not enact any decree unless it be right and reasoned in accord with the religion and opinion of Torah.

In another article,[56] Rabbi Herzog distinguishes between (1) religious and civil law regarding enactments and (2) new and complementary enactments:

> With regards religious law we are powerless to enact anything contrary to the Talmud and *Possekim*. . . . Obviously, in every case it is within our power to deliberate on the basis of the existing legal material, and this we do, so that in certain cases we arrive at a lenient conclusion though at first sight it would appear that we ought to have decided stringently. *But this is not by virtue of enactment.* It is the result of penetrating understanding of the sources and determination of the exact facts of the case. This is not so with regards civil law in which we may, within limitations, promulgate enactments.

In regard to new and complementary enactments, he says, "We do not only require enactments in the field of Civil law, but also complementary enactments. Enactments that will complement, due to the changes in the economic, business and industrial machine, the kernels that already exist in the Chosen Mishpat . . . but which require development."

Temporary Legislation

The Beth Din did not hesitate to use drastic "emergency" powers —
Hora'ath sha'ah, temporary legislation — when this was considered
warranted either to set wrong aright or by the exigencies of
the moment.[57]

A poignant example of setting wrong aright is recorded in the
Mishnah. The case involved the sacrifice of birds required to be
brought by a woman after childbirth. In some instances she is
obliged to bring several such, and the Mishnah records that
during the time of Rabban Shimon ben Gamaliel, traders took
advantage of this to raise the price of doves.[58] The Mishna
records:[59]

> Once in Jerusalem a pair of doves cost a golden dinar.[60] Rabban
> Shimon ben Gamaliel said: "By this Temple, I will not suffer the
> night to pass before they cost but a silver dinar." He went into the
> court and taught: if a woman suffered five miscarriages that were
> not in doubt, she need bring but one offering, and she may then
> eat of sacrifices, and she is not bound to bring the other offerings
> [for the remaining four cases]. The same day the price of a pair of
> doves stood at a quarter dinar each.

Rabban Shimon's action, though not without scriptural base,
was against the law, but he relied on the power of the court to
enact special temporary legislation when necessary.[61]

Hora'ath sha'ah is not a power granted only to the prophet;[62] it is
also within the compass of authority of the Beth Din.[63] Meiri, in
his commentary to Sanhedrin[64] when discussing the statement
of the Talmud[65] to the effect that "we seat in the Sanhedrin only
one who knows how to render the reptile [unclean according to
the Torah] clean by bringing proof from the Torah," says:

> It seems to me that this statement means that if they [the members
> of the court] become aware of the spread of offences against a law
> of the Torah in their time, they may enact new laws, or add or
> subtract as a temporary measure, so long as they bring some
> indication for their deed from the words of the Torah. Similarly,
> the Geonim write concerning the laws of the Talmud, that Rabbis
> or Geonim have the authority, on but scant grounds, to make
> general or specific innovative decrees and institutions in order to
> do away with unseemly practice that may be evident in their
> times. In such matters, the great commentators write that the

Talmud was given only to those possessed of the expert tradition, or to those endowed with correct reasoning and the ability to weigh clearly. A curtain is however drawn [in regard to this matter] before most people. Only one who is outstanding in his generation as to knowledge, erudition, correct dialectic, and is of settled mind, is fit for it."

Granted the conditions as to the personality of one who is enabled to employ *hor'ath sha'ah*, there are further factors governing its use.

A responsum of Hai Gaon[66] limits the authority to employ *hora'ath sha'ah* to that which is of public concern,[67] but not if the unseemly matter is affected and remains within the province of the individual. Ri Migash[68] holds, however, that such action is also possible in the case of the inveterate wrongdoer, while, if there is a possibility that others will learn from or be influenced by his example, the authorities[69] agree that extraordinary measures may be taken against him.[70]

The most crucial factor in connection with the employment of this instrument is as stressed by Maimonides[71] that this is indeed temporary legislation only. It cannot determine the halachah for generations since, were it to be of permanent nature, the prohibitions "Thou shalt not add thereto, nor diminish therefrom"[72] would be infringed.

The Mental Milieu of the Posseck

There are many more ethical principles structured into halachah; for example, the doctrine that "the Torah had pity on the money of Israel."[73] Nevertheless, it is important to bear in mind that many halachic decisions, in widely dispersed fields, are based on unarticulated ethical premises that are hidden from sight by logical and legal form. Many ethical doctrines of wide importance are found in no express enactment or halachic opinion, yet they form the mental milieu of the *possek*.

Suffering to Animals

The halachah is that the duty to avoid causing suffering to living things is Biblical.[74] The Midrash[75] says, "Just as God shows mercy to man, so too has He shown mercy to cattle . . . and in the same way that God had compassion upon the cattle, so too was God filled with mercy for birds."[76]

Harm to Humans

It is certainly so of avoiding bringing suffering or harm on a fellow human being. Rabbi Z. H. Chajes points out:[77]

> No action could be traced to the Torah which could cause even the slightest injury to the individual, still less to the community. Many legal decisions and definitive halachoth were formulated by virtue of this principle.[78] This is so even in connection with the death penalty for criminals, the severity of which towards transgressors is held to be an act of mercy to the world at large.[79] Yet, even in reference to this type of punishment, the Rabbis have deduced from the passage: "Thou shalt love thy neighbour as thyself,"[80] known by them as the great positive principle in the Torah, that we are to choose an easy death for the condemned,[81] and wherever the Rabbis were in doubt as to the kind of penalty to be imposed [upon the guilty] they deduced from the said passage that it is the court's obligation to reduce it to a minimum and, in the case of the death penalty to choose the easiest and least humiliating death.[82]

Capital Punishment

It must further be pointed out in this context that though capital punishment is prescribed in the Torah for so many infringements, it is recorded that in practice this penalty was so rarely prescribed that a court that in fact inflicted it even as rarely as once in seven years[83] is termed "murderous."[84]

This fact is certainly not due, as some writers have held, to opposition on the part of the rabbis to capital punishment. "Do not say: since the man is already dead, why should we punish murder with murder."[85] And again, "The judges shall not argue: the victim is dead already, what profit will accrue from killing another? But the murderer must be executed."[86] "And all the mitzvoth which he [the murderer] did during his life are of no weight before this sin, and they will not save him from judgement";[87] "[f]or mercy upon such sinners is cruelty to people."[88]

Rather is it due to the inherent spirit of halachah that, on the one hand, stressed the gravity of the infringement by declaring the extreme penalty, while at the same time it tempered usage[89] by means of a legal framework that tended to render the threat innocuous in all but the most extreme of cases[90] because of both the possibility of human error and the irreversibility of the punishment once executed. This did not, however, mean that capital punishment was placed in abeyance. On the contrary, in the public interest,[91] on circumstantial evidence alone,[92] and even in purely religious matters,[93] it was occasionally employed until late in the Middle Ages. There is no hint in halachah of the humanist arguments for the abolition of capital punishment.[94]

The Individual and General Good

The remarks of Chajes with respect to injury to the individual do not mean that the individual will not at times feel disgruntled, or think that he has been wronged, or consider that in the particular instance the halachah has failed to recognize and regard "his good" as he sees it. Maimonides[95] points out that since the law is in the first instance directed toward the general good, it is impossible for it not to ignore that injury might be caused to the individual in its application. In the light of his words, it seems that in such circumstances the individual must discover his personal "good" in the greater good of the community. He cannot expect his personal needs to be given precedence.

Certainly, nothing in the Torah can be detrimental to man's spiritual well-being. "And I am of the opinion," writes Rabbenu Nissim,[96] "that it is impossible for there to be any kind of loss to the soul from that which is decided by the Sanhedrin." As the Talmud itself exclaims,[97] "Now if the Holy One Blessed be He, does not bring any harm even by the animals of the righteous, by the righteous themselves how much more so!"

The words of Rabbenu Nissim are in no sense to be construed as implying a kind of infallibility to the Sanhedrin. In Leviticus, chapter 4, they are the first to be taken to task for their errors. He means simply that Chazal, in conforming to halachah, could not in the very nature of things bring about spiritual harm in society. Second, that in following the directive of the Sanhedrin, with whom the Torah reposes for interpretation and application, no spiritual harm can accrue to one who carries out their words even if it should so happen that they have erred.[98]

Chaim ben Attar[99] explains that the reason the Torah adds the words "And show thee mercy, and have compassion upon thee, and multiply thee, as He hath sworn unto thy fathers,"[100] in lieu of fulfillment of the mitzvah to destroy the idolatrous city, is because

> such a deed would naturally give rise to an element of cruelty in man's heart. . . . He therefore promises to bestow upon them the quality of mercy. And though naturally the deed should result in making them cruel, the Source of mercy will influence them with a renewed power of mercy to counteract and void the strength of the element of cruelty resulting from the deed.

The Sanctity of Human Life

The sanctity of human life in halachah is paramount, and all is put aside in deference to it.[101] The source of the law regarding *pikuach nephesh* is "Ye shall keep My statutes and Mine ordinances, which man shall do and live by them,"[102] to which the Talmud comments,[103] "shall live by them but not die because of them."

The Gemmara there quotes a Baraitha to the effect that "one who is zealous in this (i.e., in saving life) is praiseworthy whilst he who enquires is a murderer," meaning that in cases of *pikuach nephesh,* one must immediately react and not waste precious time with unnecessary queries,[104] so that Maimonides, in relation to the sabbath (and this is obviously so of other instances as well), frames the halachah as follows:[105] "It is forbidden to hesitate[106] in breaking the sabbath for a dangerously ill person, for it is written: "And live by them, and not die by them." Hence, you learn that the ordinances of the Torah are not vengeance but mercy, loving kindness, and peace for the world. And of those free thinkers who consider this desecration of the sabbath and forbidden, the verse says,[107] "Wherefore I gave them also statutes that were not good, and ordinances whereby they should not live."

A further source for the directive to set everything aside when faced with *pikuach nephesh* is deduced by the Talmud[108] from the verse[109] "Wherefore the Children of Israel shall keep the sabbath, to observe the sabbath throughout their generations"; said the Torah, "[D]esecrate for him one sabbath so that he will observe many sabbaths."[110]

The entire concept of *pikuach nephesh* was expressed beautifully by R. Tanchum of Noi when he said, "A lamp is called a lamp, and the soul of man is called a lamp. It is better for the lamp kindled by man to be extinguished [on the sabbath for one dangerously ill], rather than the lamp kindled by the Holy One, Blessed be He."[111]

Halachah does not only stress the saving of another's life, even against his will,[112] but also the care and respect that one must show toward one's own life. One is forbidden to place oneself in any kind of unnecessary danger or risk,[113] to injure or to debase[114] oneself.[115]

Life and limb are given in trust, and they may be taken only by He who gave them.[116] Man is not the ultimate master of himself. Halachah disagrees thoroughly with the assertion (and its implications) of John Stuart Mill[117] that "[t]he only part of the conduct of anyone, for which he is amenable to society, is that which concerns others. In the part which merely concerns himself, his independence is of right absolute. Over himself, over his own body and mind, the individual is sovereign."

Together with the prophet Ezekeil, halachah asserts "all souls are Mine,"[118] and, though one may beseech God to take his soul, as did the prophet Jonah,[119] he may do nothing to bring about his demise.[120]

Life is a sacred gift to be used and not to be destroyed. The appreciation of the sanctity of life leads to the appreciation of the dignity of the human being, to integrity, and to living in such manner as the verse "And thou shalt love thy neighbour as thyself" dictates. As Hillel said,[121] this is not an abstract injunction to love, which cannot be commanded; it refers to living and doing for others, for those to whom one should bear the love that can only result from selflessness on their behalf. "Do not do unto others that which is hateful unto yourself, this is the whole Torah," for the rest is learning what is to be done and how to do it.

When Life Becomes Ethically Meaningless— *Kiddush Hashem*

In the previous section, we stressed the uncompromising attitude of halachah to the sanctity of human life and its preservation. With equally uncompromising equanimity, halachah faces the problem as to when life is to be given up rather than supported, since continued preservation would negate the very ideals for which life was given.

Halachah defines the exact point beyond which life becomes ethically meaningless and intolerable and is hence to be forfeited by the individual.

The heart searching, pain, and suffering surrounding this problem are evident throughout the Responsa literature that deals with the many practical queries presented to the *Gedolei Hador* for decision. It must ever be borne in mind that these questions, posed with various intensity throughout Israel's long and tortuous history, were practical problems, the answer to which was acted on. The respondent could not and did not avoid the tragic decisions imposed on him by cruel circumstance, and Israel, loyal to God and to Torah, accepted proudly the sacrifice of *Kiddush Hashem*.

It is difficult for our generation to imagine the heroism required for such loyalty. We appreciate such heroism as that performed on the battlefield in wars supposedly engaged in for idealistic purposes, but that such demands should be part of regular existence is almost unfathomable by our minds. We saw it during the holocaust and try to shut it out, but, though there were times and climes where the readiness for *Kiddush Hashem* was less evident than others,[122] it remains an inescapable fact and factor of Jewish history.

Kiddush Hashem embraces the fundamental strata of the Jewish soul that sees God, the eternity of the soul, the transient nature of this world, and man's task to serve Him as the basis of human existence. A soul so imbued, from infancy, accepted voluntarily the supreme sacrifice entailed in "With regards every transgression of the Torah if they said to one: 'transgress and do not be killed,' he should transgress and not allow himself to be killed; except for idolatry, immorality[123] and murder."[124]

Transgression of these, though under duress, involves denial of the root of existence and as such forms the boundary of human life.

Kiddush Hashem within the Framework of Statehood

Kiddush Hashem has acquired a broader halachic, practical dimension with statehood. For, in addition to the three cardinal sins,

situations calling for self-sacrifice by the individual, as opposed
to an actual combat situation, are manifold. Consider for a moment the lot of Eli Cohen, "Our Man in Damascus,"[125] or the
problem faced by the Israeli government as to whether to trade
terrorists for lives held prisoner in Uganda[126] or in a school in
Ma'aloth. What of Israel's prisoners of war dying under torture,
and how indeed are we to view the suicide at Massada?

There are many halachic problems involved, but they stem in
these instances from the relation of the individual to his people
and his responsibilities toward them. It is a dimension of *Kiddush
Hashem* grounded in statehood, in a sense of collective responsibility[127] as contrasted with the responsibility of the individual
conscience before God. It has been very much in evidence since
the rebirth of the state of Israel. "And he shall live by them,"[128] so
long applied primarily to the individual, has, with statehood,
become reinvested with its corporate nature.

Chief Rabbi Goren, in a radio broadcast,[129] stressed this when,
in discussing *Kiddush Hashem* today, he remarked that, in the
main, the possekim refer to situations in which the problem
faced is the life of one individual as opposed to the life of another
individual.[130] They do not refer to the context of a continuous
state of war waged unremittingly against the state or people
of Israel.

In stating the criteria for self-sacrifice within this context to be
"opposing the intent to harm the people or the state and its
instruments," Rabbi Goren analyzed the problem of Entebbe in
the hypothetical instance of there having been no Jew aboard the
hijacked plane, and he said that even in such an instance, since
the purpose of the terrorists was to bring pressure on Israel,
Kiddush Hashem is involved, since this is part of the unremitting
war being waged against the people and the state.

Medicine, Doctor, and Patient

We cannot conclude this chapter without noting a further practical
and vital field of halachah in connection with human life.

While the healing art is not only sanctioned but made obligatory
on those able and competent to practice it, halachah has much to
say both to the doctor and surgeon as well as to the patient.[131]
While the doctor may not refrain from practicing medicine out of
fear that he may cause harm to the patient,[132] nor may the patient

refuse medical or surgical aid deemed necessary by competent medical opinion,[133] halachah does not abandon the many ethical problems that arise in medical practice to the conscience of the physician.[134] Both doctor and patient are bound by halachah, which alone decides as to the ethic of particular practice.

We have already mentioned the sacrosanct nature of life as well as the fact that the human being is not the "master" of his body. These basic principles govern the halachoth concerning such pressing ethical problems as birth control, abortion, euthanasia, heart transplants, experimentation on humans, the volunteering of one's body for medical, scientific research, as well as a host of questions of lesser weight.[135]

Halachah safeguards the integrity as well as the sanctity of human life and dignity in spite of the individual, and at the same time it sets the bounds that may alone be considered legitimate medical practice. By judging medical practice against the yard stick of absolute standards of morality and human worth, it ensures that life is not forfeited or prevented by the whim and fancy of either a self-centered, fickle society or the burning desire for medical progress at all costs.

In spite of the towering achievement of heart transplantation, halachah was not blind to the fact that in performing these transplants, "donors" forfeited moments of their lives at the hands of the surgeons performing the operations. By what moral or ethical criterion did the surgeons decide that A's life could be shortened in order to prolong that of B? In a survey conducted among leading heart specialists throughout the world, many of them in fact communicated to me their misgivings, stating that they were seriously perturbed in the matter since reliable criteria of death were not available and heart transplants in fact involved the shortening of the life of the donor, who was in most cases not a donor in any real, voluntary sense but was merely dubbed as one by the operating surgeon or hospital staff.

Moments of Life

Halachah rightly insists that the human being is unable to differentiate between years and moments of life. Life is an indivisible entity beyond scaling in terms of human values. Once the human being designates to himself the ability to weigh and to fragment it into meaningful, worthwhile and less meaningful and less worthwhile segments, there remains no objective value to life at all. Without objective value, all restraint is removed, and humans may do unto humans as they see fit. This generation has witnessed the tragic consequences of such an attitude. Can *scientific* progress be justified at such a cost? We ought never to forget that the experiments conducted on human beings by the Nazis were perfectly valid *scientific* experiments!

Like considerations affect the problems of both euthanasia and abortion. The distinction between the two is only in the degree of "taking life" that is involved,[136] but there is no difference in principle. Particular halachic criteria afford recognition for the legitimacy of abortion in certain circumstances, but these must be determined by competent halachic authority dealing with the individual case; euthanasia not at all.[137] In no case is the matter left in the hands of the doctor or the parents themselves. The argument that a woman enjoys right absolute over her body and may hence decide for an abortion is totally rejected by halachah, which declares, "All souls are mine."[138]

Questions such as the standard of living, economic circumstances, and the like, which figure largely in parents' considerations, play no part at all in the halachic decision. The infinite value of life is only degraded when weighed or considered against a background of selfish, or even not so selfish, desire and convenience.

Who can say that his needs are more important than another's life? If one is obliged to forfeit his life rather than take that of another, can material[139] considerations sway halachah even to consider preventing life?[140]

We would do well to ponder the words of the *Zohar*[141] that, when describing the virtues that sustained the people in Egypt and rendered them worthy of redemption, states, "[T]hough it was decreed that every son born be cast into the river, there was none among them who killed a fetus in the womb of a woman."

Notes to Chapter Four

1. Deut. 4, 8.
2. Isa. 51, 7.
3. Yalkut Shimoni, to 1 Samuel, No. 120.
4. Deut. chap. 21, 1–9.
5. Eccl. 7, 16.

6. 1 Sam. 22, 17.
7. Eccl. *ibid.*, 17.
8. Cf. also Bamidbar Rabbah, 21, 5, concerning David and Channan ben Nachash.
9. We may note that the halachah also decried overrighteousness in more general and everyday affairs. For example, basing himself on Arakh. 23b. the Sepher Chassidim, No. 397, says, "One who owes money to others and has none of his own should not buy books, nor give charity, nor hire scribes nor present candles to the Synagogue. Of this the verse declares: 'I hate robbery with the burnt offering (Isai. 61, 8).' " The translation is based on the play of words occasioned by *ba'avlah* – with iniquity – and *ba'olah* – with the burnt offering, found in the Talmud. See also Maim. Yad, De'oth 5, 12.
10. San. 7a.
11. Vide supra beginning chap. 3.
12. *Loc. cit.*, p. 53.
13. Ex. 18, 20.
14. Makk. 13b,
15. Maimonides, Commentary to the Mishnah, Arrakh. 1,3. Maimonides points out there, however, that if one is liable to capital punishment by royal decree, the king may grant amnesty if he wishes. The only analogous institution to granting amnesty known to Jewish law, may, I think, be found in the return of the unintentional murderer from the city of refuge on the death of the High Priest, Nos. 35, 28. The parents of the rebellious son, Deut. chap. 21, may forgive him, Sot. 25a. But the Sanhedrin may not act with clemency toward the rebellious elder, for this would result in the increase of contention in Israel; *ibid.*
16. B.M. 58b., etc.
17. Deut. 6, 18.
18. Commentary *ad loc.*
19. I wonder how serious R. Jair Chaim Bachrach, Chavoth Jair No. 192, was when in commenting on the Talmudic statement, Erub. 21b – "Perchance you might think that if the words of the scribes have substance they ought to have been committed to writing? Hence the verse, Eccl. 12, 12, says: Of making many books there is no end, i.e. it is impossible to write them all down, Rashi" – he says, "This is questionable. Is the hand of God short that it cannot write a book like that of Maimon [the Yad HaChazzakah] in which all the Mitzvoth of God and their details are included!"
20. Levit. 19, 16.
21. *Ibid.*, 18.
22. *Ibid.*, 16. Without delving into the ramifications of this verse, we shall quote the text of the Shulchan Aruch on the verse in order to illustrate how varied in practice are its detailed applications. This is, of course, also true of the other verses quoted so cryptically by Nachmanides. The Shulchan Aruch, Choshen Mishpat, 426, says, "One who sees his fellow drowning in the sea, or being attacked by robbers, or wild beasts, and he is able to personally save him, or hire others to save him, but does not; or if he heard that a non-Jew or an informer was planning to do him harm, or an informer was planning to do him harm, or was preparing a trap for him and he failed to

reveal this to his fellow; or if he knew that non-Jews or violent people were about to come upon his fellow, and he was able to dissuade them and change their intentions toward his fellow but did not, and like instances, has transgressed 'neither shalt thou stand idly by the blood of thy neighbor.' " The extensions are obviously legion and they are all "committed to the heart"! See also infra, this chap. note 132.

23. Levit. *ibid.*, 14.
24. *Ibid.*, 32.
25. B.M. 108a.
26. Taan. 16b.
27. Yoma 86a.
28. B.M. 30b.
29. See Yalkut HaGershuni on Liphnim Mishurath HaDin.
30. I.e., doing more than the law demands, but in no sense abrogating it; see chap. 3 supra, note 22.
31. "The Torah could not have intended *kufra* as the *lulab* since this plant is spiky and lacerates the hands, and its ways are the ways of pleasantness"; Succ. 32a, and commentaries thereon.
32. See *Encyclopedia Talmudith,* Vol. 7, pp. 712–715.
33. See *ibid.,* pp. 716–723.
34. Yoma 22a.
35. Sot. 32b.
36. See B.K. 49b; 96a; 110; B.M. 5b; Ket. 3b; etc.
37. See Choshen Mishpat, 1, and commentaries thereon.
38. See S. Albek, *Dinei Mammonoth BeTalmud* (Devir, 1976), Introduction, pp. 47 ff., and note 68.
39. B.M. 93a.
40. Responsa Rashba, Pt. 2, No. 268.
41. Mordechai to B.M. chap. 4, Halachah 18; Responsa, Chacham Zevi, No. 61.
42. Kontress Dinei Mammonoth, chaps. 4 and 2. Cf. also the remarks of Z. H. Chajes, *Introduction to the Talmud,* ch. 15, (Shechter's ed. p. 119). Cf. also Maggid Mishnah, Hilchoth Shechenim, end.
43. Responsa, Pt. 3, No. 398.
44. *Ibid.,* No. 412.
45. See Responsa, Mahrashdam, Choshen Mishpat, No. 398, etc.
46. Noda Biyehuda, Tinyanna, Choshen Mishpat, No. 40.
47. Responsa, Hithoreruth Teshuvah, Pt. 2, No. 44, section 1. Also Chacham Zevi, No. 61, end. See also Rema, chap. M., 331, 1, on the meaning of "established usage."
48. Kidd. 19b; B.M. 51a. etc., and all codes.
49. Responsa, Ribash, No. 399; Tashbatz, 159. See Aruch Hashulchan, Choshen Mishpat, 2, 3.
50. Rashba, Responsa Pt. 5., No. 178; Asheri, Responsa, 55, 10, Mahri Weil, No. 133.
51. See Chatham Sopher, Responsa, Yoreh De'ah, No. 13, at length.
52. An interesting historical enactment, reiterated successively and incorporated by many Kehilloth, refers to the virtual "outlawing" of child labor and exploitation. See Moshe Fiendling, Techukath Ha'Avodah, Jerusalem, 1945,

pp. 86–87. This, long before such enlightened legislation was undertaken in Western Europe.

53. Quoted by Menachem Alon, Hachekikah Hadathith (Tel Aviv, 5728), p. 158.

54. See Alon, *ibid.*, pp. 159–169.

55. Quoted by Rabbi E.Y. Waldenberg, Hilchoth Medinah, Pt. 1, p. 261.

56. "Legislation and Law in the Jewish State," in Yavneh, *Religious Academic Journal*, 1949.

57. See Tosaphoth to Nazir 43b, s.q. Vehai, end.

58. One who arbitrarily raises prices or engages in price fixing to the detriment of the community is called a *rusha*, Meg. 17b. He transgresses the verse: "And your brother shall live with you," which means that one must *enable* his brother to live with him; Meirath Einaim to Choshen Mishpat, 231, 25, note 43.

59. Kerit, 1, 7.

60. Equivalent to twenty-five silver dinars.

61. See the commentaries *ad loc.* Cf. Ket. 15a. bottom and Rashi thereon.

62. For the details with regard to a prophet, see Yad, Yesodei HaTorah, 9, 3, and infra chap. 6 of the present study.

63. Tosaphoth to Sanh. 89b s.q. Elijah; supra note 57; and Yad, Mamrim 2, 4.

64. End of chap. 1.

65. Sanh. 17a.

66. Quoted in Tur, Choshen Mishpat, 425

67. This seems also to be the opinion of Maimonides; see, Yad, Mamrim 2, 4.

68. Responsa No. 161; also Mahram of Lublin, Responsa No. 138.

69. Sema to Choshen Mishpat 2, note 3; Shach there, note 2, and Thumim there, note 4.

70. Cf. also Rema to Choshen Mishpat 35, 14 to the effect that regarding quarrels and injuries arising from them, or slanderous and scurrilous bickering and talk, we do not need to follow the rules of evidence in order to establish the facts.

71. Yad, Sanh. 24, 4; Mamrim 2, 4.

72. Deut. 13, 1.

73. R.H. 27a. See *Encyclopedia Talmudith*, Vol. 11, pp. 240–245, on this principle. On the related considerations of the amount of loss involved, see *ibid.* Vol. 10, pp. 32–41.

74. Rema to Choshen Mishpat 272, 9. See Responsa, Mahri Assad, Y.D. No. 164, at length. Minchath Chinuch, and Mahram Shick to Mitzvah 80.

75. Devarim Rabbah 6, 1.

76. On the basis of this comparison, Birchei Joseph to Chosen Mishpat 7, note 35, states that it is forbidden to appoint two persons of differing temperament to work together since "even with animals the Torah was careful to avoid distressing them and said, "Thou shalt not plough with an ox and an ass together, Deut. 22, 10."

77. *The Student's Guide through the Talmud*, translated by Jacob Shechter (London: East and West Library, 1952), p. 131.

78. Thus Chazal declared, A.Z. 31a. "We do not decree anything upon the community unless the majority of the community is able to uphold and accept it."

79. See Yad, San. 11, 5.
80. Lev. 19, 19.
81. Torath Cohanim to Levit. 19, 19.
82. San. 45a; 52a.
83. According to some, once in seventy years.
84. Mishna, Makk. 1, 10.
85. Sifri to Deut. 19, 13.
86. Yad, Sanh. 20, 4.
87. *Ibid.*, Rozeach 4, 9.
88. Moreh Nebuchim, Pt. 3, chap. 39.
89. But did not actually abolish capital punishment, which did not in fact cease to be practiced in isolated instances until late in the Middle Ages. See Responsa, Asheri, 17 No. 8; 21 No. 9; Judah Asheri, 75; 58, especially in Spain—"It is normal practice in the cities of the west, to put to death [the censored text reads: to punish] . . . Maim. Yad. Hobel Umazzik 8, 11."
90. The same is true of the laws concerning the rebellious son. Deut. 21, 18–21; and of the city that served idolatry; *ibid.*, 13, 13–19; the laws concerning which were never carried out, San. 71a, and they were written only so that "one would expound Torah and thereby earn reward"; *ibid.* The Talmud there explains that the law of the rebellious son is an instance of sentencing the son because of what will ultimately become of him. Though such sentencing was never carried out in practice, it does, however, find a practical echo in the laws pertaining to *Rodeph,* one who pursues with the intent of committing murder, who may be prevented even at the cost of his, the pursuer's life, Ber. 58a, etc. During the Middle Ages, the *massur,* the informer who delivered Jews or their property into the hands of the government, was considered a *rodeph* and was occasionally sentenced for his intention to inform. The law that "whoever kills him first has earned merit" being applied to him, see Ribash, Responsa 239, and others. In regard to the idolatrous city, some authorities hold that this was the case with Sodom, hence the extreme punishment meted out there; see R. Joseph Rozin VeToratho, Samuel Kreutzer, in *Zaphenath Pa'ane'ach* (Jerusalem, 1967), p. 4. It seems to me that the law to destroy a town that does not provide educational facilities for its children, Sabb. 119b. and Rashi ad loc. falls under the category of the rebellious son, the severity of the law obviously considers what will eventually become of such a town, but it was probably not actually acted on. Maimonides, Yad, Talmud Torah, 2, 1 understands the Talmudic text differently from Rashi.
91. Maimonides, Sanh. 24, 4.
92. Tur, Choshen Mishpat, 2.
93. San. 46a; Tur, 425, on the authority of Hai Gaon.
94. The late Chief Rabbi Isaac Herzog in *Legislation and Law in the Jewish State,* bases his objection to capital punishment in the state of Israel on solely halachic grounds.
95. Guide, Pt. 3, chap. 34.
96. Derashoth, Derashah 11.
97. Yeb. 99b; Ket. 28b; Hull. 5b.
98. See, e.g., Tosaphoth to Sabb. 4a s.q. Kodem, etc.

99. Commentary Or Hachayim to Deut. 13, 18.

100. Deut. 13, 18.

101. The concepts of *pikuach nephesh* are exceptionally broad, and they have received extension and depth with reference to life in present-day Israel. See the relevant articles by the late Chief Rabbi Herzog and others in *HaTorah VeHamedinah*, Vols. 1–14; Responsa, Saul Israeli, Amud Hayemini, no. 17 etc.

102. Lev. 18, 5.

103. Yoma 85.

104. Ritzba, in a responsum quoted by Or Zarua, holds that this is entirely dependent on the circumstances, and there are obviously many occasions when a *she'elath chacham* is necessary. Ritba, ad loc., has the reading in the Talmud, "And one who is asked ought to be ashamed." He explains that the one asked is the teacher of halachoth, and he ought to be ashamed at not having taught the laws of *pikuach nephesh* thoroughly to his flock so that they would have no need to waste time asking questions when occasion arises.

105. Yad, Sabb. 2, 3.

106. For this reason all that has to be done is to be done by *Gedolei Yisrael*, who fully understand that *pikuach nephesh* is a mitzvah, and they will not have the hesitations of an ignorant person who might possibly think to himself that he is transgressing the Sabbath by doing what has to be done. See the commentaries ad loc. The force of Maimonides' argument was brought home to me when, on visiting soldiers wounded during the Yom Kippur War, I came across several who were convinced that they would not recover since they had "desecrated" Yom Kippur by fighting!

107. Ezek. 20, 25.

108. Yoma *ibid.*

109. Ex. 31, 2.

110. The *possekim* explain the differences between the two sources. See, e.g., Ramban, *Torath Ha'adam*, ed. Chavell, p. 29. She'iltoth, Ha'amek She'elah, Bereshith no. 8, etc. It is, however, interesting to note that Maimonides employs this source with regard to the powers of the *Beth Din* to enact a *Hora'ath Sha'ah* in a "sick" society. He says, Yad, Mamrim 2, 4, "Similarly, if they thought fit to temporarily suspend a positive commandment, or to transgress a prohibition in order to bring back many to religion, or to save many of Israel from stumbling in other things, they may act in accord with the need of the hour. In the same way as a doctor cuts off a hand or a foot so that he may live, so *Beth Din* instruct, when necessary, to transgress some of the mitzvoth temporarily so that they should all be preserved. This, as the former Sages said: desecrate for him one Sabbath so that he may observe many Sabbaths." Cf. our remarks on *hora'ath sha'ah* supra, in this chapter. See the Responsa of the late Rabbi Y. I. Weinberg, Seridei Esh (Jerusalem, 1962), Pt. 2, No. 8, for a practical application of this theme.

111. Sabb. 30b.

112. I.e., one is in duty bound to prevent another from committing suicide. Sifri to Deut. 22, 2 Piska 223, translates the verse: "You must restore him to himself." See also San. 73a. Maharam of Rothenburg, Responsa No. 39,

states expressly that one is so bound even though the one in danger shouts "do not save me." See, Kelei Chemdah to Ki Tzetze, Section 6, at length.

113. Choshen Mishpat, 427. But when the risk is in order to save another, one should not be overscrupulous or overcautious out of consideration for one's own safety; Mishnah Berurah, 329, note 19. See also Pitchei Teshuvah to Yoreh De'ah 252, note 1, and infra in this chapter.

114. Halachah insists that even verbal self-abasement is forbidden; hence we learn, Sheb. 36a, that even one who curses himself transgresses a prohibition.

115. Or one's wife. Making one's wife foolish in the eyes of others provides her with legitimate grounds for divorce; Ket. 77a.

116. One is not allowed to take his life even when in danger of losing his life in any event, Yam Shel Shelomoh, B.K. chap. 8, Siman 58. If, however, one is afraid that because of torture one will be forced to sin, one is allowed to take his life; Tosaphoth to A.Z. 18 a.s.q. Ve'al. But see Shach to Y.D. 157 note 1, where two opinions are quoted on this. See also Shevuth Ya'acob, quoted *ibid.*, Pitchei Teshuvah, note 8.

117. *On Liberty* (Gateway, 1955), p. 13. The premises of Mill's contention to the effect that one's personal actions are unlimited and are to be unhampered unless they cause harm to others are hardly tenable in modern society. The state's interference cannot in practice be confined merely to conduct that is, in Mills's words, "calculated to produce evil in someone else."

118. Ezek. 18, 4. See, Ridbaz to Yad, San. 18, 6 and Maimonides Rotze'ach 1, 4.

119. Though one may do nothing to bring near the end, one may in fact pray for the demise of one who is suffering unbearably and seems beyond hope; Aruch Hashulchan to Yoreh De'ah, 355, 3.

120. Maimonides, Yad, Yesodei HaTorah 5, 4, considers even one who allows himself to be killed rather than transgress a mitzvah for which *Kiddush Hashem* is not enjoined, as liable for his soul. But see Kesseph Mishneh ad loc., and Rabbenu Nissim to Alfasi, Sabb. 49a, where this view is expressly refuted. This subject is comprehensively treated by Chief Rabbi Obadaiah Joseph in Yabia Omer, Responsa, Pt. 6, Sect. Yoreh De'ah No. 13, pp. 181–189. He quotes there the opinion of Nachmanides, Milchamoth, San. 74a, who, in agreeing with Maimonides, holds that one who so allows himself to be put to death, transgresses: "And surely your blood for your lives will I require (Gen. 9, 5)" and claims that we do not find that it is considered pious for one to refuse medical aid on the Sabbath. Other authorities, Tosaphoth, Asheri, Meiri, etc., hold, however, that *Kiddush Hashem* is by its very nature to be differentiated from other mitzvoth, and the normal criteria of *pikuach nephesh* do not apply to it. This is obviously so also of war, when the normal considerations governing *pikuach nephesh* cannot be applied and one is obliged to lay down one's life in circumstances that in peacetime contexts would be forbidden.

121. Sabb. 31a.

122. See the remarks of S. B. Urbach, *Pillars of Jewish Thought*, Pt. 3, p. 15.

123. I.e., the forbidden sexual relations enumerated in Leviticus chaps. 18 and 20.

124. San. 74a.

125. On the problem of fulfilling mitzvoth by a spy, the Talmud itself seems most emphatic; he is free from all religious obligations since discovery would certainly lead to his death. The Talmud records, Taan. 22a. "Why have you no *tzitzith*, and why do you wear black shoes [as is the custom of the non-Jews]? I come and go among the non-Jews, so that they will not realize that I am Jewish, and when they enact decrees, I inform the Rabbis. Such a one, said Elijah, is a son of the world to come." He obviously did not fail to observe only the mitzvah of *tzitzith*. Cf. also with regard to R. Reuben b. Istrabuli, Mciloh 17a., and Kesseph Mishnah to A.Z. 11, 3.

126. On the fact that besides the terrorists themselves, Ugandan soldiers were also killed in the action by Zahal, see Or Sameach, Rotzeach 1, 8, from whom it is abundantly clear that these soldiers aiding the terrorists are considered *rodefim* and are fully responsible for the consequences.

127. As exemplified by the brothers called the Martyrs of Lud, B.B. 10b; Taan. 18b, who sacrificed themselves to save the community. See Pitchei Teshuvah, Yoreh De'ah, 157 note 8, who quotes Yeshuoth Yaacob who permits one to sacrifice himself though he could have made his escape, so that those unable to escape from the hopeless situation would learn from his example and sanctify the Name, with fortitude. It is hardly difficult to discover present-day parallels. In other situations, Chavoth Yair, Responsa No. 213, holds that one who can escape from captivity should certainly do so and he is not obliged to consider the plight of those remaining behind. I am not, however, certain if Chavoth Yair would agree to one escaping if this were to endanger the lives of those remaining behind – provided his own life were not endangered by remaining. Might he not be considered a *rodeph* in such circumstances?

128. Lev. 18, 5.

129. On Kol Yisrael, August 2, 1976.

130. "Who says that your blood is redder . . ."; Pes. 25b.

131. See the survey, "Healing in Halachic Literature after the Talmud," in *Researches in the Responsa Literature,* I. Z. Cahana (Jerusalem, 1973), pp. 126–162.

132. Nachmanides, Torath Ha'adam, ed. Chavell, p. 41. According to many authorities, a doctor who withholds medical aid transgresses: "Thou shalt not stand idly by the blood of thy fellow"; Lev. 19, 16.

133. Responsa, Mor Uketzia on Orach Chayyim, No. 228, and, according to Melecheth Machsheveth, p. 79, *all* rishonim.

134. Shevuth Ya'acob, Responsa, Pt. 3, No. 75, permitted the use of a medicine in the case of one hopelessly ill, though it was not definitely known whether it would effect a cure or hasten death. He adds, however, the rider: "To be very cautious, to consult with all available medical opinion and to act in accord with the majority opinion *with the agreement of the rabbi of the town.*"

135. E.g., plastic surgery; see, Bakshi Doron, Torah She'baal Peh, 18, pp. 58–61.

136. A survey of the detailed halachic considerations affecting many aspects of abortion and its numerous borderline cases is found in Jacob Ginzberg, *Mishpatim LeYisrael,* pp. 223–243.

137. "All agree that one who kills a sick, dying person is liable"; San. 78a. So also Maimonides, Roze'ach 2, 7. Neither may one do any act that brings death closer, Mishna, Sabb. 151a; Rema to Yoreh De'ah 339, 1. It is possible that permission to cease medical treatment in such cases may be deduced from the words of Rema there; however, this requires a decision by Gedolim.
138. Ezek. 18, 4. Cf. note 118, supra, this chapter.
139. Responsa Levush Mordechai, No. 28.
140. For a résumé in English of the halachic considerations governing abortion when health hazards exist for either mother or child, or in instances of pregnancy as the result of rape or incest, see David M. Feldman, *Birth Control in Jewish Law*, pp. 284–294, and the authorities quoted there.
141. Exodus p. 3b.

5

The Oral Law and the Bible

In order to obtain perspective into the nature of halachic thinking, we must attempt to gain further insight by glimpsing the
Torah through the eyes of the halachist. Once we begin to see the
Torah from within, through halachic eyes, we will more fully
appreciate the modes of thought, the incessant, vibrant flow of
halachah, its tensions, and its creativity. We may achieve this by
delving a little into the fundamental nature of the "givenness" of
halachah. The essence of halachah lies in its givenness and it is
this principle that permeates all of its parts, governs all of its
thinking, and is responsible for every vestige of its authority.

The Content of Revelation

It is necessary to try to understand the nature of the revelation at
Sinai. To be more precise, how does halachah visualize what was
communicated there by God? We may begin by asking ourselves
the question the potential proselyte asked of Shammai:[1]

> It happened that a non-Jew came before Shammai and asked,
> "How many Toroth do you have?" "Two," he replied, "a written
> Torah and an oral Torah." Said he, "As to the written Torah I
> believe you, but as to the oral Torah I do not. Convert me on
> condition that you teach me the written Torah." He rebuked him
> and put him out with the builder's cubit[2] that was in his hand. He
> [the gentile] then came before Hillel, who converted him.[3] The
> first day he taught him "aleph, beth, gimmel, daleth." On the
> morrow he reversed the order of the letters. Said he, "But yester-
> day you did not teach me so?" "Did you not then rely upon me,"
> he replied, "rely upon me also as to the oral law."

The difference between Hillel and Shammai was one of temperament, but both were unequivocal as to the content of revelation. Revelation was unique in that the scope of God's communication at Sinai was not limited to or delineated by the written word. It did not constitute a concretely defined circumscribed communication in writing. The very opposite was the case. "Said R. Jochanan: 'the Holy One, Blessed be He, only made the covenant with Israel with regards the oral Law, for it is written:[4] "For by the mouth of these words,[5] I have made a covenant with thee and with Israel." '[6] Or again, "Things were said orally and things were said in writing and we do not know which are more favored. When the verse states: 'For by the mouth of these words I have made a covenant with thee and with Israel,' we must conclude that those communicated orally are favored."[7]

Far from being crystallized within the compass of the Written Word, the communication was vibrant, dynamic, and pregnant with possibilities for those who gave ear as well as sight. For such, the relation of the Written Word to what they heard was as

> the relation of short notes on a full and extensive lecture on any scientific subject. For the student who has heard the whole lecture,[8] short notes are quite sufficient to bring back afresh to his mind at any time the whole subject of the lecture. For him, a word, an added mark of interrogation, or exclamation, a dot, the underlining of a word, etc., etc., is often quite sufficient to recall to his mind a whole series of thoughts, a remark, etc. For those who had not heard the lecture from the master, such notes would be completely useless. If they were to try to reconstruct the scientific contents of the lecture literally from such notes, they would of necessity make many errors. Words, marks, etc., which serve those scholars who had heard the lecture as instructive guiding stars to the wisdom that had been taught and learnt, stare at the uninitiated as unmeaning sphinxes.[9]

Two Toroth

The two Toroth stand side by side, the one unintelligible without its fellow, the other grounded mnemonically in the wisdom of the Written Word. The two *together* are termed Torah, and it was this complete Torah that was received by Moses and transmitted from generation to generation. "Moses received Torah from Sinai and transmitted it to Joshua, and Joshua to the elders, and the elders to the prophets and the prophets transmitted it to the men of the great assembly."[10]

> She [Torah] is one to her mother[11]—to Knesseth Yisrael who received her,[12] as they said:[13] 'These are the statutes and ordinances and laws [Heb. Toroth] which the Lord made between Him and the Children of Israel in Mount Sinai by the hand of Moses.'[14] "The statutes" refers to the methods of exposition.[15] "The ordinances," these are the laws, "and the Toroth"—this teaches that two Toroth were given to Israel, one written one oral. "In Mount Sinai by the hand of Moses," this teaches that the whole Torah, its halachoth, details and explanations were given by Moses from Sinai.

Much more is intended here than the mere complementary nature of the written and oral laws expressed by K. Kahana when he says:

> The written law presents to us the legal institutions and their nature, and the nature of rights and duties. The oral law teaches us the practical application of these institutions and the working out of rights and duties in social conduct. It should be recognized that, vital as it is to extract the principles of law, something further is necessary—their application to human experience . . . . There is in the Torah an organic body of rules and principles with an inherent power to grow. The machinery for its development is the oral law. It is essential to concentrate on bringing out abstract statements of important principles but there would be no point in stopping there. Principles acquire full meaning only when they are applied to cases.[16]

Accepted that the two laws are complementary, their connection expresses yet a more fundamental relationship, since even "the abstract statements of important principles" can only be drawn in very limited fashion from the bare scriptural text.[17] Halachic eyes see the connection on a deeper level, as follows.

We have already pointed out in a previous chapter that the written Torah, as the Word of God, nay, as His Name, in fact contains all, so that the total substance of the oral law is implicitly contained in the written Torah. Halachah in exploring the written Torah taken either on its own or in the light of the oral law but reveals what is implicit. Halachah in all of its detail and ramification is laid bare in a text in which it in fact preexists and requires but to be brought forth.

In light of this, we may understand the approach of different schools of commentators whose aim was to elicit the harmony, the organic oneness of the written and oral laws within the biblical text.

To what degree this is illustrated successfully by the halachic commentary is beside the point. The essential unity and integrated harmony exist;[18] this is the common fundamental approach. The diversity to be found from commentary to commentary results from the different systems of exegesis employed, as well as from the predilections and insights of the particular author.

The earliest halachic textual commentaries that we have are the *Mechilta* to Exodus, *Sifra* to Leviticus, and *Sifri* to Numbers and Deuteronomy. These follow a verse-by-verse exegetical scheme by which the halachah is drawn from the text. In the main this is achieved by employment of the hermeneutic rules of R. Ishmael enumerated at the beginning of the *sifra*.[19]

Source or Hindsight?

The question arises as to whether the exegetical halachic commentary is actually discovering the source for the particular halachah in the text, or, since the halachah is in any event known by oral tradition, "hindsight" is employed to discover a textual base by employing the rules by which Torah is to be interpreted?

There are, of course, numerous instances, such as those halachoth that are termed *Halachah le'Moshe meSinai*[20] that are independent of Scripture, but a hint is nonetheless found for them in the wisdom of the Written Word, where this distinction does not apply, as there are others where Scripture plain and simple is the source.[21] But what of the vast majority of halachoth?

We may put the question another way. The Book of Ezra records[22] that "Ezra set his heart to seek—*Lidrosh* the law of the Lord, and to do it, and to teach in Israel statutes and ordinances."

The root *darash* in connection with the Torah signifies the exposition of Torah, its explanation, and commentary, and in this sense the root is employed throughout rabbinic literature. The entire context of the passage and chapter indicates attention to the verse with the object of teaching the people how their lives had strayed from the path of God. This is graphically illustrated by the fulfilment of the mitzvoth of *Succoth* immediately following and the general return to religious practice recorded there. The question is, on what exactly is Ezra engaged? Is he illustrating to the people how the halachah, forgotten or ignored by them, is implicit in the Torah, which they revered, or is he drawing the practical halachah from the text?

The same problem faces all who study the Talmud and its related literature, every page of which is replete with biblical references. What exactly is taking place before the eyes of the student in the Beth Hamidrash of the Tannaim and Amoraim? Are they studying Bible, or are they studying halachah?[23] Or is it perhaps a particular combination of both? In other words, what exactly is the relationship between the halachah and the text of the Torah?

Malbim and the Literal Meaning of the Text

In regard to this basic problem, two distinct schools of thought are evident. These may be typified by Meir Leibush Malbim, author of *HaTorah VeHamitzvah*, and Chaim ben Attar, author of the commentary on the *Or HaChayim*, respectively. Malbim wrote extensive and detailed commentaries on the Mechilta, Sifra, and Sifri as well as commentaries to all the books of the Tenach. First published was his work on the Sifra, which he prefaced with an introduction called "*Ayeleth Hashachar.*" In this introduction, he presents 613 rules by which the exegetical methods of Chazal are fully worked out.

By means of these rules, Malbim shows how "the exposition of Chazal is in fact the literal meaning of the verse, and is implicit in the depth of language and foundations of Hebrew speech," so that "the entire tradition as transmitted at Sinai" is in fact *literally* expressed in the Written Word. According to Malbim, the oral tradition was the orally transmitted literal commentary of the Torah.

Or HaChayim, Explanation by Means of the Halachoth

On the other hand, *Or HaChayim*[24] sees the unity of the written and oral laws in a different light. He says:

It is true that the entire word of Torah was told to Moses, and no Sage can know more than he knew. And though one join all the generations of Israel, from the giving of the Torah until the time when the earth shall become filled with knowledge, together, there is nothing new of which Moses was unaware. The difference is, however, that God gave Moses the written and oral laws, and the Lord, Blessed be He, in His wisdom noted in the Written law the entire oral teaching that he had told to Moses *but He did not inform Moses where all He had given him orally was hinted in the Written Torah.* It is the task of the Children of Israel, toilers in Torah, to bestow a place in the Written Torah upon all the halachoth, mysteries and expositions told to Moses at Sinai. This is the reason why you find that the Tannaim compiled Torath Cohanim [*Sifra*] and Sifri etc. All their exposition of the verses *is by means of the halachoth,* which they enshrined in the perfect Written law of God. And until this day, the sacred task of the student of Torah is to examine the verses carefully and resolve them by means of the statements which are the oral law.

According to this view, the oral law is the basis for understanding the written law, but, while all is contained in the written law, it is not produced from it.

Nachmanides, Literal Meaning and Halachic Exposition

There is an interim view, that of Nachmanides. In discussing the thirteen rules of R. Ishmael,[25] he comments on the general rule that "the verse does not lose its literal sense" as follows:

Farbeit, do we not find that all the Midrashim dealing with the mitzvoth depart from the literal sense of the verse? But the Midrash of Chazal does not in fact disregard the literal sense of the verse. All the *ethim* and *gammim* are inclusions and the verse embraces all. For the meaning of "the literal sense of the verse" is not as those lacking in understanding or as the Saducees would have it. The Book of the Torah of God is perfect there being no superfluous or deficient letter, all were written with wisdom, and they did not consider a midrash on *the essence of the mitzvah* as negating the literal sense . . . . Similarly, in every instance that they expounded parable and proverb, both are true, the inner sense as well as the outer expression, and if the Sages had a received tradition [to go beyond the text in their exposition] they did not consider this as a departure from its literal meaning.

Thus, the interpretation of the verse by means of the rules is the meaning intended by the Torah. The essence of the Midrash halachah is the deeper realm and expression of the literal meaning of the text. Far from the literal meaning being confined to the outer crust of the text, the Sages showed us how the plain meaning reaches organically inward toward deeper levels. This is, of course, not the same as saying, as does Malbim, that halachic exposition reflects the literal, linguistic, grammatical, and stylistic meaning of the text.

According to Malbim, full knowledge of these would theoretically suffice for the deduction of the entire detailed structure of halachah from the Written Word. According to Nachmanides, the tradition of the Sages reveals this deeper level, but without their tradition we could easily miss it. According to *Or HaChayim*, the discovery of halachah in the written text has nothing to do with the literal meaning of the verse. It is related to the all embracing "other faces" of Torah, which by its very nature as the Word of God must contain all of the truth that God wishes to impart to man. Thus, Nachmanides in fact forms a bridge of compromise between the two approaches. His remarks in the introduction to his commentary on the Torah:

Everything that was said in prophecy, from the Work of the Chariot[26] and the Work of the Beginning and that which was received by the Sages . . . is all written clearly in the Torah or hinted in its words, or in the numerical combinations of its letters, or in the form of the letters written according to law, or the letters whose form is different, or the ends of the letters. When Moses ascended on High, he found the Holy One, Blessed be He, binding crowns to the letters. What are these for? he asked. Said He, there will in the future be one who will expound from them mounds of halachoth.

It is clear that Nachmanides accepts the premises of *Or Ha-Chayim*; he deviates only as to what is called *peshat*, the literal meaning of the text, distinguishing between the tradition of the Sages and the results of study by the individual scholar, and in this he is equally far from the opinion of Malbim.

Asmachta—Mnemonics

Allied to this discussion is that on the notion of *asmachta*. This is the term used throughout rabbinic doctrine and enactment in the written text of the Torah.[27] *Asmachta* is employed in accord with the exegetical principles of Torah, to which it has to conform, and Chazal did not employ an *asmachta* unless they discovered some intimation for it in the verse. But they would not have interpreted the verse in this way had they not received the particular instance as halachah.[28] Thus, Maimonides,[29] after explaining that the halachoth termed *Halachah LeMoshe miSinai*, laws received by Moses at Sinai, though of biblical standing, are not hinted in any verse, or tied to one, nor can they be discovered by logical reasoning,[30] continues:

> They queried and said: how can you claim that the halachic standards of measurement—*shiurim*, are *Halachah LeMoshe Mi-Sinai*, are they not hinted[31] in the verse:[32] "A land of wheat and barley, and vines and fig trees and pomegranates, a land of olive trees and honey?"[33] The answer is, that in fact the rules of standards are *Halachah leMoshe miSinai*, and there is no way of discovering them by logical reasoning, and they are not intimated in the Torah,[34] but this precept was pegged to this verse mnemonically. And this is the sense of their oft repeated statement: the verse is but an *asmachta*.[35]

Obligatory Nature of *Asmachtoth* Decided by Sages

The opinion that *asmachta* is employed solely as a mnemonic device, or to reinforce known halachoth, presents only one view. Ritba[36] puts forward the view, which incidentally extricates Malbim from the otherwise knotty problem posed for him by *asmachta* as understood by Maimonides, that indeed everything is contained in the Torah, but laws that are only *hinted* there are called *asmachta*.

Such laws are intimated in this way because they bear a very special position in deciding practical halachah by the Sages.

> With regards everything that has an *asmachta* from the verse, the Holy One, Blessed be He, intimated that it is *fitting* to act so, *but He did not make it obligatory*. He turned it over to the Sages [for

consideration and decision]. And this is quite clear and true, and
not as those who explain the *asmachtoth* simply as mnemonic
devices determined upon by the Sages but that the Torah did not
in fact intend them. Farbeit! Such a theory should be confined to
oblivion and not mentioned, for it is the way of the Minnim.[37] But
[the truth is that] the Torah intimated them and handed [the
question of] their obligatory nature over to be determined by the
Sages, as it is written:[38] "And thou shalt do according to the word
which they shall declare unto thee from that place which the Lord
shall choose; and thou shalt observe to do according to all that
they shall teach thee." Hence one finds that in every place the
sages bring proof, or intimation, or an *asmachta* for their words
from the Torah, meaning to say that they are not inventing anything new, but the entire oral law is hinted in the written Torah,
which is perfect. Farbeit that it should lack ought."[39]

Kalman Kahana[40] shows that this interpretation of *asmachta*
applies also to ordinances that are of solely rabbinic origin, as
Ritba himself says,[41] "The Torah taught Moses at Sinai that the
Sages would so enact in the future," and he quotes several
authorities in support.

The text of the Talmud[42] would seem to support this view.

Further, said R. Chiyya bar Abba in the name of R. Jochanan: what is
meant by the verse: "[And the Lord delivered unto me the two tables
of stone written with the finger of God] and on them was written
according to all the words which the Lord spoke with you in the
mount"?[43] This teaches that the Holy One, Blessed be He, showed
Moses[44] the fine points of Torah, and the fine points of the scribes,
and what the scribes would innovate in the future—and what are
they? [For example],[45] the reading of the Megillah [on Purim]."

Prophet and Sage at Sinai

As does that of the Midrash,[46] which states:

R. Isaac said: The prophets received from Sinai the messages they
were to prophecy to future generations; for Moses told Israel: "But
with him that standeth here with us this day before the Lord our
God, and also with him that is not here with us this day."[47] It does
not say "that is not here standing with us this day," but just "with
us this day"—these are the souls that will one day be created; and
because there is not yet any substance in them the word "standing" is not used of them. Although they did not yet exist, each one

received his share [of Torah], for so it says: "The burden of the word of the Lord to Israel by Malachi."[48] It does not say "in the days of Malachi," but "by Malachi," for his prophecy was already with him since Sinai, but hitherto permission was not given to him to prophecy, . . . So Isaiah . . . Not only did all the prophets receive their prophecy from Sinai, but also each of the sages that arose in every generation received his [Torah] from Sinai.[49]

"Turn it over, turn it over for all is contained therein," and this is precisely what the scholar does, in the light of the "personal" portion of Torah that he received from Sinai.

But the Torah did not become many Toroth. In the words of Kohelleth,[50] "The words of the wise are as goads, and as nails well fastened, the gatherings of the scholars, they are given from one shepherd." On which the Talmud comments:[51]

"The gatherings of the scholars," these are the sages who sit in groups and engage in Torah. These say "unclean," these, "clean." These forbid while these permit. These void and these render fit. Perchance one might think to himself "how then can I learn Torah?" Therefore the verse concludes, "they are given from one shepherd." One God gave them, one leader said them from the Mouth of the Lord of all works, Blessed be He, for it is written:[52] "And God spoke all these words." So you, make your ear like a hopper and acquire an understanding heart to follow the words of those who say "unclean" as of those who say "clean." The words of those who forbid as the words of those who permit. The words of those who void and the words of those who render fit.

These and These Are the Words of the Living God

Both opinions, seemingly contradictory, are of the essence of Torah. "Both these and these are the words of the living God."[53] For, though there is no doubt before heaven[54] the Torah is no longer in heaven,[55] it was given to man who, within the guidelines laid down for the study of Torah and its unfolding, is free to come to that conclusion to which his powers of reasoning lead him. And, as Maimonides points out,[56] it is unreasonable to suppose that all minds should think exactly alike and arrive at exactly the same conclusions.

In practical halachah, the majority opinion is to be followed. In theory, the words and opinions of the minority are as faithfully recorded, studied, pondered, and discussed as are those of the majority ruling[57] since these are also Torah.[58]

Revelation and Freedom

The unfolding of Torah from within by interpretation or by drawing forth its depths on the basis of search and inquiry within the framework of norms handed down by tradition constitutes the fulfillment of the Divine Torah set before the people at Sinai. The organic relationship between revelation, on the one hand, and the freedom, nay, the injunction,[59] to delve into it and to render decision, on the other, ensures the viability, dynamism, and continuous development of halachah as a living organism. The juxtaposition of the two enables and in fact leads to creativity. The tension often encountered between the written and oral laws, as the diversity of opinion within the framework of halachic discussion, provides ever undiminished stimulus to be creative. But it is not only this. Rather, it is this within the compass of life lived with the sense, awareness, tension, and challenge of the immanence of God, who continually demands of man that he unravel that which He thought fit to reveal.

Notes to Chapter Five

1. Sabb. 31a.
2. See Maimonides, Talmud Torah 3, 11.
3. See Shach to Yoreh De'ah 268, note 23.
4. Ex. 34, 27.
5. I.e., that which was by word of mouth only.
6. Gitt. 60b.
7. Jer. Peah 2, 4.
8. I.e., that Torah SheBa'al Peh precedes the written law. On this subject, see, Judah Copperman, Introductory Chapters to Meshech Chochmah (Jerusalem), pp. 8–11.
9. Commentary of Samson Raphael Hirsch to Ex. 21,2. English ed., trans. Isaac Levy (London, 1956).
10. Aboth, 1, 1.
11. Songs 6, 9.
12. Tosaphoth Yom Tov to Aboth *ibid.*
13. Torath Cohanim, Bechukkothai.
14. Lev. 26, 46.

15. I.e., the method of deducing laws from the written word by means of language analysis and by means of the hermeneutic rules by which the Torah is to be expounded; see infra in the present study.

16. *The Case for Jewish Civil Law in the Jewish State* (Soncino Press, 1960), p. 35.

17. See, e.g., the remarkable attempt of Dr. A. Jacobus, *Chukkath Hatorah* (Jerusalem, 1966).

18. "We are thus led to recognize that even without the above mentioned methods of exegesis these precise interpretations were already known as ancient traditions transmitted orally from Sinai; for how otherwise could such a law as the taking of the 'fruit of a goodly tree' at the Feast of Tabernacles have been given to Moses in general terms without instructing him in detail regarding the nature of the fruit and in what manner he should carry out the command. Whether to take it to cover the *sukkah* or to have it merely grasped by the hand. The same thing will apply in connection with the ordinance of the *tefillin*. Surely it could not be left in the bare form of Scripture, 'frontlets between your eyes,' without adding further elucidation in detail as to what they consist of as well as the method of carrying out the command. Such explanatory details, therefore, must have been given clearly to Moses in connection with every precept, and this in spite of the fact that the rabbis endeavored to deduce them from Scripture by means of the exegetical rules. Surely, if their only source had been the biblical inferences quoted one might justly ask, how were these precepts practiced before these exegetical rules were formulated? Was the precept of *tefillin*, for example, not properly practiced before these methods of biblical exposition were devised? The fact is that neither Moses, Phineas, Joshua, Samuel, nor the elders ever had any doubt about the explanatory details of the written precepts, because they were all handed down from generation to generation by oral tradition as received at Sinai. The Rabbis merely sought to find biblical support for them." Chajes, *Student's Guide*, p. 13.

19. These rules are discussed and explained below, Appendix 1.

20. The laws called *Halachah le'Moshe miSinai* are discussed below in this chapter.

21. See Hag. 11a: "When in doubt in connection with leprosy study the verses, if in case of *Ahaloth*, study the Mishnah," and the gloss of Meromei Sadeh thereto. On the pitfalls of such use by a possek, cf. Piskei Uzziel, No. 22, pp. 117–118. On the use of the Biblical text in cases where no rabbinic precedent exists, see J. Copperman, introductory chapters to Meshech Chochma.

22. Ezra, 7, 10.

23. In the reverse situation, i.e., study of Bible with the Rabbinic commentary, e.g., with Rashi, one is considered to be engaged in study of the oral law; see Reuben Margolies, Nephesh Chayyah, Siman 238, etc.

24. Commentary to Lev. 13, 37. Cf. also R. Moses Chaim Luzzatto, *Ma'amar Ha'ikkarim* (Mossad Harav Kook, 1949), p. 33.

25. Sepher Hamitzvoth, Root 2. See also Responsa, Kol Mevasser, Pt. 2, No. 23, on the literal meaning of the verse and the halachah derived from it.

26. Ezekiel chap. 1.

27. E.g., "It is actually a Rabbinic law, and the Biblical text is merely quoted in support, Hull. 64b." "This is in fact a *Halachah leMoshe miSinai*, and Joshua

pegged it to a verse, Tosaphoth to Yeb. 71b. s.q.Lo." "Before Ezekiel came and told us this, who had stated it? But we have it by tradition and Ezekiel came and stated it explicitly, San. 22b." "R. Nathan says: From here there is a hint in the Torah for the song of the Levites, but it was explained in detail by Ezra, Sifri to Num. 18, 3."

28. Kiryath Sepher, Introduction, chap. 1, sect. 9.

29. Introduction to the Mishnah, ed. Rambam Le'am, pp. 30–31.

30. This is the major identifying characteristic of such halachoth. It should, however, be noted that there is a further use of the terminum *Halachah leMoshe miSinai*, for, as pointed out by Asheri to Mikva'oth, 1, it is occasionally used in the sense of "this is as if it had been a *Halachah leMoshe miSinai*." Cf. also, Bertinoro to Terumoth 2, 1; Tiff. Yisrael, Yoma 2, note 19.

31. As stated by the Talmud, Ber. 41a.

32. Deut. 8, 8.

33. The Talmud, *ibid.*, explains the relevance of each of the seven fruits mentioned in the verse, to one of the halachic standards of measurement.

34. The verse intending merely to list the fruits for which the land is noted and praised.

35. Given, however, a *Halachah leMoshe miSinai*, the verse is to be interpreted in its light, regardless of the literal sense. See Yoma 32a. Said R. Hisda, etc., where the order of service on Yom Kippur as received by *Halachah leMoshe miSinai* determines the interpretation of Scripture.

36. Commentary to R.H. 16a.

37. See Responsa Kol Mevasser, by the Gaon R. Meshullam Ratt, Pt. 2, No. 21, and No. 22, sect. 5, on Ritba's use of this expression.

38. Deut. 17, 11.

39. On this basis, we are able to comprehend the various degrees of severity attached to particular halachoth in connection with which the Talmud employs an *asmachta*; see Peri Megadim to Orach Chayyim, Petichah Kollelleth, Pt. 1, sect. 20; as also the rule that "one may not [always] compare the decrees of the Sages to each other," for in some cases they felt the need to be stricter in regard to the intimation of the Torah than in others.

40. Chekker Ve'iyyun (Tel Aviv, 1960), pp. 15–17.

41. On Erub. beginning of chap. 2, quoted by Kahana *ibid.*

42. Meg. 19b.

43. Deut. 9, 10.

44. "Showed" but did not give to him to hand on as definite halachoth; Tosaphoth Yom Tov, Introduction to Commentary on the Mishnah.

45. Torah Temimah to Deut. 9, 10, note 3.

46. Exodus Rabbah 28, 6.

47. Deut. 29, 14.

48. Mal. 1, 1.

49. See the comment of Azulai to the Haggadah of Pessach, Simchath Haregel (Lemberg, 1864), p. 16b, to the effect that no one is able to expound that part of Torah that was given to another at Sinai.

50. Eccl. 12, 11.

51. Hag. 3b.

52. Ex. 20, 1.

53. Erub. 13b; Gitt. 6b.

54. Gitt. *ibid.*

55. B.M. 59b, see supra, chap. 3, note 9.

56. Introduction to Mishnah, *ibid.*, pp. 36–37.

57. The minority opinion is not, however, without all weight in practical halachah; see Eduyoth 1, 5 and commentaries. Also Rashi to Ketuboth, 57a, s.q. Ha Kamashma Lan. "Furthermore, one should know that with regards the individual opinions, not accepted by halachah, but which are accepted to bolster custom, permission is granted to the decisor to be *aided* by them when need arises, for example in cases of *iggun*, or pain, or loss." Z. H. Chajes, *The Works of* (Jerusalem, 1958); Darchei HoRa'ah, p. 227. In particular, see his remarks, *ibid.*, p. 231, on *Hephsed Merubeh*. See also infra, chap. 11 of this study at length.

58. Cf. the remarks in chap. 3 supra, on the Rebellious Elder, who may teach his view.

59. Semak, Additional Mitzvoth, No. 9, considers the rendering of a halachic decision the fulfillment of a positive precept based on Levit. 10, 11.

6

Prophecy and Law

Paradoxical Relationship

Prophecy is intimately bound up with revelation. According to Chazal, each prophet received his prophecy at Sinai, as did each Sage his potential measure of Torah.[1] Despite this, the relationship between halachah and prophecy is paradoxical. Though Torah is from heaven, prophecy is allowed no entry into the realm of halachah. On the other hand, halachah alone decides who is a prophet, when one is considered a prophet, when the individual is obliged to listen to a prophet or to one claiming to be a prophet and when not. Furthermore, halachah alone determines the legitimate limits of prophetic activity and decides whether and when he is a true or false prophet.

Phenomenon of Prophecy

The phenomenon of prophecy as such is of no interest to halachah. The manner of divine manifestation is considered appropriate subject matter for metaphysics, while the preparation of the prophet for his calling is subject to both metaphysical and quasi-halachic/ethical considerations. It is the content of prophecy, the authority and activity of the prophet, with which halachah is concerned.

A True Prophet?

It is an important fact that though the Torah states,[2] "If there arise in the midst of thee a prophet . . . and he give thee a sign or a wonder," the Biblical prophets are not recorded as having performed such a sign or miracle in order to gain acceptance or recognition for their calling. We do not, of course, argue *ex silentio* that no such sign was given. On the contrary, since no mention is made of such activity, it seems that the procedure for prophetic legitimation was well known and accepted.[3]

However, we may reasonably ask, how can one ever be certain that one is indeed in the presence of a prophet? The answer given by halachah is astounding. It is, in fact, that we may never know. Even to pose the question is to miss the point of the passage[4] enjoining one to hearken to the prophet's voice, as well as to miss the essential point of halachah. In keeping with the general theory of halachah already outlined, so in connection with the prophet. Halachah does not ask, is this a true prophet? Halachah asks, *when must I act as if in the presence of a true prophet* and when not? And it is this question that is clearly and unequivocally answered by halachah.

> It is possible for him to perform a sign or a wonder and yet not be a prophet . . . nonetheless, it is a mitzvah to hearken to him. Since he is a great man, sage and worthy of prophecy we accept his presumption,[5] for in such a case were we enjoined, as we were enjoined to decide law by the word of two witnesses, though it is possible that they testify falsely. Since they are in our eyes worthy, we accept their worthiness.[6]

Prophetic Opinion on Law

The sense of the passage is that even in the case of witnesses, we do not know absolutely that the truth conforms with their testimony, yet the Torah enjoined us to act on their word; otherwise, we could never decide a case. So when one claims to be prophet, if he fulfills the preconditions for prophecy, we accept him as a prophet, and we are enjoined to hearken to him without hesitation or deviation.[7] Halachah removes the problem of prophecy from the realm of belief and places it squarely in the sphere of action. Whatever misgivings the individual may have, he is certain as to what he must do.

The conditions that establish one as a prophet and enable a prophet to retain credence as such are outlined by Maimonides.[8] They are, briefly, impeccable personality and conduct, the performance of a sign, foretelling[9] an event in its exact detail, that he does not contradict the words of Torah or attempt to interpret them by prophecy rather than by the canons of received tradition, and that he admonishes to observe Torah. If he proffers his *prophetic* opinion on a halachic controversy or attempts to opine by prophecy in regard to any tradition, he is a false prophet, and no sign or piety can avail him.

Only the human intellect applied to halachah and its principles is valid halachah. Inspiration, even of the prophet, has no place there for Torah is no longer in heaven.[10] "From the prophet you are to seek a sign, but you are not to seek a sign as to Torah, of which it is written:[11] 'By the law which they shall teach—*yorucha*, thee.' "[12]

The Talmud[13] relates that

> three thousand halachoth were forgotten during the days of mourning for Moses. They said to Joshua: "Ask." "It is not in heaven," he replied. They said to Samuel, "Ask." "These are the mitzvoth[14] — no prophet may say anything new from now," he replied. . . . When Moses our teacher was about to depart to Gan Eden he said to Joshua: "Ask of me all of your doubts." Said he, "Master, did I then leave your side for a moment and go elsewhere! Did you not write of me:[15] "And his attendant Joshua son of Nun, a young man, departed not out of the tent"? Whereat Joshua became faint and he forgot 300 halachoth and there arose seven hundred doubts in his mind, and Israel wished to kill him. Said the Holy One, Blessed be He, to him: "To tell you [what you have forgotten or what is now unclear to you] is impossible, go and divert them with war," as it is written:[16] "Now it came to pass after the death of Moses the servant of the Lord, the Lord spoke unto Joshua son of Nun, Moses' minister . . . go over . . ."

Temporary Abrogation of Law by a Prophet

A prophet is recognized as such without investigation if he is proclaimed a prophet by an already recognized prophet.[17] However, he forfeits his status as a prophet on infringement of any of the aforementioned conditions.[18] The exception lies in the directive of an established prophet to suspend or transgress a biblical law, or halachah, temporarily, *hora'ath sha'ah*.[19] Provided he stresses the *temporary* nature of the abrogation, he is to be heeded.

In his preface to the commentary on the Mishnah, Maimonides elaborates this principle as follows:

And I will tell you a story by means of which this principle will be clarified. Suppose one whose prophecy is established tells us on the Sabbath to arise, men and women, to kindle fire, prepare weapons of war, gird our weapons and fight the people of a certain place on this Sabbath day, and take spoils and capture their women. It would be our duty, as commanded in the law of Moses to rise immediately, without delay, as enjoined by him and do all that he commanded, energetically and with abundant love, with no hesitations or waiting. And we should believe that every-thing we do on that day, though it be the Sabbath, whether kindling fire or other work, killing and war, is a mitzvah for the fulfillment of which we may hope for good reward from the Holy One, Blessed be He. This, since we acted upon the word of the prophet, to do which is a positive precept as the verse states,[20] "Unto him ye shall hearken." Upon which the received tradition is:[21] "In connection with everything,[22] if the prophet says: "trans-gress the Torah, hearken unto him, except for idolatry." That is to say, that if he should say, worship only this day, this idol, or burn incense to this star only at this time—he is to be put to death and one must not hearken to him.

Now if a righteous, God fearing man, well on in years, should think to himself: "I am old, advanced in years and so many years have passed and I never transgressed any of the command-ments, how can I arise on this day, the Sabbath, and transgress in matters forbidden on pain of stoning, and go and fight? I have no longer strength to do good or evil. Surely there are others who can take my place to do this!" Such a one is a rebel and transgresses the word of God, and is liable for death at the hand of heaven for transgressing that which was enjoined by the prophet. And he who commanded the observance of the Sabbath, He is the same who commanded to hearken to the words and decrees of the prophet, and one who transgresses his word is liable as mentioned. It is to this that the verse[23] refers in saying: "Whosoever will not hearken unto My words which he shall speak in My name, I will require it of him." Even so, should one tie an unnecessary knot[24] on this Sabbath, he is liable to be stoned.[25]

Now this same prophet, who enjoined us to do what he com-manded on the Sabbath and we fulfilled his word, were he to say to us: "The permitted walking distance beyond the city limits on the Sabbath is two thousand cubits less one, or two thousand and one cubits," and support his opinion by saying that he was so informed by prophecy, not by investigation and logical reasoning, we know that he is a false prophet and he is to be put to death.

In accord with this illustration you should weigh everything enjoined by the prophet, and everything that you find in the Bible in connection with a prophet who [seemingly] acted contrary to a mitzvah. This principle is the key to the entire subject [of the influence of prophecy on the performance of mitzvoth and their explanation]. And in this alone is the prophet different with regards mitzvoth, from other people.

But as to investigation, logical reasoning, and understanding the mitzvoth, he is as the other sages, who, though they lack prophecy, are his equals. When a prophet holds an opinion, and one who is not a prophet holds a [contrary] opinion, and the prophet says that the Holy One, Blessed be He, informed him that his opinion is true – do not listen to him. If a thousand prophets, all as Elijah or Elisha hold one opinion, and a thousand sages opine differently, follow the majority, and the halachah is in accord with the thousand and one sages and not the thousand honored prophets. And so we find:[26]

"I swear, even if Joshua himself were to tell me so, I would not consent or hearken to him!" and:[27] "Were Elijah to come and say that *Chalitzah* is performed with the shoe, we would hearken; with a sandal, we would not."

This means that one may on no account add to, or detract from the performance of a mitzvah, by means of prophecy. In like wise, a prophet who testified that the Holy One, Blessed be He, informed him that the law with regards a certain mitzvah is so, and the reasoning of that sage correct, is to be put to death as a false prophet. As we have already explained, no Torah was given after the first prophet [Moses] . . . and it is no longer in heaven.

God does not allow one to learn [halachoth] from the prophets,[28] only from the sages, men of logical reasoning and opinion. He did not say: and you shall come to the prophet who will be at that time, but: "And you shall come to the priests and levites and to the judge who will be at that time."[29]

Prophetic Innovation

The Talmud[30] learns from the verse[31] "These are the mitzvoth which the Lord commanded Moses for the Children of Israel in mount Sinai" that "no prophet may innovate from now."[32] Meaning that apart from the irrelevancy of prophecy for the process of halachic decision, the prophet may neither establish a new mitzvah nor annul one already given. Chatham Sopher[33] explains that this limitation on prophecy is actually the basis of Torah. Without it there would be no Torah:

> For it has already happened, as declared by the *min*[34] "Since you were exiled from your land, the Torah of Moses has been removed and another book has been given" . . . and the prophet of the Ishmaelites did so, and Sabbethai Zevi declared that the mitzvoth have all been changed, mitzvoth becoming prohibitions and prohibitions, mitzvoth. Now, though we would reject such an approach with regards the Torah as a whole, nonetheless no mitzvah would remain as given.[35] Anyone could claim that he dreamed in a dream that this fat is forbidden, this permitted . . . therefore, the Holy One, Blessed be He, made it a basic principle that no prophet may innovate with regards mitzvoth.

Emphatically, Chazal stress,[36] "Forty-eight prophets arose in Israel and they neither detracted from, or added ought[37] to that which is written in the Torah."[38]

The functions of the prophet are then restricted, other than in the event of a *hora'ath sha'ah*, to matters of public (or private[39]), general concern and welfare.[40]

Four Grades of Prophecy

Nonetheless, we find halachic mention both during Talmudic times and beyond, of four grades of "prophecy" in connection with halachah.[41] These are prophecy, *ruach hakodesh*, *bath kol*, and dreams—these besides the revelation of Elijah[42] and the particular connotations of "The secret of the Lord is upon him" discussed in a previous chapter.[43] In view of these sources and their apparent conflict with the principles outlined earlier, we must take cognizance of a number of halachic distinctions.

The exact site of the altar in the Temple is crucial for valid sacrifice, and it cannot be altered.[44] It is the spot from where the dust of Adam was gathered,[45] so that man's atonement is at the site of his creation, there Noah sacrificed and there Isaac was bound. When the exiles returned from Babylon, they were unable to determine its exact position. The problem was solved by the prophets among them.[46]

The question[47] is solved on the basis of the commentary of the Sifri to the verse[48] "But unto the place which the Lord your God shall choose out of all your tribes to put His name there, even unto His habitation ye shall seek and thither thou shalt come. Search and you will find, and afterward the prophet will tell you." From which it appears that the Torah itself placed the problem of the altar within the province of the prophet.

Chatham Sopher[49] employs this principle in regard to all the Temple appurtenances and the changes in construction from Tabernacle to First and Second Temples. As he shows, this realm was *ab initio* placed within the purview of the prophet.[50]

Exceptions to the Rule

Z. H. Chajes[51] shows that halachah excepts from the rule, instances where Elijah merely determines the prima facie facts of the matter under discussion.[52] This enables halachah then to be decided according to rule.[53]

The Messiah

Withal, it is clear that prophecy has no function in the realm of practical halachah.[54] This fact is again pressed home by Maimonides who, when discussing the Messiah and his qualities, states,[55] "He will be greater in wisdom than Solomon, and a great prophet close to Moses our teacher." Close to Moses, but there is no second to Moses, who alone is called[56] "the father of wisdom and the father of prophecy." Only one prophet received or will receive Torah through the media of prophecy, and he cannot be imitated by any other prophet, even by the Messiah.

The final words of prophecy, spoken by Malachi immediately before heralding Elijah, are[57] "Remember the words of Moses My servant, which I commanded unto him in Horeb for all Israel, even statutes and ordinances." While the Midrash[58] declares that the Messiah will come to bestow mitzvoth on the Nations, and while he is so occupied, Israel will be engaged in studying Torah from the mouth of the Holy One, Blessed be He.

Between Prophecy and Halachah

While halachah sets norms, standards, and bearing for the individual and society, the prophet, who is the moral voice in society without practical authority either in halachah or in government, reproves, castigates, and demands submission[59] so that decency and integrity do not remain but empty phrases. But he is more. While halachah carries the people onward stage by stage, the prophet leaps ahead, revealing vistas and portraying the horizons toward which halachah shepherds its flock. The soaring sight of the prophet invests each stage with timelessness, with infinity and grandeur. The prophet comforts and assures that setback and tragedy, that fall and failure are not permanent but that they are mere stages on the road to a better life, when the spirit of God will invest mankind. This world, says the prophet, is just over the horizon if only you will hearken to His voice—today.

Aggadah

Though we have no prophecy, we have a reflection of its soul and flight of spirit in both halachah and aggaddah.

Aggadah in its various forms is for the individual spirit what prophecy was for the people.[60] In the aggaddah the individual soars to spiritual heights. His intuitions and insights are free to roam and explore, at will. No bonds of time or space fetter him. His soul delights in the mysterious Universe of the Creator, in contemplation of matter and of spirit. He yearns for a glimpse of eternity and is vouchsafed it.[61] He is borne on the wings of reflection and understanding, and he knows that, elusive as it is, there is indeed meaning to life, to living and history.

Uplifted, he returns to reality to reimmerse himself in the concrete, of necessity to surge forward to a better future. The present is no longer drab. It glistens with light, with spirit, for he has found the way to capture the pulse of infinity and live it in practice—halachah.

Aggadah and halachah together enable the mystic soul to live concretely. They ensure that practical affairs are suffused with spirit. Both manifest meaning and purpose in existence. Together they lead inexorably to heavenly days on earth.

Tempered by aggaddah, the halachic personality is rendered sympathetic to the actual plight of society and individual, and this plight is amply reflected in halachic ruling. "We must mortgage our soul," writes the late Chief Rabbi Isaac Herzog,[62] "to free the woman from her distress," and the genius of halachic intellect is activated by and brought to bear on the problem of a suffering soul.

Tempered by love for Am Yisrael and love for Eretz Yisrael, and the vision of rebirth and the salvation of Israel, the late Chief Rabbi Kook wrote[63] in connection with the problem of *shemittah* year,[64] "Certainly every *ba'al hora'ah* is obliged to ever set his sight and his heart upon the welfare of Israel, and he is not to worry if one temporarily suspends a mitzvah because of the force of circumstances . . . when such a course is possible according to the canons of Torah."

What degree of unbounded humanity, feeling, sympathy, understanding, and encouragement suffuse the arch halachist Maimonides, when he writes on *Kiddush Hashem* to the desperate, suffering communities of his time. Who else so identifies himself with the plight of those forced to apostacy, bringing halachic light and succor to a tragic generation!

Notes to Chapter Six

1. Exodus Rabbah, 28, 6. The text of the midrash is quoted supra, toward the end of the previous chapter.
2. Deut. 13, 2.
3. Isaiah 41, 22–23, taunts the idolators with the exact demands of the Torah for the verification of the aspirant to prophecy.
4. Deut. 18, 15.
5. I.e., since he fulfills the preconditions of a claimant to prophecy; see Maimonides ad loc.
6. Maimonides, Yesodei HaTorah 7, 7.
7. See Responsa, Chatham Sopher, Even HaEzer, Pt. 1, No. 95; Pt. 2, No. 131.
8. Yesodei HaTorah, chaps. 7–10.
9. At least three times; Turei Even.
10. B.M. 59b.
11. Deut. 17, 11.
12. Jerushalmi, Ber. 1, 4. *Yorucha*, from the root *lehoroth, hora'ah*, to render practical halachic decision. Rashi to Ket. 7a, defines *hora'ah* as the rendering of decision by means of a received tradition or by the logic of one's wisdom.
13. Tem. 16a.
14. Levit. 24, 37.
15. Ex. 33, 11.
16. Josh. 1, 1 ff.
17. Yesodei HaTorah 10, 5; Deut. 34, 9; 2 Kings 2, 15.
18. He is considered a false prophet only from the time he infringed, but the validity of his prophecies and activities until that time are not impugned; the Gaon of Vilna, quoted by Meshech Chochmah to Deuteronomy, p. 272.
19. The temporary suspension by the prophet is only effective when he says that he was told prophetically to act so. So, Minchath Chinuch 516, on Maimonides' opinion. Others hold, however, that this qualification is un-

necessary; Tosaphoth to Yeb. 90b. s.q. Veligmor. See Avodath Hamelech to
   Yesod. HaT. 9, 3.
20. Deut. 18, 15.
21. San. 90a.
22. Even murder; see Ridbaz, Responsa, Pt. 2, No. 652; also Klei Chemdah to
   Deut. 13, 4.
23. Deut. 18, 19.
24. I.e., one not required for the war effort enjoined by the prophet.
25. Maimonides here enumerates a cardinal principle of halachah with numerous practical ramifications. To continue with M.'s example, this principle forms one of the basic problems and pitfalls for an observant Jew
   serving in the Israeli army. The exact dividing line between the permitted
   and the forbidden on the Sabbath in order to maintain security and pre-
   paredness is very hard to determine. But it is the crux of the permission to
   do that which is permitted. The story is still told in the Israel Air Force of the
   fighter pilot (later killed in combat) who would fly on the Sabbath but
   refused steadfastly to carry his handkerchief to the plane. This halachah is
   clearly stated in the Mechilta: Said R. Judah b. Bythra: If non-Jews sur-
   rounded Eretz Yisrael, and Israel profaned the Sabbath, they may not say:
   since we have profaned part of it, we may profane the remainder of the day.
   For the verse teaches: those who profane it shall surely die; Ex. 31, 14. Even
   for the twinkling of an eye, those who profane it shall surely die.
26. Hullin 124a.
27. Yeb. 102a.
28. Z. H. Chajes, Darchei HaHora'ah, *loc cit.*, p. 251, points out that though we
   may not learn halachah from the prophet, this is only so when the prophet
   intends to teach halachah by means of prophecy. We may, however, deduce
   the halachah from the incidental remarks of the prophet when he is engaged in delivering reproof or teaching ethics, since these incidental remarks but reveal to us what the halachah was, or ought to have been, in the
   time of the prophet, and the prophecy was never intended to teach halachah directly. Of this nature are the deductions, Ber. 31 from the Prayer of
   Channah. See also gloss of Chajes to Nedarim, 22b.
29. Deut. 17, 9.
30. Sabb. 104a; Meg. 3a; Tem. 16a.
31. Levit. 27, 34.
32. I.e., from the time of Moses onward, but Moses himself was able to employ
   miraculous means to discover the truth of halachah; see Yoma 75a, in
   regard to the manna.
33. Responsa, Orach Chayim, No. 208.
34. Sabb. 116b. The *min* referred to seems, from the context of the passage to
   have been one of the early Christians.
35. It is instructive that the Jerusalem Talmud, Sabb. 13, 3, states on this same
   verse (Levit. 27, 34), "This teaches that if one performed them according to
   law they are mitzvoth, if not, they are not mitzvoth."
36. Meg. 14a.
37. Since all the enactments and decrees are not additions but fences around
   the law, see Maimonides, Mamrim, chap. 2. Rashi to Meg. 14a, raises the

problem of the institution of Channukkah and says that since the events it commemorates happened after the cessation of prophecy, no problem of its institution by a prophet arises. Since the need to celebrate the event is deduced *a fortiori* (see following note) there is also no problem of adding a mitzvah to the Torah; Ritba ad loc. In any event, since *ab initio* the mitzvah of its celebration was declared to be of Rabbinic origin, this problem does not exist; see Maimonides *ibid.*, Halachah 9.

38. On the problem of Purim, since Mordechai and Esther were prophets, Meg. *ibid.* the Jerusalem Talmud, Meg. 1, 5 holds that its enactment was the fulfillment of a specific ordinance of the Torah. So also Saadyah Gaon, Sepher HaMitzvoth. In the opinion of Nachmanides, to Deut. 4, 2, the celebration of Purim at the time was deduced *a fortiori*: "If from slavery to freedom they uttered song, how much more so from death to life," as explained in the Talmud, Meg. *ibid.* The problem raised by the Jerusalem Talmud revolves only around the determination of Purim as a *permanent* festival since no prophet may innovate. See Responsa, Kol MeVasser, Pt. 1, No. 21; Ha'amek She'elah to Sheilta 26, Sect. 1. Following this train of thought, other authorities hold that the problem regarding Purim affects only the demand of Esther to be written for public reading, as the Sepher Torah, Meg. 7a, and Tosaphoth s.q. Ne'emrah, end; and it is to this problem that the Jerusalem Talmud answers with a biblical verse. Because of the reasoning *a fortiori*, Chatham Sopher, Responsa Orach Chayyim, No. 163, end, holds that a community or an individual may determine to hold a festival on the day they were delivered from danger. Malbim in his commentary to Esther, 9, 31–32, probably bases himself on similar reasoning in his striking, original solution of the problem. In another Responsa, Orach Chayyim, No. 208, Chatham Sopher stresses that the actual holding of such a festival on deliverance, is a biblical injunction, its content, Rabbinic. See also *ibid.* Yoreh De'ah No. 233; The Responsa of R. Zadok HaCohen, Tiffereth Zevi, Yoreh De'ah 27, 6; and R. Yerucham Perle, Sepher Hamitzvoth of R. Saadya Gaon, p. 516. This entire discussion and the sources quoted are, of course, extremely relevant to the problem of establishing Yom Ha'atzmauth as a festival. Peri Chadash, O. H. 496, sect. 14 end, would perhaps agree in this case since it is a matter affecting Klal Yisrael and not merely a community.

39. For example, Saul did not hesitate to visit Samuel to seek aid in finding his lost asses, 1 Sam., chap. 9.

40. Yesodei HaTorah, 9, 2.

41. There are more than four grades of prophecy. See Leviticus Rabbah 1, 14 and Bereshith Rabbah 44, 6, where ten grades of prophecy are enumerated. These, however, refer to actual prophecy, whereas we are here concerned with four degrees of holy inspiration. See Bachya to Deuteronomy 33, where these are discussed.

42. Reuben Margolis in his lengthy introduction to *Responsa from Heaven* by R. Jacob of Merose (Mossad Harav Kook, 1959) collected the relevant source material from the Talmudim and later responsa on this topic. He shows that indications from dreams were not discarded out of hand even by Achronim. He shows, *ibid.* p. 40, note 8, that achieving true halachic

decision by reasoning process alone is superior to the revelation of Elijah. Interesting to note in this connection is the statement of R. Chayim of Volhozyn in his introduction to Sifra De'tzeniutha, to the effect that the Gaon of Vilna continually refused the aid of heavenly *maggidim* in the study of Torah. He declared that Torah must be understood only by unaided study and immersion within it. A detailed study of the dream in halachah is to be found in Torah Shelemah to Bereshith, sect. VaYeshev, pp. 1403–1405.

43. Supra, chap. 2. See also Mishpetei Cohen, No. 96, p. 206 ff., on the inspiration of the Ra'abad. Azulai, Yair Ozen, 1, paragraph 15, holds that when the scholars in a particular generation are unable to reach a decision, it is permitted to enquire from heaven, and they may act in accord with that which is shown to them, as Ra'abad records: "The Holy Spirit appeared in our Beth Hamidrash." Nonetheless, if a scholar still persists, he may persist since "it is not in heaven."

44. Maimonides, Beth Habechirah, 2, 2.

45. Jerushalmi, Nazir, 7, 2.

46. Zeb. 62a.

47. Responsa, Mishpetei Cohen, No. 92.

48. Deut. 12, 5.

49. Responsa, Yoreh De'ah No. 236.

50. Chatham Sopher, *ibid.* and 208, is also of the opinion that, irrespective of the halachic problems affecting the construction of the Temple nowadays, we are in any event unable to rebuild the Temple unless so bidden by a prophet. Minchath Chinuch, 95, does not, however, agree with this stipulation. The general halachic problems and considerations concerning the rebuilding of the Temple are thoroughly discussed in Mikdash Melech, R. Zvi Pessach Frank (Jerusalem, 5728).

51. Torath HaNevi'im, chap. 2.

52. See Pes. 13a; Yeb. 35b; Sabb. 108a, etc.

53. Further distinctions may be found in Mishpetei Cohen, *ibid.* See also *Encyclopedia Talmudith*, Vol. 2, s.q. Eliahu; Vol. 5. s.q. Bath Kol; Vol. 7, s.q. Divrei Chalomoth.

54. The oft-found remark that Elijah will determine this matter is to be understood as Torah Temimah to Levit. 27, 34, note 216—that the spirit from on high will stir him so that the foundations of wisdom will be revealed to him and he will be able to decide by the ways and on the foundations of Torah.

55. Yad, Teshuvah, 9, 2.

56. Meg. 13a.

57. Malachi 3, 22.

58. Shocher Tov, 21.

59. "He [Daniel] was not a prophet since he was not sent to castigate Israel. But he attained prophecy, since he saw visions by means of the Holy Spirit", Tosaphoth HaRosh to Meg. 3a.

60. This is not, of course, to minimize the role of aggaddah in the life of the people as a whole.

61. "Said R. Jose b. Chalaphta to R. Ishmael his son: 'Do you wish to see the Divine Presence in this world? Engage in Torah in Eretz Yisrael.' Shocher Tov, 105."

62. Responsa, Hechal Yitzchak, Eben Ha'ezer.
63. Shabbath Ha'aretz, Introduction, p. 64.
64. Quite apart from the present halachic solution to the problem of the *shemittah*, I am personally convinced that the ultimate solution lies in the adoption of a seven-year plan embracing all the aspects of Israel's economy and gearing them all to the cessation of forbidden agriculture during *shemmittah*. Development could absorb agricultural workers during the *shemmittah* year, the water economy of the country much improved by the saving, which would enable replenishment of resources. Exports and imports could be geared accordingly, and with modern freezing methods there would be no shortage of fresh fruit and vegetables. Given the continued prolific fructivity of the country, agricultural exports might be continued, with careful planning. The details are, however, a problem for the experts.

7

Eretz Yisrael—A Law unto Itself

The Halachic Effects of Eretz Yisrael

The relationship between the halachah and Eretz Yisrael is not to be seen in terms of "the laws of the country" alone. Eretz Yisrael is a halachah, a law unto itself. It is invested with a "personality" that produces halachic effects.

The law not to deliver unto his master a bondsman that is escaped from his master unto thee[1] applies only to a slave who fled to Israel from beyond its borders[2] and he gains his freedom "because of the respect due to Eretz Yisrael."[3]

The reason that no *hallel* is recited for a miracle that took place outside Eretz Yisrael[4] is that a *kahal,* a community of Israel, is said to exist only in Eretz Yisrael but not outside it. Hence Jews outside Eretz Yisrael are considered as individuals, and no *hallel* is recited for a miracle performed for an individual.[5] Similarly in regard to *hora'ath beth din.*[6]

The normal laws of acquisition do not apply to the land, which may not be sold in perpetuity;[7] hence, even when occupied by non-Jews, the Jewish title to the land remains unaffected.[8]

The sanctity of the Temple area and Jerusalem is due to the Divine Presence that rests there, and this is never nullified[9] whether Jews live there or not; hence, though desolate, one is nonetheless obliged to treat the area with respect; and the original prohibitions regarding entry into the Temple area retain their force.[10]

The Talmud[11] permits one childless after ten years of marriage to divorce his wife or enjoins on him to take another[12] in order to fulfill the duty of procreation. The years spent together by the couple outside Eretz Yisrael do not count, since they lacked the merit of Eretz Yisrael.[13] The merit of Eretz Yisrael entitles a murderer fleeing there from abroad to a new trial.[14]

The halachah devolves on the people from on High and passes through them to the very ground on which they stand endowing it with an independent status that enables it to dispense merit, renders it entitled to respect and to be held sacred, ensures that it does not lose its character as the national home, that it cannot be bartered and is responsible for creating a community of Israel. Halachah penetrates deeply, and, in entering as it were the very crust of Eretz Yisrael, it cuts a broad swathe through its various levels.

Ten Sanctities

The Mishnah[15] says, "There are ten degrees of holiness. The Land of Israel is holier than any other land . . . The walled cities . . . Within the wall of Jerusalem[16] . . . The Temple Mount . . . The Chel . . . The Court of the Women . . . The Court of the Israelites . . . The Court of the Priests . . . Between the Porch and the Altar . . . The Sanctuary . . . The Holy of Holies . . ." If the *kedushoth* mentioned are counted, we find eleven, not ten. R. Hai Gaon[17] replies that Eretz Yisrael itself is not counted among the ten sanctities, since these ten "all refer to the respect due to places . . . but not to Eretz Yisrael as a whole . . . each of the ten sanctities gives rise to distinctive laws."

The Sanctity of the Land
and the Sanctity of Its Mitzvoth

The sanctity of Eretz Yisrael per se is to be distinguished from the sanctity arising out of the mitzvoth applicable to and arising from residence within it. On the one level, Eretz Yisrael is, as it were, a *hechsher mitzvah*, a necessary background and preparation for observing mitzvoth; on the other, it is sacred in essence. This, explains R. Kook[18] in the same fashion as Torah, though preparing and bringing one to observe mitzvoth, bears an intrinsic, superior sanctity stemming from its essential creation.

Residence There

He explains there[19] that this is the reason why residence in Eretz Yisrael is of equal weight to all the mitzvoth of the Torah.[20] The elemental sanctity of the Land is realized by residence, by being there. Hence, one living outside Eretz Yisrael lacks contact with it and is "as if he had no God."[21] "Said R. Jochanan: the verse:[22] 'Better a dry morsel and quietness therewith,' refers to Eretz Yisrael, where, one who resides though he eat only bread and salt is assured of the World to Come."[23]

The mitzvoth dependent on the land result from being there, but failure to observe such a particular mitzvah, challilah, does not detract from the elemental sanctity engendered by actual physical presence. It is a failure on a different level.

The fact that prophecy is possible only in Eretz Yisrael,[24] that the very land itself is polluted by murder[25] and by immorality,[26] is related to this level of essential sanctity that inheres in the land, as explained by HaTorah VeHamitzvah there.[27] For these ([murder] idolatry and immorality) are not, in the first instance, mitzvoth dependent on being in the land at all,[28] and one is obliged to observe them everywhere, yet only in connection with idolatry and immorality does the Torah say that the land will vomit you out. "Now the verse[29] mentioned 'the doings of the Land of Egypt,' for they practiced all these abominations, yet the Land of Egypt did not vomit them out . . . but the entire matter is grounded in the [spiritual] degree of the land and its sanctity."[30]

On this basis, we may suggest a solution to the difficult problem of the omission by Maimonides from his list of precepts of the mitzvah to settle in Eretz Yisrael. Nachmanides lists this in his additional precepts No. 4. Maimonides does not list it since residence in the land is sine qua non and is not to be equated with the particular precepts and obligations arising from it.[31]

Borders

The fundamental distinction between Eretz Yisrael per se and the mitzvoth to which it gives rise enables us to understand clearly the many practical halachic discussions centering on the borders of Eretz Yisrael. Basically, there are three sets of borders: the first, the borders promised to the patriarchs; second, those conquered by Joshua; and third, those occupied by Ezra and the people who returned with him from Babylon.[32]

The borders as promised to the patriarchs are the borders within which the unchanging, everlasting[33] sanctity of the land inheres. The discussion of the Tannaim regarding the duration of the sanctity[34] resulting from Joshua's conquest and Ezra's resettlement refers to the obligation to perform the particular mitzvoth that arise from habitation of the land.[35] Since *this* sanctity is created by human beings and their obligations after conquest or settlement, it may be terminable with defeat and exile from the land.

Conquest and Possession

Some authorities hold that the fact of conquest automatically brings about the obligations of the mitzvoth dependent on possession of the land,[36] others that the erection of the sanctuary brought them about.[37] According to the latter opinion, even though the sanctity of the Temple and Jerusalem is never nullified, because of the Divine Presence that ever resides there,[38] the sanctity stemming from the mitzvoth dependent on the land is rendered null without them.[39] Hence the Rabbinic status of these obligations nowadays.[40]

Maimonides[41] differentiates between the sanctity that resulted from the conquest by Joshua and that which resulted from the resettlement by Ezra. The sanctity of the former was dissolved by the conquest of Nebuchadnezzer, whereas that of the latter was never rendered null.[42] The logic for differentiation between conquest and settlement is difficult to comprehend and has not been satisfactorily solved.[43] Chatham Sopher[44] offers a fundamental solution. He explains that conquest may supersede conquest, but throughout Israel's history *chazzakkah*, the actual possession commenced by Ezra, never ceased. There were always some Jews in the land so that the original *chazzakkah* never came to an end. He bolsters this view with the fact that Maimonides himself[45] asserts that it is a Divine Promise that the land would never be denuded of Jews. Were this to happen, the Jewish calendar would be invalidated.[46] The difference between the two sanctifications is then to be found in a fact of history—a fact of history that is of the essence of Jewish existence, since "If, farbeit, no Jew were to remain in Eretz Yisrael, though there be Jews outside it, this is called the extinction of the people."[47]

My late grandfather, of blessed memory,[48] basing himself on the opinion of Rishonim[49] to the effect that the essential observance of Mitzvoth is in Eretz Yisrael, explains that this is also true of the study of Torah. Though the Yeshivoth in Babylon were hundreds of years old and enjoyed continuity and tradition, they were nonetheless in exile and as such lacked the "air of Eretz Yisrael" essential for the fullest acquisition of Torah by the soul. Only in Eretz Yisrael, the land sought by the eyes of God continuously, are the finest and deepest sensibilities aroused by Torah and Mitzvah.[50]

Halachah is not satisfied with obliging those in residence to observe the mitzvoth dependent on possession of the land. It obliges one to make every effort to be in the land. R. Jacob Emden writes:[51]

And I am ever amazed that Israel, so stringent with themselves with respect to the minutiae of mitzvoth, which they go to great lengths and expense to observe as perfectly as possible, yet belittles and is indolent with regards this delightful mitzvah, the pin upon which the entire Torah is suspended . . . . [I]t behooves every Jew to make a determined resolution to go up and dwell in Eretz Yisrael, at least if he is able to make some kind of a living there.

In explaining the mitzvah to live in Eretz Yisrael, Nachmanides[52] elaborates on the major points embraced by the mitzvah, halachoth that are obligatory on Israel for all time. These are the duty to wrest the land from foreigners[53] and possess it, the personal mitzvah to live there, that it is forbidden to leave the land empty or desolate,[54] and that one may not engage in conquest of other territories before Eretz Yisrael is completely in Jewish hands.

Aliyah

Since living in Eretz Yisrael is a personal mitzvah, one may go on aliyah even against parents' wishes.[55] The fact that it is a mitzvah gives rise to an immediate state of permanence to one coming there so that one who hires a dwelling in Eretz Yisrael is immediately obliged to affix a *mezuzah*,[56] though abroad one is free from this mitzvah for thirty days.[57] It is also considered a mitzvah to dedicate a home in Eretz Yisrael but not in *chutz la'aretz*.[58]

Even according to those opinions that disagree with Nachmanides as to the obligation nowadays to conquer the land and settle there,[59] Avnei Nezer[60] explains that such difference of opinion exists only so long as a foreign power is responsible for the country and prevents entry there. But a community or an individual who has permission of entry is certainly in duty bound to fulfill this mitzvah. He also states[61] that the problem is only one of conquest from without, but there is no doubt at all as to the right of self-defense on the part of those already there, and there is no shadow of infringement even of the lone opinion in the Talmud[62] that "they may not go up in force" until the time of the Messiah. According to this opinion, generally concurred in, there is no doubt whatsoever regarding the obligation on each individual to settle in Israel today.[63]

If the situation is such that as a result of aliyah he will become impecunious and have to live on charity, Maharit,[64] Rashbash,[65] and others hold that he is free from the mitzvah. Even in such a case, Avnei Nezer[66] is doubtful since this mitzvah is of equal weight to all the mitzvoth. He is certainly obliged to go to the expense of at least one-fifth of his capital in order to go there since this sum is the limit determined for fulfillment of all positive mitzvoth.[67] However, one who is able to work for a living is not necessarily bound by this limit in order to fulfill a mitzvah, and he may well be obliged in some cases to spend all of his capital in fulfilling it,[68] there being no danger of his having to beg since he can work.

Neither can the religious situation in Israel today be considered adequate motive for remaining abroad since "One should ever dwell in Eretz Yisrael even in a city with a non-Jewish majority, rather than abroad even in a city with a Jewish majority."[69]

In any event, though the situation is far from ideal religionwise in Eretz Yisrael, one should not exaggerate or draw false conclusions from this situation vis-à-vis aliyah:

For with all the shadows there are great lights that cannot be ignored, for Medinath Yisrael today is the world centre of Torah . . . thousands are engaged day and night upon its study, and Torah is returning to its own. For there is no Torah as the Torah of Eretz Yisrael. 'Said the Holy One, Blessed be He: a small group engaged in Torah in Eretz Yisrael is more beloved before Me than a great Sanhedrin abroad.' Thousands educate their children to Torah and mitzvoth . . . and many indeed are groping and seeking Torah guidance . . . and there is a famine for the word of the Lord.[70]

In searching for reasons why not to go on aliyah,[71] we would do well to remember that the needs of Am Yisrael and the challenge of rebuilding and defending the state take precedence over every other claim on the loyalty of Jewry's sons and daughters. The Jewish people as a people has every right to demand, and it does demand, of its children, to be in Israel. It demands that they come and shoulder the burden, that they come and face the challenge. In this demand the state has all the authority of the halachah behind it. As the Midrash (Lev. R. 25.5) states so poignantly, when Israel were about to enter the land, Moses said to them, "Let *every one of you* take up his spade and go out and plant trees."

Yeridah

It goes without saying that one who is already there is forbidden to leave; thus, Maimonides[72] codifies the law concerning *yeridah* as follows:

> It is forbidden ever to go out of Eretz Yisrael except to study Torah, to marry or to deliver from the non-Jew. Then he must return. Similarly, he may go out for business but it is forbidden to live abroad. And though, in the instances stated, it is permitted to go abroad, this is not the measure of the pious, for Machlon and Kilyon[73] who were leaders of their generation, and went out only because of great distress, became liable to extinction before God.

Reaching Out Beyond the Borders

The halachah of Eretz Yisrael reaches out and imposes itself distinctly, and this in the most important fields, on those who have not yet fulfilled the mitzvah of aliyah. Such essential institutions as ordination[74] and the fixing of the calendar are only valid if done in Eretz Yisrael[75] or if Jews reside there.[76] The function of the courts, the *Batei Din*, outside of Eretz Yisrael are in many important matters dependent on the assumed delegation of authority to act, by those ordained there.[77]

In what manner are they to remember it [the Temple]? Though those who live in the East, or in faraway isles require rain during the summer solstice, they do not pray for rain except when Eretz Yisrael requires rain. For if you say that they should pray for it when they need it, even in summer, they will come to think of themselves as if they are in their own land. But they must see themselves as guests with their heart directed to Eretz Yisrael.[78]

That all Israel are surety for one another is a direct consequence of being in the land, "for the land welds those who dwell therein into a single unit, hence they became surety for each other only when they crossed the Jordan and entered Eretz Yisrael."[79] This is intimated in the Talmud, which states[80] that in regard to *hora'ah*, follow the majority of the inhabitants of Eretz Yisrael, for these are considered a community, the others not.
Avnei Nezer adds:[81]

Now it is obvious that though Israel is in exile, the surety for one another, remains. The reason is that though in exile, their place is in Eretz Yisrael, and when we are in another country we are accounted as exiles for this is not our place. Our place is only in Eretz Yisrael and it is a mitzvah to dwell there. Hence it is considered as if we are all there, though we are not there in fact. Nonetheless, that is our place.

Simply put, the Halachah says there is no other place that is his. Hence the unity and brotherhood of Israel, the responsibility of Jew toward Jew, is inextricably bound up with Eretz Yisrael, which reaches forth and embraces all of its scattered children.

Notes to Chapter Seven

1. Deut. 23, 16.
2. Gitt. 45a.
3. Responsa, Sha'arei Tzedek, Kobetz Teshuvoth HaGeonim, Gate 6, No. 12.
4. Meg. 14a.
5. Responsa, Tzophenath Pa'anech, No. 143.
6. Horayoth 3a. This is not, however, so in regard to every law requiring a *kahal*. Some laws require the physical presence of the majority of Israel in Israel for the constitution of a *kahal*, e.g., the law of the Jubilee, Arach. 32b; *Challah*, Ket. 25a; and this is so according to Maimonides of all tithes, Yad, Terumoth 1, 26; for the building of the Temple, Chinuch, mitzvah 95. Nonetheless, in regard to matters bearing on Klal Yisrael as a whole, even the minority, living in Israel, has the law of Klal Yisrael, see Get Mekushar,

notes to Mizrachi on SeMaG, p. 134b. A good example of this is quoted by R. M. Z. Neriah in his discussion of *Hallel* on Yom Ha'Atzmauth. The institution of the fourth *berachah* of the *Birchath Hamazon, Hatov VeHametiv* was the result of bringing the dead of Bethar to burial, Ber. 48b., from which we see that since the event was of national significance and importance, it was considered by Chazal as an event of Klal Yisrael. See also Responsa Be'er Yitzchak, Orach Chayyim, No. 14, sect. 2.

7. Levit. 25, 23.

8. Responsa of R. Nachshon Gaon, quoted in Responsa, Mahram of Rothenburg, No. 536.

9. Maimonides, Beth Habechirah 6, 16. See Responsa, Kol Mevasser, Pt. 2, No. 43, s.q. Min HaHalachoth, and s.q. Midbarech Naveh.

10. *Ibid.*, 7, 7 Mishneh Berurah to 561, 2. Even according to Ra'abad who holds that there is no *kareth* for entry into the Temple site nowadays, the prohibition remains. See Mishpetei Cohen, No. 66. Tuketchinsky, Sepher Eretz Yisrael, p. 71. Also Mikdash Melech, pp. 34–36, and notes of Hararei Sadeh, 4–7, *ad loc.*

11. Yeb. 64a.

12. Torah Temimah to Genesis 16, 3, note 2.

13. See also R. H. 16b.

14. Makk. 7a. "Perhaps this will help to find a way to exonerate him, Rashi." Similarly, see Sho'el Umeshiv, Tinyana, Pt. 3, No. 87, in regard to a *Katlanith*.

15. Kelim 1, 6–9.

16. "Jerusalem enjoys two sanctities, one as a walled city, the second as Jerusalem itself, Responsa, Mahrit, Choshen Mishpat, No. 37." So also Minchath Chinuch, 362. Special sensitivity toward Jerusalem is evidenced in the Midrash, Exodus Rabbah, end, which records that there was a special accounting house outside Jerusalem, and anyone who wished to make up his accounts would repair there that he might not make his reckoning in Jerusalem and possibly become grieved or distressed there. For Jerusalem is "the joy of the whole earth, Ps. 48, 3."

17. In a Responsum, quoted by Eshtori Haparchi, Kaftor Vapherach, chap. 10 (Edelman, 1852), p. 39.

18. Shabbath Ha'aretz, Introduction, p. 61.

19. *Ibid.*, p. 62.

20. Sifri to Deut. 12, 29.

21. Ket. 110b.

22. Prov. 17, 1.

23. Midrash Mishlei, 17.

24. Mechilta to Bo, Introduction, section commencing: In the Land of Egypt. See also Rashi to Ezekiel 1, 3.

25. Nos. 35, 33.

26. Levit. 18, 25; 28.

27. To Sifra, paragraph 150, in Malbim's ed.

28. Nachmanides to Levit. *ibid.*

29. Lev. *ibid.* 3.

30. Nachmanides *ibid.* See the relevant remarks of R. Moses Hagiz in Sephath Emeth, pp. 30–31.
31. This may be compared with the stand of the commentators to Sepher Hamitzvoth, No. 1, who justify the omission by Halachoth Gedoloth of the mitzvah "to believe in God." He does not list it, they claim, since it is a sine qua non, without which no mitzvah is possible, and hence it cannot be included in the list of particulars arising from it. The fact that Maimonides does list the mitzvah to believe is explained to refer not to belief itself but to particular forms of its expression, i.e., specific, detailed activities.
32. The precise delineation of these different sets of borders is a matter of both Rabbinic and scholarly contention and embraces a literature unto itself. We cannot enter into this question here, although it is fraught with actual problems such as the observance of the second day of Yom Tov beyond the confines settled by Ezra, and the observance of the specific mitzvoth dependent on Eretz Yisrael, in these same areas.
33. Responsa, Chatham Sopher, Yoreh De'ah, No. 234.
34. Meg. 10a; Hag. 3b, Yeb. 81b; Hull, 7a; etc.
35. See Eshtori Haparchi, Kaftor Vapherach, chaps. 10 and 11 at length.
36. Chazon Ish to Shebi'ith, 3, 1.
37. Rashi to B. M. 89a; Nachmanides to Levit. 26, 42.
38. Maimonides, Beth Habechirah 6, 16.
39. Tosaphoth to Yeb. 82b, s.q. Yerushah.
40. There are, however, strong differences of opinion on this matter, some authorities holding, for a variety of reasons, that these obligations are also today of biblical standing. See Shulchan Aruch, Yoreh De'ah 331, 1; and *Encylopedia Talmudith*, Vol. 2, p. 218, notes 128, 129, and the authorities quoted in the following section there, pp. 218–222 on each of the mitzvoth dependent on the land. Current Responsa on this problem are voluminous.
41. Yad, Terumoth, 1, 5; Beth Habechirah 6, 16.
42. Nonetheless he holds that the mitzvoth of the land are Rabbinic, Terumoth 1, 26, since only a fraction of the people returned.
43. See Kesseph Mishnah *ad loc.* and the note to Terumoth 1, 5 in the Rambam Le'am ed.
44. On sugyoth, to Hullin 7a.
45. Sepher Hamitzvoth, mitzvah 153.
46. Maimonides *ibid.* Yad, Kiddush Hachodesh 5, 13.
47. Responsa, Yoreh De'ah No. 234.
48. The Gaon, Rabbi D. Rabinowitz of Mohilev and Sunderland, Ne'um David, manuscript.
49. Rashba, Responsa 194, Ra'abun; see also Addereth Eliahu to Deut. 8, 1.
50. He explains several difficult Talmudic passages on this basis. Cf. also the gloss of R. Jacob Emden to Sanhedrin 97a.
51. Introduction to Siddur Ya'abetz.
52. Positive mitzvoth, No. 4.
53. Though there is no objection to foreigners living there provided they eschew idolatry, Maimonides, Issurei Biah 14, 7. See also *ibid.*, Avodah Zarah 10, 6 and Mishneh Lemelech to Ma'achaloth Assuroth 11, 7. The foreigner is also entitled to social benefits, Maimonides, *ibid.*, 10, 12.

54. There are numerous halachoth that deal with the development, fructification, beautification, and preservation of the land, e.g., B.K. 90, on cutting down trees; Tamid 29, on destroying its fruit; Arachin 33, on turning arable land into gardens or the reverse, the former because of the reduction of farm land, Mishneh Lemelech to Shemmitta 13, 5, the latter because it destroys the beauty of the town, Rashi. The Talmud records, San. 102b, that the reason Omri merited kingship was because, in spite of his wickedness, he added a town to Israel. The town was Samaria, the center of idolatry that brought about the exile, yet he is still accounted meritorious for having built it and thereby contributed to the mitzvah of developing and settling the land. Additional environmental considerations, bearing on the quality of life, are scattered throughout the Mishnah, Talmud, and Codes.

55. Mahram of Rothenburg, Responsa, Berlin, No. 79. Responsa Mabit, Pt. I, No. 139.

56. Men. 44a.

57. See Yoreh De'ah 286, 22.

58. Jerushalmi, Sot, end of chap. 8. According to Avnei Nezer, Y.D. 455, acquiring a property in Eretz Yisrael, though still resident abroad, is accounted a partial fulfillment of the mitzvah to settle there. So also Mahrit, Responsa Pt. I, No. 131.

59. The disagreement is only in regard to the obligation to wage war in order to capture the land, not as to the mitzvah to live there. The opinion expressed by R. Chaim Hacohen, Tos. Ket. 110b, is rejected by virtually all authorities.

60. Responsa, Yoreh De'ah, 454, 56.

61. Ibid. 54.

62. Ketuboth, end.

63. Chacham Zevi, Responsa, No. 41, and others hold, however, that there is no power to enforce this mitzvah; it is dependent on him alone. But see Imrei Shemuel, to Se'aroth Eliahu, p. 26, note 1, who holds that this mitzvah is enforceable.

64. Responsa, Pt. 2, No. 28.

65. Responsa, No. 2.

66. Ibid., 8.

67. See Rema, Orach Chayyim, 656.

68. See Biur Halachah, ibid., s.q. Afilu, eight lines from the bottom.

69. Maimonides, Melachim, 5, 12. and see ibid., Ishuth 13, 19.

70. Obadaiah Joseph, Responsa, Yabia Omer, Pt. 6, Orach Orach Chayyim, No. 41. See also Imrei Shemuel loc. cit., p. 29, end of note, to the effect that it is halachically illogical not to go to Eretz Yisrael out of fear that one may fail to perform mitzvoth there. Similarly Ya'abetz, Introduction to his Siddur, Sulam Beth El, p. 28.

71. R. Moses Hagiz listed all the "modern" reasons for not going on aliyah, two hundred years ago in his wonderful little book, Sephath Emeth, and he decries them all. It may be noted that nowadays there is no halachic objection to the ownership of property in Israel by Levites; see the letter of the Gaon R. Saul Moshe Zilberman, of Verishov, printed in Piskei Teshuvah, Pt. 2, p. 4.

72. Melachim, 5, 9; See also Tosaphoth to Avodah Zarah 13 s.q. Lilmod.

73. Ruth, chap. 1.
74. Though the original, traditional ordination ceased in the time of the Talmud, it could only be validly performed in Eretz Yisrael. San. 14a, Maimonides, Kiddush Hachodesh, 3, 4.
75. Maimonides *ibid.*, chap. 1, end; chap. 5 end.
76. See supra, notes 45, 46, and 47.
77. B.K. 84b, Choshen Mishpat, 1, and Commentaries thereon.
78. Mishnath Rabbi Eliezer, ed. Enelow, sect. 3, p. 50.
79. Mahral, quoted by Avnei Nezer, Responsa, O. H. 314.
80. Horayoth 3a. See supra, note 6, this chapter.
81. Responsa, Yoreh De'ah, 126.

II

The Study of Talmud

8

Talmudic Logic — Sevara

Peculiar Construction of the Talmud

Now that we have begun to fathom some of the fundamental amalgams of the halachic mind, we are better able to understand the essential nature of the "peculiar" construction of the Talmud and also to grasp something of the problematic form adopted by halachic codes. For it is in these that the basic outlook outlined in the previous chapters is expressed. I shall preface my remarks by quoting a brief section of the Talmud. On highlighting some of the aspects of this, we shall, it is hoped, gain some of the visual and mental aids necessary for continuing our discussion.

The Talmud says:[1]

And she acquires her freedom by divorce or her husband's death. As for divorce, it is well, since it is written:[2] "then he shall write her a bill of divorcement"; but whence do we know [that she is freed by] her husband's death? It is logic — *sevara:* he [the husband] bound her; hence he frees her.

But what of consanguineous relations, whom he binds, and nevertheless does not free?[3] But since Scripture decreed that a *yebamah* without children is forbidden [to the outside world], it follows that if she has children she is permitted. Yet perhaps, if she has no children she is forbidden to the world but permitted to the *yabbam,*[4] whereas if she has children she is forbidden to all?

But since Scripture states that a widow is forbidden to a High Priest,[5] it follows that she is permitted to an ordinary priest.[6] Yet perhaps [she is forbidden] to a High Priest by a negative injunction, and to all others by an affirmative precept?[7] What business has this [alleged] affirmative precept? If her husband's death has effect, let her be entirely free; and if not, let her remain in her original status?[8]

Why not? It [sc. her husband's death] withdraws her from [the penalty of] death and places her under [the interdict of] an affirmative precept. For this may be analogous to consecrated animals rendered unfit [for sacrifice], which originally [before they become unfit] involved a trespass offering[9] and might not be sheared or worked with; yet when they are redeemed, they no longer involve a trespass offering, but may still not be sheared or worked with?[10]

But [it is known] since Scripture said:[11] "[And what man is there . . . his house,] lest he die in battle and another man take her." To this R. Shisha, son of R. Idi, demurred: Perhaps who is meant by "another man": the *yabam* [but not others]?

Said R. Ashi: there are two answers to this: firstly, the *yabam* is not designated "another man": and furthermore, it is written:[12] "And if the latter husband hate her, and write her a bill of divorcement . . . or if the latter husband die," thus death is compared to divorce: just as divorce completely frees her, so does death completely free her.

The stages followed in solving the problem posed by the gemmara are:

1. It is logical to assume so—*sevara*. That is, logical reasoning alone is sufficient to prove that the marriage tie, though biblical, is voided in this instance.
2. The gemmara proves that the logic advanced is, by analogy, insufficient.
3. Two scriptural bases are involved, and logical possibilities are raised in objection to each.
4. Against the logical objection an analogy to consecrated animals is drawn with the purpose of substantiating the previous logical supposition.
5. A further scriptural proof is forthcoming.
6. This is objected to on possible exegetical grounds.
7. These possible grounds are refuted.
8. The final solution is found on the basis of one of the hermeneutic rules of Torah interpretation (*hekesh*).

Let us be quite clear about our subject. The Talmud is discussing the very serious problem of voiding the marriage bond and hence freeing a woman hitherto tied in marriage, to marry another at will. No small or insignificant matter, since were she to take up liaison with another before the dissolvement of her previous marriage, she would incur capital punishment as an adultress.[13] The gemmara attempts to solve the problem in three ways: by logical reasoning, by scriptural proof, by Scripture as interpreted by hermeneutic rule.

Dominance and Force of *Sevara*

While all three methods are legitimate, it is important to note their order. Logical reasoning—*sevara*— precedes actual scriptural proof. Furthermore, had the logical reasoning been sustained, no scriptural base would have been sought; the *sevara* would have sufficed. The first fundamental point to note, therefore, is the force of the *sevara*, as the Talmud exclaims in other places:[14] "Why do I require scriptural proof? It is logical—*sevara hi!*" If a *sevara* exists, Scripture has no need to teach that which I could know by logic.

Now this is not only so in attempting to solve the problem outright. It is also true, as stage four shows, in regard to voiding a logical objection and reinstating a previous objection raised against the plain meaning of Scripture.

This is in fact only another way of saying that *sevara* has biblical force, a fact that the Talmud[15] emphasizes most clearly even in relation to life itself: "How do we know that one should expose himself to death rather than commit murder? It is a *sevara* viz., who knows that your blood is the redder."[16]

Reverting to the order of the argument of the gemmara, scriptural proof precedes that proffered by hermeneutic means, but in the last resort it is these, and not the plain meaning of Scripture, that are found to be adequate to free the woman for remarriage. It must, therefore, be concluded that both *sevara* and hermeneutic rule carry scriptural force.[17] Once this is appreciated, the argument of the gemmara flows smoothly but for one seemingly incongruous link—the analogy drawn from the case of consecrated animals.

We must, however, bear in mind that the gemmara is not superficially comparing the two laws. It is seeking a common unit of thought, of logical premise from which to draw a conclusion, and from this standpoint the incongruity disappears.

Unity and Cohesion of the Deeper Levels of Logical Construction

This kind of analogy is common in the Talmud; see, for example, B.K. 24a., where problems in torts are queried from teachings concerning *zab*, or Sabb. 59b., where problems of Sabbath and ritual impurity are taken together and so forth. It but reflects the unity of the deeper logical construction and cohesion of halachah. It is this deeper level which shows how concepts employed in halachah are reducible to others, and how various concepts and principles are logically or functionally related to others in halachic reasoning.[18] "One who asks a question [in the Beth Hamidrash] out of context, should say: "I have asked out of context," 'so the opinion of R. Meir. But the sages say: "there is no need, for the entire Torah is one subject.' "[19]

Such analogy forms one of the basic, if not the dominant structural strata of the responsa literature, particularly in regard to those problems for which no actual halachic precedents are readily available.

Ritba in his commentary to our passage explains the connecting link between the two cases as follows. At the base of our problem is a woman who by presumption is forbidden to marry another. She is known definitely to have been married and was therefore forbidden absolutely to any other person, and until we know definitely that this presumption has been voided, it remains in force. Now the factor that gave rise to the presumption (i.e., the husband who died) no longer exists. Does this remove the presumption?

In seeking to answer this question, the Talmud looks for an analogous case of presumption. Such a case must start off with a presumption of forbiddenness, similar to that of the married woman, and, by reason of a change in status, the presumption must be known to be voided in its entirety. This is found in the instance of consecrated animals whose secular use was entirely forbidden but, on redemption from the Temple treasury, though forbidden expressly by Scripture for shearing and work, no longer involve the transgressor in the original penalty for working with them.[20]

The basis of the entire section is the *sevara*, and this permeates all of its parts as well as its extensions when the passage is studied together with the commentaries. The Talmud uses and applies logical reasoning to all the available material. Every deduction, every implication, every *sevara* is examined. The *sevara* delves beneath the surface to find logical connection where none would seem, at first sight, to exist.

The Way of the Talmud

This is the way of the Talmud. Nothing is taken for granted and it seeks its own bases on grounds of logic. The Talmud is in fact so constructed that the central points of each section, and of every opinion, must be discovered and analyzed by the student himself. To study Talmud one must become involved in the logical reasoning called *sevara*. This is gemmara, as Rashi[21] explains: "Gemmara is dependent upon *sevara*, for they used to expound the logic of the Mishnah and gather together and engage in it. This is the format of the gemmara arranged by the Amoraim." On this the Talmud there says, "One who has learned Bible and Mishnah but has not ministered the sages [i.e., engaged in gemmara, Rashi] is an *am ha'aretz*."

Who Is an *Am Ha'aretz*?

In discussing this, R. M. A. Amiel[22] quotes the following letter written by the Gaon R. Moshe Mordechai Epstein of Slobodka (Later of Hebron) to his colleagues:

> There is study and there is study. We find that Chazal said[23] that one who is asked a question of halachah in one tractate, even in the tractate Kallah,[24] and he can answer it, is called a sage. Whilst of Rami bar Poppa they told[25] that he did not wish to include in a quorum for Grace after meals one who had studied Sifra, Sifri, and Mechilta, and that he considered him to be an *am ha'aretz* because he had not ministered to scholars. How far apart they are! This one studied a single tractate and is called a sage, whilst this one studied the entire shass and is called an *am ha'aretz*. Because the essence of Torah knowledge is not in wide knowledge and familiarity with texts. The essence is the *sevara* and the understanding of the subjects. As they said:[26] "The reward for study is given for *sevara*." If one is expert in the practical knowledge of an halachah, but is unaware of its logical bases, he cannot say that he lacks part of it; he lacks it completely, because the essence is in the *sevara*.
>
> By means of the underlying *sevara*, deduction of further halachoth is affected radically, hence they said:[27] "The tannaim[28] destroy the world," meaning, as explained there, that they decide halachoth on the basis of the Mishnah studied but since they did

not learn gemmara, the contradictions, queries and answers, nor did they plumb deeply the inner depths of the problems, they were unable to decide halachah.

This being so, even one who studied the entire shass but was not versed in the methods of *sevara*, is called an *am ha'aretz*. See for example, Gittin 6b. where they said: "Because a man does not know this rule of R. Isaac, is he therefore not a great scholar? If it were a rule established by *sevara* we might think so, but this is an oral tradition and he had [simply] not heard it."

Sevara is the objective[29] analytical tool of halachah and by its means the expansion or limitation, the essence and fundamentals, the direction and purpose of a given halachah are determined. It is fluid rather than absolute, since as Nachmanides says:[30]

All who study our Talmud know that no final proofs can be adduced to settle disputes among its commentators, nor in the main are there irredeemable questions. For in this wisdom there is no certain confirmation, as there is for example in mathematics or in geometry. But we shall try with all our strength, and it will suffice in any controversy to oust an opinion by weighty *sevaroth*.

The *sevara* compels even when there is no actual Talmudic weight in its support—"his earlier words are logically correct, and the *sevara* would seem so. Though there is no proof for it in the Talmud."[31] And again, "That opinion though without Talmudic support, is convincing enough by itself, and is correct."[32] However, while *sevara* is sufficient to decide problems raised by the Talmud and not resolved therein,[33] it is insufficient when the Talmud itself declares *Teku*— the matter is undecided,[34] for then he would be arguing against the Talmud itself, which by closing the discussion with the terminum *Teku*, intended that the matter remain a case of doubtful prohibition for all time.[35]

So it is for the Talmud, so for its commentators and so also for all who take up its folios. It is also so when one studies halachah with the object of rendering a practical directive. Leaving aside the norms, criteria and hierarchy of authority in such matters, the decisor—possek—is still faced with the problem of sifting his material and deciding the relevance of precedent to the matter in hand. He must weigh the evidence carefully, compare minutely and decide if and in what measure and on what basis his problem is analogous to a decision already rendered or not. He can only do this if, in addition to commanding the necessary textual material, he is fully versed in halachic *sevara*.

The Problem of Codifying Halacha

It is this problem that has dogged codifiers of halachah since codes first began to be formulated in the earliest times. A code purports to represent authoritative decision. To be so goes entirely against the grain of halachic thinking and development. This was expressed tellingly in one of the early codes[36] by R. Tanchum b. Chanilai, when he said, "Had the Torah been given in the form of clear-cut decisions [leaving no room for differences of opinion] there would have remained no ground upon which the decisor could stand." As also in Midrash *Tehillim:*[37]

> Said R. Jannai: the words of Torah were not given as clear-cut decisions but, on everything that the Holy One, Blessed be He, said to Moses, He would tell him forty-nine ways in favor of "clean" and forty-nine in favor of "unclean." Said he, "Master of the Universe can we stay the clarification of the halachah?" "Turn after the majority,[38]" He replied.

Furthermore, a code not only acts as a standard; it tends to crystallize its subject matter and impede the organic growth of its material. It interferes with the theoretical legal processes at work within a viable and dynamic system. There may be excellent reasons for compiling codes, but halachah is in fact more at home without one.[39] This problem faced all the codifiers of halachah and was variously overcome by them. It is, however, the basic reason for the striking diversity evidenced from code to code.

Between Ra'abad and Maimonides

To Maimonides' remarks in his preface to Mishneh Torah to the effect that "I have called this code Mishneh Torah because a person may read the written law first and then read in this book and know from it the entire oral law without studying any intermediate work," Ra'abad comments:

> His [M.'s] intention was constructive but it has failed to be so, for he has forsaken the method of all previous codifiers who brought

proof for their decisions and quoted their authorities, from which practice great benefit was derived. For it often happens that the dayyan, relying on a certain authority, decides to permit or prohibit; if, however, he would have known that there exists a more important source, he would have decided in its light. And now, I do not know why I should leave my received decision and proof for the sake of this compiler. If he who disagrees with me is greater than I, all well and good, but if I be greater than he, why should I annul my reasoning for his? And furthermore, there are matters concerning which the Geonim disagree with one another and this compiler chose to decide according to the one opinion and included it in his code. Why should I rely upon his choice if I do not agree with it? And [I am at a disadvantage because] I do not know who is his opponent, whether it is fitting to argue with him or not.

For Ra'abad, pessak is integrally related to the give and take of halachic discussion. But Maimonides, as pointed out by Migdal Oz,[40] "deals in his code only with that which is explicit in the Talmud but not with what may be deduced from it." Maimonides himself declared in a responsum to the sages of Lunel,[41] "We will not forsake an explicit statement in the Talmud and decide on the basis of the give and take of halachic discussion." This is true also of Maimonides regarding his numerous quotations from the Jerusalem Talmud that he prefers when this is more explicit than the Babli.[43]

Asheri[44] is equally outspoken in the matter. He says:

Similarly all those who render decisions on the basis of Maimonides' words [in the Yad] make mistakes. Since they are not adept in gemmara to know the source of his words, they mistakenly permit the forbidden and vice versa. For he [M.] did not do as other compilers who brought proof for their words and indicated their sources in the gemmara, from which one could fathom the bases and the truth. But he wrote his work as one prophesying from God, without reasoning and without proof so that whoever reads it thinks that he understands it. But this is not so. For if he is not expert in gemmara he understands nothing of its [i.e., of the Yad] depth and true perspective, and he will stumble in judgment and in rendering decision from it unless he finds proof in the gemmara. And so I heard of a great man in Barcelona[45] who was expert in three Orders of the Talmud and said: "I am amazed by those who have not studied gemmara, but read the books of the Rambam, of blessed memory, and render decisions from his books thinking that they know them." He added, "I know of myself that with regards the three Orders that I have studied, I understand when I read his books, but as to his work on sacrifices and seeds, I don't understand them at all. And I know that this is true of them with respect to all of his works."

Early Criticism of the *Shulchan Aruch*

The original opposition to the *Shulchan Aruch* of R. Joseph Caro was similarly motivated, so that while the Rema in his introduction writes, "And I saw all his words in the Shulchan Aruch as if given by Moses from God and the students who follow will drink of his words [as if they are] unanimous, with the result that they will set at nought the custom of [other] countries," and R. Joseph b. Lev[46], Rosh Yeshivah in Constantinople, forbade his students to study the works of Beth Joseph because they would lead to a lessening of the wide familiarity with the primary sources. R. Yom Tov Zahalon[47] wrote that R. Joseph Caro made the *Shulchan Aruch* only for youngsters and *amei ha'aretz*.[48]

Others[49] considered the *Shulchan Aruch* as an index to Caro's Magnum Opus, Beth Joseph, study of which alone enables one to decide halachah responsibly. R. Abraham Danzig of Vilna, himself the author of two brief, popular presentations of two parts of the *Shulchan Aruch*, writes in the preface to Nishmath Adam:

> Though our masters, the authors of the *Shulchan Aruch*, indeed set for us a table laden with delicacies . . . we nonetheless lack a mouth to eat and to enjoy. For, as is known, the Master of Israel, the Beth Joseph's main work is the Beth Joseph on the Tur, as is the Darchei Moshe the main work of Isserles. In those works they fully explained the running, living sources of their words, while the *Shulchan Aruch* presents only indications for one who has thoroughly studied Tur and Beth Joseph to undertake brief revision . . . but they never intended anyone to decide the halachah from the *Shulchan Aruch* alone.

The Responsa Literature

Side by side with the code literature is the responsa literature.[50] This latter is in fact the embodiment of pristine halachic thinking applied to day-by-day problems. In the responsa, each problem is tackled on the basis of Talmudic grassroots principle that is developed through commentary, codes, and other responsa until the final conclusion is reached.

It is in the vast responsa literature that one witnesses the halachic process alive, alert, and dynamic.[51]

Historically, the streams of code and responsa were never divorced from one another. Those who compiled codes also wrote responsa, while the conclusions of the responsa were embraced by and incorporated in the later codes and glossaries.

Nowadays, when studying *Shulchan Aruch* in conjunction with its commentaries and glossaries, many of which are printed alongside the actual text of the *Shulchan Aruch*, one in fact becomes engaged in the halachic process since the accompaniments to the text indeed argue, discuss, dissect, and analyze the *Shulchan Aruch* on the basis of primary texts and contemporary sources as well as in the light of contemporary problems. So in fact the codes themselves, while bringing order and classification into the tremendous mass of halachic material available, were never static, were continually updated, and succeed in retaining contemporary viability and relevance.

Presenting Halacha in Modern, Accessible Legal Form and Format

Our discussion of halachic codes and the responsa literature bears a sequel. There is a growing genus of literature, on a fundamental, vexing problem in modern Israel. Leaving aside the actual question of replacing present Israeli law by halachah, if, for argument's sake, such a transformation were possible, now, how would one actually set about instituting halachah as the law of the state? To put the question another way: Is it possible to present halachah in modern, accessible legal form and format?

The problems are indeed legion, for we are not here seeking a method of creating a hybrid system shot through with the kind of fundamental contradictions that result from grafting systems of law on one another. We are seeking to define a method of accessibility and presentation that would enable halachah to take over the entire corpus of legal life in a bourgeoning, dynamic, and viable society. The problem falls naturally into two distinct spheres, each of which inheres its own problems: first, the present state of halachah regarding legal problems already dealt with more or less exhaustively by halachah and, second, the spectrum of problems that, arising from conditions of modern life, have not yet been so treated in halachah.

The raw material to cope certainly exists, but the theoretical, structural background is more fully developed in some spheres than in others, so that we do not merely have to search the records—we have to reexamine basically entire spheres of halachah in the light of the numerous problems posed by present society. In traditional terms, these particular problems require authoritative, classical responsa that would set out the basic norms to be applied, and that could assume halachic test case validity. This in much the same fashion as the towering achievement toward the end of the previous century, of R. Isaac Elchanan Spector, concerning the problems of *Aguna*. Piecemeal efforts in the form of numerous halachic monographs and studies have appeared during recent years. For the most part, the material is, however, scattered in responsa, the publications of the religious courts, journals, and pamphlets, but no real coordinating discussion within the framework of authoritative halachic groups of scholars and possekim has taken place.

It would seem that a fully coordinated, organized, long-term project is called for. Such a project should assign groups of recognized halachic scholars to particular problems and spheres of law. The groups would investigate, analyze, and formulate the fundamental halachic norms to be applied to the problem in practice. Such a framework is entirely feasible within the organization of already existing institutions. Coordination and planning are lacking, as also the essential task of defining the areas of law and the problems to be dealt with.

The work of such groups would in no way interfere with the traditional dynamism of halachah, its processes, or its instruments, and the results, which would be independent halachic results, could easily be presented in modern, accessible format. Publication would be unified and in accord with predetermined standards and systems of presentation, and would take place only after independent discussion and criticism by halachic authorities not primarily engaged in the group study.

Within the framework of an approach such as that outlined, the enormously difficult problem of the present state of the sea of halachic material with which it is impossible for the nonexpert (and for many experts) to cope would in time be obviated. At present one of the major problems lies in the largely amorphous, scattered, and conglomerate nature of the material of halachah. Several attempts have been made in the past and are presently being conducted in order to overcome this terrifying obstacle. To my mind, this problem could well be left alone at the present time and the resources devoted to its solution more usefully employed. Were the previously described scheme to be adopted, the problem of lack of accessibility would solve itself almost as a by-product of the main task of the groups. It is possible to assign to a competent member of each group the task of drawing up a fully referenced and cross-referenced index of the subject under study by his group, as their assignment progresses. The indexes, prepared in accord with predetermined plan, directive, and criteria, could then be integrated by computer, so that eventually a full reference index of halachah would automatically emerge.

The functions of the proposed project would be primarily administrative and advisory, as follows:

1. Determination of the fields for study
2. Determination of the composition of the groups, which would work in their own locale and within existing settings
3. Developing machinery for ensuring work progress within the groups
4. Handling study group results for independent discussion and criticism
5. Determination of standard format for publication
6. Preparation of manuscript for publication
7. Publication
8. Determination of indexing criteria
9. Production of an integrated, cumulative index
10. Distribution

The value of the proposal lies, first, in shifting the emphasis of activity to the actual grappling with problems. Second, the problems dealt with will be treated on strictly halachic initative, grounds, and considerations and will be free from admixture of systems grounded in concepts and modes of thought strange to halachah. Third, the present instruments of halachah will not be affected in the slightest. What will emerge will be an original, strictly halachic codex dealing with modern problems, prepared by expert halachists, and presented in modern, accessible format. In addition, in the course of time a thoroughly cross-referenced integrated index of halachah will become available.

Notes to Chapter Eight

1. Kiddushin 13b. Translation of the passage is taken from the Soncino Translation of the Talmud, Kidd., pp. 55–56.
2. Deut. 24, 1.
3. A woman may not marry her father-in-law even after her husband's death. Thus the interdict which he imposed on her by marriage remains even when he dies.
4. In order to prevent erasure of the dead man's name, see Deut. 25, 6.
5. Levit. 21, 14.
6. And by the same reasoning, to all other men.
7. Levit. 21, 14 is in the form of a negative injunction, the violation of which is punished by flagellation (malkoth), whereas that of an affirmative precept goes unpunished by biblical law. Tosaphoth suggests that the affirmative precept may be the verse, Gen. 2, 24: "Therefore shall a man . . . cleave to *his* wife," implying but not to his neighbor's wife (cf. San. 58a.). An interdict implied by an affirmative precept is itself regarded as such, and not as a negative command.
8. As a married woman she is forbidden to others by a negative precept under pain of death; Levit. 18, 20; 20, 10; Deut. 22, 22. There are no grounds for supposing that her husband's death leaves the interdict but changes its nature.
9. For secular use, e.g., plowing with them.
10. See Bek. 15a. This proves that a certain fact may leave the interdict but change its penalty. And the same may apply to the husband's death.
11. Deut. 20, 7.
12. Deut. 24, 3.
13. Levit. 18, 20, etc.
14. Ket. 22a; B.K. 46b; Nid. 25a.
15. San. 74a.
16. I.e., his life is not less valuable than yours; hence if one is ordered to take life under threat of being killed himself, he should face that threat rather than commit murder. See Rashi to Pes. 25b.
17. See the discussion on the status of laws derived by means of the rules, in TaR YaG, by the present author.
18. While some principles apply only in limited areas of halachah (e.g., *muktza*, which applies only to sabbaths and festivals), others are broader in scope (e.g., agency, which is common to as diverse a spectrum as divorce, fiscal matters, personal status, mitzvoth, sacrifices, etc.). Yet others, such as the rules of presumption, embrace even wider fields.
19. Tosephta, San. 7, 5.
20. The surface problems of the passage have now been cleared up. The commentaries treat the passage in relation to a variety of additional problems, but these need not detain us here. I would, however, on the basis of

the responsa of R. Joseph Rozin, Eben Ha'ezer, 34, 36 suggest that the difference between the two answers of the Talmud reflects a difference of opinion as to what exactly frees the woman. The first answer is satisfied that the act of dying is the dissolving agent in marriage, while the second answer, in deducing death from divorce, considers that lack of the essential components of marriage, i.e., a husband and wife, bring about its dissolution. A practical difference arising from this theoretical standpoint would seem to arise in the case of a married man who undergoes a heart transplant, since he may be considered technically dead prior to receiving the donor heart. What is his wife's status after he has received it? Must he rewed her? See Eben Ha'ezer, 17, and Birchei Joseph thereon at length. Also *Sho'el Umeshiv*, 3d ed., Pt. 2, No. 131.

21. To Ber. 47b. s.q. Shelo.
22. Hamiddoth Lechekker Hahalachah, Vol. 1, Introduction Sect. 15.
23. Kidd. 49b.
24. Which is short and not difficult; Rashi.
25. Ber. 47b.
26. Ber. 6b.
27. Sot. 22a.
28. The tannaim here referred to are those who used to learn mishnayoth and baraithoth by heart for recitation in the Beth Hamidrash where they were used as "texts" for study.
29. R. Yair Chaim Bachrach, Responsa Chavoth Yair No. 94, queries the opinion of Rishonim to the effect that we do not decide the halachah in accordance with the view of R. Eliezer b. Hyrkanus since he was placed under the ban (Rashi) or because he was of the school of Shammai (Tos.) saying, "Why should he lose because of this? And even one who was judged a rebellious elder why should we not decide according to his opinion if he spoke well and achieved the truth? . . . Such considerations cannot in any wise alter the truth of the halachoth . . . and they did not *fine* R. Meir in determining the halachah because he received his tradition from (the apostate) Aher (Elisha ben Abuya)." With respect to R. Eliezer cf. also Rashba to Sabb. 130b; Tosaphoth Harosh to Nid. 7b. The responsa are replete with such phrases as "one cannot countenance persons in halachah," etc. Enlightening in this respect is the fact that though Maimonides enjoys unparalleled awe and veneration, the possekim do not hesitate to decide against his opinion. See I. Z. Cahana, loc. cit., pp. 8–88, where the source material is liberally portrayed.
30. Quoted by Amiel, *ibid.* sect. 16.
31. Yam Shel Shelomoh, Gitt. 1, 31.
32. *Ibid.*, Yebamoth 3, 14.
33. *Ibid.*, B. K. 2, 5.
34. *Ibid.*
35. *Ibid.*, Betza 1, 43. Not all possekim agree with this stipulation; see Ein Zocher. s.q. *Teku*.
36. Tractate Sopherim, 16, 5.
37. 12, 4.
38. Ex. 23, 2.

39. Though the commentaries there interpret the statement differently, the words of the Talmud, Tem. 14b, that "Those who write halachoth are as those who burn the Torah" would seem to stress the point made in the text.
40. To Nizkei Mammon, 2, 19.
41. Nos. 32 and 15.
42. See also Peri Chaddash to Yoreh De'ah, 99.
43. See Biur Hagra, To O. H. 547, 5. Also Ridbaz to Shemmittah Veyovel, 9, 8.
44. Responsa, Klall 31, 9.
45. The reference is to R. Shelomoh ben Adereth, Rashba.
46. See Azulai, Shem Hagedolim, Ma'arecheth Hasephorim, s.q. Beth Joseph.
47. Responsa, 47.
48. Cf. also Yam Shel Shelomoh, Hullin, Introduction.
49. See I. Z. Cahana, *Researches in the Responsa Literature*, p. 94.
50. The responsa literature, embracing several thousand volumes, is generally considered to commence with the eighth-century "Sheiltoth" of R. Achai Gaon. See I. Schepansky, *Eretz Yisrael in the Responsa Literature*, Vol. 1, p. 14, notes 1 and 2.
51. This is not entirely so of the responsa of the Gaonic period. See Schepansky, *ibid.*, p. 19; but also *ibid.*, p. 34, notes 8, 1.

9

Sevara and Dialectic—Pilpul

We have already indicated the profound importance and role of the *sevara* in the Talmud. This and the following chapter will discuss some of the varied forms taken by the *sevara* through many centuries of Talmudic study.

The essential use of logical argument in the Talmud lies in the investigation of the truth of assertions and opinions, testing them and discussing them critically. This dialectic is called pilpul.

The Importance of Pilpul haTorah

The importance of pilpul haTorah cannot be over-estimated. There are those who find its origins in the patriarchal period.[1] So much so, that "When óne is called to the [final] judgment, he is asked . . . did you engage in the pilpul of Torah?"[2] For it is by pilpul that one acquires Torah,[3] and "If God forbid, Torah should be forgotten in Israel, I could," said R. Hanina, "restore it by my pilpul."[4]

The Talmud recognizes full well that pilpul could be something of a two-edged sword and that unrestrained or unchanneled it could well lead away from truth. "Perhaps you are from Pumpeditha, where they draw an elephant through the eye of a needle!"[5] The sages did not hesitate to say that "as great as one's sharpness is the mistake that he makes"[6] or "relying on his ingenuity, he did not study it carefully."[7] Such expressions only serve, however, to stress the mainstream of pilpul as the normative method of Torah study.

Pilpul and Practical Halachah

The mean between pilpul and practical halachah was carefully preserved—"If it is a halachah, we accept it, if a deduction there is an answer"[8]—so that logical reasoning alone could never suffice to override an accepted halachah.[9]

Untrammeled pilpul was never allowed to intrude on practical halachah. The realms of theoretical discussion and pessak were kept distinctly apart. Hence they said[10] that since "it was impossible to fathom the ultimate opinion of R. Meir," whose sharpness and acumen were celebrated and who would advance as many reasons for as against, his colleagues refrained from determining the halachah in accord with his opinions.[11]

The problem of drawing the final halachah from the discussion of halachah is considered a quite distinct discipline[12] with particular requirements. Chacham Zevi[13] expresses this forcefully when he says, "This was also questionable in my eyes, to seek advice from a lamdan with respect to any hora'ah. I have never done so hitherto."

Likewise, R. Naphtali Zevi Yehudah Berlin[14] expresses himself to the effect that:

> On the contrary, when one is responding in a matter of practical halachah one delves deeper into the matter than when one is merely studying the subject. There is also greater aid from heaven in rendering a practical decision,[15] while the gemmara[16] states: "We do not learn the halachah either from theoretical study, or from [having witnessed] practice, but only from being told that such is the practical halachah," study the commentary of Rashbam thereon.[17]

In the height of the age of untrammeled pilpul, Mahri Bruna[18] distinguishes between study and hora'ah as follows:

> Certainly when we are engaged in pilpul and study with acumen . . . then we weigh everything and bother with fine differences and distinctions as one who draws an elephant through the eye of a needle. But to decide a law, or permit something forbidden, one may do neither of these without clear proofs, burnished and clarified from the plain meaning of the sugya, but not as the result of such kinds of distinction.

The Approach of the Commentaries to the Talmud

The dialectic method of the Talmud was preserved and passed from generation to generation with but little change. Amiel[19] notes that this constancy is so evident that if, for example, we were to insert many of the passages of the Tosaphoth into the Talmudic text, we would more than likely be unable to see any difference between the texts, they are so alike in style and spirit.

Balanced and controlled, the major discernible emphasis on the part of the masters lies in the employment of dialectic with a view to enabling one to reach practical decisions. In this capacity the dialectic is constrained within a framework of down-to-earth logic that succeeds in expunging artificiality and superficiality, as well as preventing the reduction *ad absurdum* of the basic norm.

Those works that deal directly with the mechanisms for arriving at such decision aside, the commentaries on the Talmud usually deal with both the theoretical and practical aspects simultaneously, with the result that the structured logical theory of the sugya becomes the guideline for implementation in practice. This may best be understood by turning our attention to the Tosaphists.

In the Beth Hamidrash of the Tosaphists

The Ba'alei Hatosaphoth, only a portion of whose work is to be found in the printed editions of the Talmud, utilized the critical tools of the Talmud to weigh its every statement. Before amplifying this subject, it is well to bear in mind the general approach of the Tosaphists to their subject matter.

Apart from several known additions of the Rabbanan Saborai who followed Ravina and R. Ashi, the Talmud was sealed by these, the last of the Amoraim, and as such it is the embodiment of the Torah Sheba'al Peh—the Oral Law in its entirety. The corollary to this, implicitly and fervently upheld by all students of the Talmud since it was so sealed, is that everything contained therein is both true and complete. The answers given by the gemmara are the best possible answers, and these were given only after every avenue of approach to the subject had been thoroughly explored. This is also true of the questions posed by the Talmud; that is only the question actually posed there is relevant. Other problems that may seem to exist within the given context and framework are not really problems at all.

The dialectic of the commentaries, including to an even more marked extent the work of the Tosaphists, is directed toward understanding why only the answer given by the gemmara is the correct and ultimate solution and why, on the other hand, the gemmara considered the actual question formulated as the sole difficulty.

Alternatives have to be carefully analyzed as do the question and answer of the gemmara itself, in order to fully comprehend the basis of the subject and the conclusions to be drawn from the Talmudic discussion. In this the Tosaphists excel, and their work opens the paths through the maze of discussion for practical halachah.

Now this approach to the Talmud was not confined to the actual folio that was under discussion. Each part of the Talmud was subjected to the same analytical scrutiny with reference also to every other passage in the Talmud, so that in fact the Tosaphists, in subjecting the Talmud to internal criticism and comparison, succeeded in transforming the vast body of the Talmudic sea into a coherent, logical whole. Not only was each section analytically at one with itself, it was shown how the section coalesced smoothly and integrated naturally into the entire corpus of the oral law.

In the words of R. Shelomoh Luria:[20]

> but for the scholars of France, the Ba'alei Hatosaphoth who made it [the Talmud] into a single ball, and of them the verse says:[21] "The words of the wise are as goads and as nails well fastened." They turned it over and rolled it from place to place, for it appears to us as a dream without solution and without solidity, this sugya saying so and this sugya saying so, the one not drawing nigh the other. [But as a result of their work] the Talmud is straightened out and bound up and all the sealed [incomprehensible passages] explained, and the content of its decisions established.

Tradition has preserved a portrait of how the Talmud was actually studied in the Beth Hamidrash of the Tosaphists:[22]

> Concerning Rabbenu Yitzchak [Ri, Baal Hatosaphoth], son of the renowned Tosaphist Rabbenu Tam's sister, who studied and taught in the Yeshivah, my French masters told me in the name of their teachers that he was well known and famous and that sixty Rabbis used to study before him. Each of these would hear the halachah that he taught, while each would study alone a tractate which his colleague was not studying [at that time]. [So that between them they covered the entire Shass]. And they would revise [their particular tractates] by heart. R. Yitzchak would not, therefore, say a halachah with which

between them they were unfamiliar. And, as the particular halachah was before their eyes, so in fact was the entire gemmara. So
that the doubts in the gemmara were cleared up. Any halachah
or statement of a Tanna or an Amora which appeared contrary in
another place, he would sit and establish according to its interpretation, as is evident to anyone who has seen their tosaphoth
and their questions and answers and commentaries and the
arguments they advance against their grandfather Rabbenu
Shelomoh [Rashi].

The method of the Tosaphists is in fact the method by which
the Talmud is studied to the present day, with the difference that
since the advent of the printing press the Shass is luckily on the
bookshelf of the scholar, and "the master of wheat whom everyone needs,"[23] and whom Ri found in sixty scholars, is readily
available. Methods of analysis have, however, undergone peri-
odic changes in both tone and emphasis, and some of these
methods succeeded in superimposing themselves for a longer or
shorter period on the traditional dialectic foundation.

The dividing line between *pilpul shel emeth* and *pilpul shel hevel*
is not and was not ever susceptible to exact definition other than
with respect to practical decisions, where practice, usage, and
precedent provide guidelines beyond which one cannot stray or
wander. Pilpul as such was never derided, but one had to be
extremely wary of falling into empty pilpul and vain acumen.[24]

Shelah, in his detailed treatment of the oral law, its categories,
and methodology, castigates such pilpul severely, and, careful
not to impinge on pilpul per se, he finally recommends the
method adopted by R. Yitzchak Kanafenton (sixteenth century)
and the rules formulated by him.[25]

These rules are based on the careful and intensive study of
the language employed by the Talmud and its commentaries,
coupled with the prior efforts of the student to fathom the sugya
for himself. R. Yitzchak insists on an exact determination of
the nuances employed and recognizes the necessary conformity
of the uses of language to the logical structure of the sugya.
These bind one another and determine the legitimate limits
beyond which dialectic cannot go. His system is well exemplified
by the Chiddushei Mahrsha and Mahram of Lublin on the Shass,
which, by careful examination of the details of the term employed, open the way to the depths of the plain meaning[26] of
the sugya.[27]

In his insistence on the efforts of the student himself to fathom the sugya and then compare his results with those of the commentaries, Kanafenton succeeds in creating a built-in critique, a "feedback system" in modern parlance, both with respect to the student and his approach to the sources and from the sources to his conclusions, the result of which is to open the door naturally to the deeper strata of the sugya.

Unrestrained Dialectic

As opposed to this method of study, there grew up almost contemporaneously with the work of Kanafenton the dialectic known as *chillukim*. Under this system, the exact terminology employed by the sugya was often disregarded, and much more freedom was granted to spontaneity, improvisation, and imagination.

The *chilluk* became part of the curriculum of the Yeshivoth, especially during the months Cheshvan-Kislev when the Rosh Hayeshivah was obliged to engage in *chillukim* daily[28] in order to sharpen the minds of the students.

Shelah opposes the use of *chillukim* strongly. He claims that in its various forms it leads to both lack of truth and absurdity. It is in fact a kind of logical antinomianism. This, because the basis of the *chilluk*, literally, distinction, developed to the point where those using it recognized neither general rules nor logically based criticism. It started and ended as a solely intellectual exercise in which neither the material forming the foundation for the dialectic edifice erected by the *chilluk*, nor its context, nor the requirements of practical halachah, succeeded in exercising restraint or modification or in giving it direction.[29]

Notes to Chapter Nine

1. Netziv; Introduction to Sheiltoth; Amiel, Hammidoth Lechekker Hahalachah.
2. Sabb. 31a.
3. Baraitha of Kinyan Torah.
4. Ket. 103b. Cf. also Tem. 16a. on Athniel ben Kenaz.
5. B. M. 38b.
6. *Ibid.* 96b.
7. B.B. 116b.
8. Yeb. 76b; Kerit. 15b.

9. See Mishnah, Negaim 9, 3. R. Judah ben Bathyra said to him, "Shall I expound it?" He replied, "If it be to confirm the words of the sages, yes" — But if not, not. Since I will not forsake the tradition of my teachers and accept your argument, Bertinoro.

10. Erub. 13b.

11. *Ibid.*

12. See Sot. 21a. and Rashi thereon. Gitt. 19a. "Because we make comparisons, shall we then act so in practice!" See also Tosaphoth to Yoma 54b. "Though I compare them, I would not act so in practice."

13. Responsa, 76.

14. Responsa, Meshiv Davar, 24.

15. See Ket. 60b.

16. B.B. 130b.

17. Ri Migash, commentary to B.B. 130b. states, "Since they told him the halachah in practice, they certainly did not do so before thorough and exact investigation. And this, our Talmud, is practical halachah since it was committed to writing only after searching investigation over several generations and underwent several recensions. And it is as if they declared by it the practical halachah for they committed it to writing for practical application." "For this reason," writes my father-in-law, the Gaon R. Isachar Tamar, "R. Ashi and Rabina are called "the end of *Hora'ah* (B.M. 86a)" — and not the end of the Talmud." Cf. also Or Zerua, Pt. 1, No. 754 — "For the Talmud was written for Hora'ah . . . ."

18. Fifteenth century, responsa, 29. See also, Yad Malachi, Kelallei She'ar Possekim, No. 32, while Rema, Yoreh De'ah 242, 30, declares: "Nowadays, [in regard to preference] one's Rabbi is not he who taught him pilpul and chillukim, but he who taught him pessak, and deliberation and trained him in the bases of truth and rectitude." "Nowadays," says Iglei Tal, Introduction, "with the oral law committed to writing, the mitzvah to teach Torah is to instruct in the methods of study."

19. Hamiddoth, Introduction, chap. 2, sect. 6.

20. Yam Shel Shelomoh to Hullin, First Introduction.

21. Eccl. 12, 11.

22. The description is from Tzedah Laderach, quoted by E. E. Urbach, *Ba'alei Hatosaphoth* (Jerusalem, 1955), p. 210.

23. Hor. 14a.

24. Cf. the remarks of Chavoth Yair, Resp. 124 toward the end.

25. Shenei Luchoth Habrith, Torah Sheba'al Peh, pp. 31–32.

26. Cf. also the Introduction of the Peri Meggadim to his commentary *Porath Joseph on Yeb. and Ket.* (Warsaw, 1898) pp. 5–6. The story is told that when the Peri Meggadim was preparing his commentary, Rosh Joseph, to Berachoth and Megillah, one of his students asked him why he bothered to write such simple things? "There will come a time," he replied, "when students will have had enough of pilpulim and they will prefer the more useful, simple explanation."

27. Penei Yeshoshua is also an ardent adherent of this method, but in his hands the system is broadened to embrace the comparative study of sugyoth and

is no longer limited to the sugya at hand. This is also true, by and large, of R. Pinchass Hurwitz in Hamakneh and Hafla'ah.

28. See Be'oholei Ya'acob, Simchah Assaf, p. 51 and note 178 *ad loc.*
29. On the entire subject of the Chilluk, its nature, and development as well as the opposition to which it gave rise, see Rabbi N. S. Greenspan, *Melecheth Machsheveth* (London, 1955), pp. 13–27.

10

The Modern Trend—Analysis

The Modern Trend and Practical Halachah

The modern age has witnessed a twofold change in the direction of the sevara. However, it appears that this development, fundamental as it is, has, as its predecessors, bypassed the path of pessak. This is evident in the works of two of the contemporary giants of halachah, R. Chaim Ozer Grodzinski and the Chazon Ish.

Though R. Chaim Ozer's work evidences traces of the influence of Volohzin and R. Chaim Brisker, and he was thoroughly adept in the new system of R. Chaim, his responsa, Achiezer, avoid its use in practical decision. Rabbi Zevin[1] surmises, in fact, that the reason R. Chaim, founder of the new learning, avoided *hora'ah* was due to his innovative method of study. In discussing this he says, "In practical *hora'ah* one cannot burst the bounds. In this field traditional methods of study are fundamental."

The sole exception to this "practical guide" seems to have been the Rogotzover, R. Joseph Rozin, who ignored completely halachic literature after the Rishonim and found all the precedents required for contemporary problems in the Talmud and Rishonim alone. It is a common trait of both R. Chaim and of the Rogotzover that they avoid discussion with acharonim and hardly mention them. Though their systems are similar and both lead away from the mainstream of traditional forms of exposition, the Rogotzover remained in the field of pessak and is one of the most prolific respondents ever, in spite of his ignoring the traditional links in the chain of pessak development.

Between R. Joseph Rozin and the Biur Hagra

There is a kinship between the Rogotzover and the Biur Hagra in
that both sought to base the halachah, and even custom, on the
words of Chazal alone. Neither argue with contemporaries; both
seek, each in his own way the basic primary sources alone. While
the Rogotzover virtually ignored the Shulchan Aruch, the Gaon
showed how, far from being a source of diversion from the
Talmudim and Rishonim, every one of its statements is contained
in Chazal. The Gaon thus succeeded in preserving the orderly,
historic progression of pessak, whereas the approach of the
Rogotzover could well prove disastrous in the hands of one of
lesser caliber than himself.

The modern changes in the use of the *sevara* were fathered by
R. Chaim Soloweicyk (1853–1918) and Rabbi M. A. Amiel (1883–
1946), respectively. Though their aims differ, it seems hardly possible that R. Amiel's magnum opus, *Hammidoth Lecheker Hahalachah*, could have been written but for the pioneering work of R.
Chaim. This is not, farbeit, to belittle in any way the tremendous
originality exhibited by R. Amiel in his wide-ranging, thorough
penetration of halachah. His work, however, which to my knowledge has not unfortunately been continued, flows as an important
offshoot directly from that of R. Chaim, which was in vogue in the
great centres of learning in Lithuania and was the major influence
on the masters in the centers where Amiel studied.[2]

Rabbi A. M. Amiel—The Intellectual Ingredients of the Halachic Mind

While R. Chaim developed analytical concepts and tools that he
applied locally, that is, directly to the subject in hand, R. Amiel
embarked on the much more ambitious project of attempting to
construct such principles for halachah as a whole. His intention
was to expound the concepts which form the intellectual ingre-
dients of the halachic mind.

In his attempts to ground the thousands of *sevaroth* employed
throughout the ages, in a limited number of major principles,[3]
sevara as a logical tool comes to be treated scientifically. Types of
sevara are classified, and with tremendous erudition and consis-
tency his classification and archtypes of *sevara* are applied to the

vast sea of the Talmud and the enormous mass of its supporting literature down to the present time.

> The number of *sevaroth* propounded since the Talmud to the present day is virtually limitless. Is it possible to assume that all these *sevaroth* are but towers flying in the air, without prior foundations? Is it possible to consider that every single *sevara* is a world unto itself without known principles which bind numbers of *sevaroth* to a single principle?
>
> The number of *derashoth* by means of which Chazal expounded the Torah in deducing halachoth also totals many thousands and yet they are all reducible to the framework of the thirteen hermeneutic rules, so that so many hundreds fall under *gezerah shavah*, so many hundreds or thousands. . . . Likewise, it is necessary to discover the *middoth* of *sevara*. For though the actual number of *sevaroth* is limitless, ultimately the *middoth* which gave rise to the *sevaroth* are certainly determined and fixed and must embrace all *sevaroth*.[4]

Philosophical Terminology

Now Amiel certainly succeeds in showing the basic structural continuity of halachic thought, but he does this by conceptualizing, to a large extent philosophically, many of the basic norms of halachic thinking. While the essential unity of Torah finds no incongruity in applying philosophical terms or concepts to halachah and jurisprudence,[5] in this usage Amiel parts with the accepted terminology of the analytical school of R. Chaim. Such "philosophical middoth" as cause and effect (middah 1), and its derivative middoth; *etzem umikreh*—essence and accident (no. 17); *bekoach*—actual and potential (no. 18), stand side by side with *metziuth vedin*—fact and law (no. 11).

It is not improbable that Amiel employs philosophical terminology deliberately in order to stress the philosophical/logical background of halachic thinking in an age that tended to look down on Talmudic study from the "olympic heights" of secular knowledge, as also to emphasize the basically rational principles of halachah.

It is perhaps instructive that in describing the simple syllogism, he says, "All men are mortal. Socrates is a man. Therefore Socrates is mortal."[6] Other halachist would have chosen Socrates specifically for his example. His treatment of time[7] is both philosophical and intensely practical.

His middoth therefore differ from those of the analytical school in number, terminology, and scope. In actual content they are not, when placed side by side with those developed by the analytical school, incongruous.

Amiel is, however, careful to point out that though "it is clear that all the foundations of logic are to be found in the bases of halachic inquiry, the sages did not employ logical terminology as such";[8] this has to be done by the student.

His work contains numerous illuminating asides. Two examples will suffice. Interestingly, Amiel finds[9] that the cast of mind underlying the Talmud Babli differs in predilection from that underlying the Yerushalmi. While the former is more given toward a mathematical type of construction, the latter evidences a bent for logical analysis. Similar distinction is to be discovered between the Rishonim of France and those of Spain. The latter tend more toward the logical-analytical approach; the former incline toward the mathematical. There is, however, no hard and fast line or rule.

With respect to systems of classification, he also discovers similar, separate trends.[10] Thus, while R. Hai Gaon classifies on the basis of definition stemming from the intrinsic logic of subjects, Maimonides in the Yad classifies on the basis of congruous subject matter, so that subjects that enjoy a common logical basis are nonetheless scattered in the Yad while they are united in R. Hai's work.[11]

R. Chaim Soloweicyk—The Factors at Work

The analytical school proper was founded by R. Chaim Soloweicyk whose method of study is called both *havannah*, understanding, and *chakkirah*, investigation.[12]

The method is strikingly similar to that employed in chemical analysis and may be briefly stated as follows. A proposition is first broken down into its component parts. Once these are established, we find that we have what are called "two dinnim," two laws.[13] Careful examination of the proposition or case in hand in their light follows, and this illustrates the manner in which each fundamental component operates within the propositional framework. The influence of each component is traced as is its modifying effect on the second component and the degree to which it contributes and shapes the composite proposition.

Once it is appreciated that two basic factors are at work, the subject matter is rendered amenable to treatment from different viewpoints. Seemingly internal incongruities disappear since these are shown to be the reflection of two and not one basic criterion. The relative weight of each of the factors may be determined as also its limitations.

The result of this is that the *sevara* in the hands of R. Chaim becomes the tool for the elementary understanding of the Talmud. It does not erect castles in the air; it lays bare the building bricks of Talmudic discussion so that one is led by R. Chaim to plumb the depths of the plain meaning of the text.

The "two laws" may refer to subject and object or, one to the article *(cheftza)* the other to person *(gavra)*. One may be active, the other passive; one general, the other particular. One may be found to refer to essence, the other to the incidental aspects of the case. One may refer to fact, the other to law. The following example[14] illustrates the method by showing that there are two laws of intention *(kavannah)* with respect to prayer, one essential the other incidental, each with its own effects on the practical halachah.

Prayer and Intention

This section is based on an apparent contradiction in the Yad of Maimonides. In Tephillah 4, 1, Maimonides lists "the intention of the heart" among the five necessities of prayer. In the same chapter,[15] he says, "How so intention. All prayer without intention is not prayer. And if one prayed without intention he must pray again with intention."

It appears, says R. Chaim, that the law requiring intention applies to the entire prayer. But, he asks, Maimonides himself[16] declares that "One who prayed without intention of heart must pray again with intention. If, however, he had intention during recital of the first *berachah* [of the *Shemoneh Esreh*] he need not [pray again]"?

R. Chaim resolves the contradiction as follows. There are two kinds of intention with respect to prayer. One, to understand the meaning of the words uttered, is basically a law of *kavannah*. The second is that one must be aware that he is standing in prayer before God, as Maimonides states:[17] "How so intention? That he clear his heart of all thoughts and see himself as standing before the Divine Presence."

This second intention is of the essence of prayer, so that if his mind is not free from other thoughts and one does not see himself as standing before God, there is no act of prayer. Such a one is acting without purpose *(mithassek)* and his activity is not considered a valid legal act. Hence, without such intention throughout the entirety of prayer, it is as if one had not prayed at all. On the other hand, if one were aware of standing before God but did know the meaning of all the words uttered, this is a specific requirement of prayer whose failure of fulfillment does not in other than the first blessing of the *shemoneh esreh* invalidate the prayer.

R. Chaim distinguishes between the essence of prayer and its secondary or accidental characteristics, and on this basis the contradiction in Maimonides is resolved, for, regarding the incidental characteristics, the halacha decides which are indispensable and which not.

The solution, while probing the depths of prayer is, it will be noted, deceptively simple. Once grasped, it is difficult to see Maimonides in any other light. This is so of the majority of the work accomplished by R. Chaim and his followers. Unforced, it has the ring of truth.

Modern Yeshivoth

The method employed by R. Chaim was taken over and extended by his students who popularized his "way of learning" in the great Lithuanian Yeshivoth. Traditional pilpul gives way to analysis, which becomes in many instances highly conceptual. The school is characterized by terminology, such as *cheftza-gavra*, or fact and law, and common modes of thought.[18] While some of its terminology borders on the philosophical, only Amiel consciously employs philosophical terms to define the principal terms of his analysis.

The great Roshei Yeshivah of Telz, Slobodka, Grodno, Lomza, Kamenitz, and others—all developed the system of R. Chaim, and through these masters the method passed to contemporary yeshivoth. This is probably the origin of limiting the curriculum in modern Yeshivoth to the Orders Nashim and Nezikin, whereas formerly the great Yeshivoth, such as Volohzin and others, would study the entire Shass, tractate after tractate. Nashim and Nezikin, as Kodeshim that also enjoys particular attention nowadays, lend themselves more readily than other orders to such analytical treatment.

Notes to Chapter Ten

1. Ishim Veshittoth, p. 175.
2. Prof. L. I. Rabinowitz of Jerusalem pointed out in a communication to me that though his father-in-law, the late Rabbi Amiel, was greatly influenced by the system of R. Chaim, he "always stated his indebtedness for his new approach in the halachah to the system of higgayon of his predecessor as Rabbi of Schwientyan, the late Rabbi Reines, one of the founders of the Mizrachi." "And," he continues, "I think you will find that Rabbi Amiel's middoth owe something to that as well as to R. Chaim, and his system may even be considered as a fusion of the two."
3. Which he called "middoth," paralleling the middoth by which Torah is interpreted.
4. Hammiddoth, Introduction, chap. 6.
5. R. Joseph Rozin did not hesitate to mingle them at will; see Zevin, *ibid.*, pp. 81 and 121.
6. Hammiddoth, ch. 5.
7. Introduction, chap. 7.
8. *Ibid.*, chap. 8.
9. *Ibid.*, chaps. 9 and 10.
10. *Ibid.*, chap. 11.
11. It should be noted that one of the features common to adherents of the analytical school lies in illustrating that scattered Maimonist dicta inhere a common logical foundation.
12. Both terms are employed by his sons in their Introduction to Chiddushei R. Chaim Halevi.
13. There are instances of three such basic laws, but these serve only to emphasize the system.
14. Taken from Chiddushei R. Chaim, Hilchoth Tephillah.
15. Halachah 15.
16. *Ibid.*, 10, 1.
17. *Ibid.*, 4, 16.
18. On the development of the school and its types of chakkirah, see the article by Norman Solomon, "Hilluq and Haqira, A Study in the Method of the Lithuanian Halakhists," in *Dine Yisrael*, Vol. 4, T.A. 1973, pp. lxix–cvi; and the relevant sections in R. Zevin's Ishim Veshitoth, T.A. 1952.

III

Halachic Authority and Its Transmission

11

The Basic Mechanism of Halachic Decision

The subject of this section is very complicated. It has not, to my knowledge been dealt with systematically in either Hebrew or English. However, without some fundamental discussion of the mechanism of halachic decision and authority and the manner in which this decision is implemented in practice, this study would remain glaringly inadequate.

The Authority of the Beth Din Hagadol

Nachmanides[1] writes:

> Even if you think in your heart that they [the Beth Din Hagadol] are mistaken, and the matter is as simple in your eyes as the difference between right and left, do as they enjoin . . . say: so did the Lord who enjoined the mitzvoth command me, to do with regards all His mitzvoth as the teachers standing before Him in the place which He would choose, instruct me *and on their understanding He gave me the Torah, even if they make a mistake* . . . even if in your eyes they seem to exchange right for left. Certainly when they call right right. For the spirit of God is upon the ministers of His sanctuary and He will not forsake His pious ones, ever preserving them from mistake and stumbling block.[2]

The Torah is given over completely to the Beth Din Hagadol for interpretation, decision, and discretion,[3] there being only a single, overriding biblical injunction in this connection, namely, "Follow the majority."[4]

The authority of the Beth Din Hagadol is absolute, "and whoever believes in Moses our teacher and in his Torah, is in duty
bound to rely upon them in all matters of religion."[5]

Maimonides continues:[6]

Whoever does not act in accord with their *hora'ah* transgresses a
prohibition—Thou shalt not turn aside from the word which they
shall tell thee, right or left[7] . . . so with regards matters learned by
them by employing one of the rules by which Torah is interpreted . . . so with respect to safeguards [*seyyagim*] which they
made around the Torah in accord with the needs of the time.
These are *gezeroth*—decrees—*takkanoth*—enactments—and *minhagoth*—customs. It is a positive mitzvah to hearken to them, with
respect to each of these three and one who transgresses any of
them, transgresses a prohibition.[8] The verse says: "By the Torah
which they shall teach thee"—this refers to the *takkanoth*, the
gezeroth and the *minhagoth* in which they shall instruct the public so
to strengthen the religion, and benefit the world. "And by the
judgment which they shall say"—this refers to matters deduced by
use of one of the rules by which Torah is expounded. "With respect
to all that they tell you"—this refers to the tradition which they
received generation after generation [literally man from man].

There is no argument in matters received by tradition [from
Moses] and wherever you find argument it is certain that the
subject of the argument is not a tradition received from Moses.

With respect to matters deduced by means of the [thirteen]
rules of interpretation, if all the members of the Beth Din Hagadol
agreed about them, then they agreed; and if they argued about
them, we follow the majority and pronounce the law in accord
with the majority. Similarly with regards *gezeroth*, *takkanoth* and
minhagoth, if some [members of the court] thought fit to decree or
to enact or to allow people to follow a particular custom and others
considered that the *gezera* or enactment should not be decreed or
enacted, or that they ought not to allow the particular custom,
they discuss the matter and follow the majority . . . .

As long as the Beth Din Hagadol existed there was no [lasting
halachic] argument in Israel. . . . [T]hey would come to the
Chamber of Hewn Stone, to the Beth Din Hagadol and enquire.
If the doubtful matter was known to the Beth Din Hagadol
either by tradition or by means of deduction from the rules,
they would immediately discuss the matter until agreement
was reached. Or they would vote and then follow the majority,
saying to the enquirers: this is the halachah,[9] and they [the
enquirers] would depart.

When the Beth Din Hagadol was abolished [halachic] argument increased in Israel. This one rendered unclean and gave reason for his opinion, this one rendered clean and gave reason for his opinion, this one forbade and this one permitted.

With the Cessation of Centralized Authority

As long as the situation described by Maimonides existed, there was no gulf between authority and its translation into practice. But this represents an ideal state of affairs. Once the Beth Din Hagadol and the unified pessak halachah obligatory on all Israel emanating from that body, ceased, two distinct, major problems arose. The one problem: how, in view of the dissentient opinions and the lack of a recognized central body who could decide by majority vote, is the halachah to be decided at all? In other words, where does halachic authority lie? The second problem is, since the cessation of centralized authority, how does any halachah come to be authoritatively accepted by the public?[10] How is anarchy obviated in practical halachah? Why in any given instance can the individual not say, "I hold with the other opinion"?[11] We assume, of course, that the individual wishes to abide and live by halachah, but how is he to choose and what is he to do?

To be viable, meaningful, and relevant, halachah must solve both the theoretical, technical problem of its authority and also the problem of inculcation and implementation. We shall see that halachah solves both problems adequately. For clarity's sake, we shall treat, up to a point, each of these problems separately, though, as will become evident, the problems, as their solution, are actually intertwined. What we shall discuss are basically two halachic processes that are inextricably coiled around one another.

Greater in Wisdom and in Number

The Mishnah[12] states:

And why do they record the opinion of the individual against that of the majority, since the halachah may only be according to the opinion of the majority? That if a court approves the opinion of the individual it may rely upon him, since a court cannot annul the opinion of another court unless it is greater both in wisdom and in number; if it exceeded it in wisdom but not in number, or in

number but not in wisdom, it cannot annul its opinion; but only if
it exceeds it both in wisdom and in number.

This Mishnah is the classical text for study of our problem. It
raises a number of difficult, basic problems. How can a later Beth
Din be greater in number than the original Beth Din of seventy-
one when this number is the maximum for a Beth Din Hagadol?[13]
What is meant by "greater in wisdom"? How can this be mea-
sured or determined?

Maimonides and Ra'abad are at variance as to the interpretation of the Mishnah. Maimonides[14] asserts, "This refers to the
number of the sages of the generation who agreed and accepted
the word declared by the Beth Din Hagadol and did not argue
against it." This interpretation raises a further problem for, as we
have already quoted from Maimonides, the authority of the Beth
Din Hagadol was absolute. What then have the other sages of the
generation to do with the matter?

Ra'abad[15] explains "in number" to refer to the age of the
members of the court. Others[16] hold that it refers to the age of the
president of the court. On this view, Aruch Hashulchan[17] explains that since all the members of the court were prolific in
wisdom, seniority had to be determined by age. Yet others[18] hold
that it refers to the number of years he studied at the feet of the
sages, while a final opinion[19] holds that it refers to the number of
students attending on the members of the court.

In regard to the condition "greater in wisdom," Maimonides
explains this to refer to the president of the court, others[20] to the
sum of the wisdom of the sages sitting in that particular Beth
Din. That is, the sages of the present court are more generally
illustrious and renowned for wisdom and eminence than those
of the previous court.

Reversing the Decision of a Previous Beth Din

Now the plain meaning of the Mishnah is that a later Beth Din
may determine the halachah in accord with the single opinion
rejected by the previous Beth Din. Had the lone opinion not been
recorded, the latter Beth Din would have been unable to act
contrary to the former on their own account. This is because no
Beth Din may nullify the words of a fellow Beth Din unless it, the
latter, be greater in wisdom and in number. Since, however, a

lone opinion exists, they are able to rely on it.[21] This does not, however, solve the problem for Maimonides as to why the lone opinion was recorded in the first place.

Furthermore, this is only so in regard to enactments or decrees. As to matters deduced by means of the rules, the latter Beth Din may revoke the decision of the former though these conditions are not present. In those instances where the former Beth Din erected a safeguard (seyyag) around the Torah, if the "fence" had, by the time of the second Beth Din, spread among Israel, it cannot be abrogated even by a greater Beth Din. So the opinion of Maimonides.[22] Ra'abad holds, however, that there is no distinction between enactments, decrees, and safeguards; a later Beth Din may never revoke the decision of a previous Beth Din once the enactment, decree, or safeguard has taken hold and spread throughout Israel.

Now besides the problem of the retention of the lone opinion, which may even determine the halachah at a later date, if under the particular conditions, a later Beth Din may set aside the ruling of a former Beth Din, why is an Amora, a teacher of the Talmud, unable to argue with a Tanna, a teacher of the Mishna, unless he finds a supporting Tanna? And why in later times, when the Talmud was sealed, was one rendered unable to argue with anything stated in it?

Kesseph Mishnah[23] answers the second query by stating that after the sealing of the Mishnah, subsequent generations (i.e., the Amoraim) accepted on themselves not to controvert the teachings of the Mishnah. Likewise, later generations also accepted on themselves a similar condition after the sealing of the Talmud.[24] This answer will only become clear after thorough discussion and solution of our first problem.

Majority and Minority Opinions

It is necessary first to analyze the principle "decision by the majority," as this operated in the Beth Din Hagadol. To follow the majority is a positive precept;[25] nonetheless, following the majority inheres a fundamental problem. What is the position of the minority opinion? Since the Torah says follow the majority, does the minority opinion disappear and merge with that of the majority so that the majority opinion becomes a unanimous opinion (in halachic terminology, this is called rubo kekulo, the majority is

as all), or does the decision, though rendered according to the
majority, fail to erase the minority opinion, which retains potency, though not acted on as a minority opinion?

There are numerous practical differences in halachah stemming from this theoretical problem.[26] The halachah[27] is that the
majority opinion is considered a unanimous opinion, and the
opinion of the minority ceases to exist[28]; hence Chajes states:

> With respect to the Sanhedrin, it is considered as if the *hora'ah*
> issued from the entire Sanhedrin [i.e., unanimously], the major-
> ity of the Sanhedrin being considered as all of the Sanhedrin. The
> minority opinion is converted to that of the majority and no
> controversial minority voice remains. This being so, even if it
> should chance that the reasoning of later sages would enable them
> to ally themselves with the previous minority opinion, they are
> unable to argue against the previous decision that issued from the
> majority . . . a decision having once issued from the Beth Din
> Hagadol becomes *Din Torah* and its words cannot be rendered null
> at any time, now or later."[29]

On the basis of Nachmanides' opinion, Chajes[30] stipulates that
the minority opinion ceases to exist only when it was actually
voided. If, however, the minority opinion was not discussed,
those holding it remaining silent throughout the discussion,
then, though the decision was issued by the majority, and it is to
be acted on, the minority opinion is not without potency.

On this basis, the conclusion may be drawn that a sage of
minority opinion who did not participate in the discussion and
vote may indeed gather around him scholars of like mind and
render the previous decision null, since in this instance the
minority voice, not having been heard, was not voted out by the
Beth Din.

Reuben Margolies[31] explains that this distinction is true only of
decisions of the courts and gatherings of the sages after the time
of the Sanhedrin. It is not so with respect to the voting undertaken in the Sanhedrin where even one who did not participate
or vote is bound by the majority opinion. On this basis several
incidents in the Talmud are clarified.[32]

Furthermore, even if the minority opinion was voiced but, in
spite of an actual majority against, no vote was taken since one
side was unable to completely refute the other, allowing some
measure of right to its claims, the minority opinion retains

validity.[33] This is certainly so when no central discussion takes place, and there is no rule to follow the majority and erase the minority opinion in such a case. The matter is left open, and a later majority may certainly decide and act even in accord with a single, previous opinion.

On this basis we are well able to appreciate why the lone opinion is recorded in the Mishnah. It is recorded in those instances in regard to which no synod was convened and no vote was taken; hence it may be adopted by later authorities for actual halachic application.[34]

Two Sanhedrins

But more so. Maimonides' assertion that the reference "greater in wisdom" refers to the number of the sages in the generation who agreed with and accepted the words of the Beth Din Hagadol intimates a further, generally concurred-in concept of the Beth Din Hagadol. On the one hand, there is the Sanhedrin of seventy-one, sitting in the Chamber of Hewn Stone; on the other, that of the sages of Israel acting together in matters not declared absolute by the decision of the seventy-one. When no formal Sanhedrin of seventy-one exists, but all the sages of the generation gather together, their decision is binding as was that of the seventy-one who sat in the Sanhedrin.[35] The direct, absolute authority of the Beth Din Hagadol passes to the collective body of the sages of Israel.

The Sealing of the Mishnah and Talmud

On this twin foundation we are now able to understand more fully the words of Kesseph Mishnah with respect to the sealing of the Mishnah and the closing of the Talmud.

Broadly speaking, the following scheme is evident in the Tannaitic and Amoraic periods. Though for the most part the period of the Tannaim is replete with individual teachers, we find that from our perspective the period may be seen as a progression from Sanhedrin to Sanhedrin in Exile, to occasional gatherings of sages, to the Mishnah. The period of the Amoraim, on the other hand, portrays Mishnah to individual scholars and schools, to the sealing of the Talmud, but we do not find synods or other gatherings of the sages.

If the principles already outlined are applied to this scheme, we find that during the period of the Tannaim, from Sanhedrin to Mishnah, there are two separate halachic trends acting side by side. On the one hand, the meetings of the Sanhedrin in exile, and the occasional gatherings of the scholars of the age, would determine halachah unequivocally. On the other, the Tannaim of the times in between, and even scholars who failed to attend the occasional synods, could and did render absolute halachic decision binding on all Israel, impossible in the majority of cases. Only with the advent of Rabbi Judah Hanassi, when the particular historic circumstances of the time enabled him to gather all the sages of the time together, was the definitive halachah of the Mishnah promulgated.

Rabbi Judah Hanassi's court was, since all the sages of Israel participated, as the Beth Din Hagadol in its time, and as each Mishnah was decided by the majority it became binding, even when they decided in accord with a lone former opinion. The recording of lone opinions in the Mishnah was due to the fact that no deciding vote was taken in regard to these halachoth, and though practice was to conform to the majority opinion, the door was left open for later scholars to adopt the lone opinion when occasion warranted and sufficiently weighty reason and reasoning presented themselves.

The Individual Tanna or Amora

The Talmud is replete with such instances. Two and more centuries pass by, the period of the Amoraim. During this period there are no synods; hence halachah is decided by general recognition of the eminence of the teacher and his school, general rules adhered to by the Amoraim, and the binding guiding pessak halachah of the Mishnah. An Amora cannot dispute with a Mishnah, since this was rendered absolute halachah by vote. He may do so when he finds another Tanna holding a contrary opinion, since in such a case the position was intentionally left open by Rabbi and his Beth Din.

Now as in the time of Rabbi Judah Hanassi, so in the time of Rabina and Rav Ashi. Once again there was an all embracing synod consisting of all the sages of the time, and over a period of sixty years[36] the mass of the halachah that had accumulated between Mishnah and that time was sifted and decided by all the sages of Israel. Hence the Talmud also is the product of a Beth Din Hagadol, and it is as such that it is binding on all Israel.

But the Talmud is even more. For it not only determines the rules of halachah, and thousands of actual halachoth, but, by the very mass of its material and precedent, it sets out to provide the *halachic* precedent and base for everything that would come after. It leaves open may sides of particular questions, all of which sides are halachically reliable and tenable for use by future generations. But principles, guidelines, directives, or norms not found within its folios do not bear its binding stamp and remain subject to other canons for authority and binding nature. Rabina and Rav Ashi were in an absolute and binding sense "the end of *hora'ah*."[37]

The acceptance spoken of by Kesseph Mishnah is in fact nothing less than the acceptance of the binding authority of the Beth Din Hagadol.[38]

The absolute authority of the Beth Din Hagadol was therefore transmitted to the Mishnah and then to the Talmud, so that the Talmud became the sole repository of definitive halachah. This factor underlies the opposition of Gedolim throughout history to rendering decision other than on the basis of the Talmud alone.

But codes are necessary and authority is transmitted. What further mechanisms come into play to ensure continuity? What element of authority underlay the actual halachah during the time of both Tannaim and Amoraim when each town, village, or area in fact acted according to the teaching of its Tanna, or its Amora, in the absence of centralized authority? And they did, of course, so act, as is evident throughout the Talmud,[39] and in such glaring examples as "In the place of R. Eliezer they would cut down trees to make coals to make iron [for preparing the blade for circumcision due on the Sabbath] on Sabbath.[40] In the place of R. Jose the Galillean they used to eat the flesh of fowl with milk."[41]

The answer lies in the principle *kiblu alaihu*, and it is to this that we must now turn. For it is the notion of *kiblu alaihu* allied to the Torah stature of the sage and teacher coupled with the absolute authority of the Talmud that is responsible for practical halachic authority.

Notes to Chapter Eleven

1. Commentary to Deut. 17, 11.
2. See the quotation from Cuzari ad loc. in Chavell's edition. Cf. our remarks on the words of Rabbenu Nissim, quoted supra, chap. 3.
3. See chap. 3, supra, in the present study.

4. Ex. 23, 2.
5. Maimonides, Mamrim 1, 1.
6. *Ibid.*, halachoth 2–4. The translation is according to Rambam Le'am ed.
7. Deut. 17, 11.
8. See TaRYag by the present author.
9. As to why the controversy regarding laying the hands on the head of the sacrifice during the festival persisted for several generations, Mishnah Hagig, 2, 2, see Reuben Margolies, Yesod Hamishnah Va'arichathah, Birurim 4, pp. 43–44.
10. For only the duly ordained may enforce their opinion, see Tosaphoth to Gitt. 88b. s.q. Liphneihem, San. 2b. s.q. Libai, to the effect that the Torah only required properly ordained judges in order to compel the litigants, but when no compulsion is involved, ordained judges are only required for the particular cases mentioned in section Mishpatim and employing the term *Elokim*, for judges. See also Aruch Hashulchan, Choshen Mishpat, 1, 1, end.
11. This claim in fact played an important part in practical halachah, in particular with respect to fiscal matters; see Choshen Mishpat 25, Shach, note 19, Thumim, Kitzur Tokfo Cohen, (Warsaw, 1881), pp. 43 bottom ff. Responsa, Mahri bar Lev, Pt. 2, No. 67; Mahrik, Shoresh 161, Kontress Hassephekoth, Pt. 6, and Pt. 5, sect. 9, end of first paragraph, etc.
12. Eduyoth 1, 5.
13. See Margolies, *ibid.* Birurim 1, on the 120 members of the Great Synod. According to our opinion, infra in this chapter, the problem is easily solved. This gathering was the second type of Beth Din Gadol and consisted of all the sages available at the time in Eretz Yisrael. Our solution also explains the reference, Jerushalmi Meg. 1, 5, to eighty-five elders.
14. Mamrim 2, 2.
15. Commentary to the Mishnah *ad loc.*
16. Ridbaz, Lileshonoth HaRambam, No. 1490.
17. Choshen Mishpat, 1, 15 end.
18. Ritba to A.Z. 7a.
19. Bertinoro on the Mishnah.
20. Ridbaz *ibid.*
21. Tosaphoth Yom Tov *ad loc.*
22. Mamrim, 2, 1–3.
23. Mamrim *ad loc.*
24. So also Ridbaz. See also Azulai, Yair Ozen, Ma'arecheth Heh, No. 51. Yad Malachi, in the rules of Alfasi, printed in Rom Talmud after the Mordechai in Tractate Berachoth, holds that this is not so of the Talmud Yerushalmi; see rule 2 there, at length.
25. Maimonides, Sepher Hamitzvoth, No. 175.
26. See Z. H. Chajes, Atereth Zevi, chap. 3.
27. Based on Horayoth 3b.
28. Chajes, *ibid.*
29. Ketzoth Hachoshen, Kontress Hassephekoth, queries this with respect to any court other than the Sanhedrin. However, Beth Joseph is of the opinion that in any court of three judges, a dissentient judge must also sign the pessak, which is then issued unanimously; Chajes *ibid.*, p. 374, bottom.

Responsa, Mishpatim Yesharim, No. 238 writes, "The law to follow the majority of judges considering the majority as all, applies only when sitting as a Beth Din, but, if scholars dispute in a particular case, even though there are other possekim who hold with one opinion to the dispute, since they do not sit as a constituted Beth Din they are considered as individuals and the law to follow the majority does not apply. The custom to decide in accord with the majority of possekim, as their opinions appear in books, has nothing to do with the principle to follow the majority. It is only that when one wishes but is unable to decide the halachah, we say that since so many possekim decided thus, it is better to follow them since this is akin to following the majority." But see Chazon Ish, Y.D. 150: "When the majority of possekim agree, we do not follow the individual possek even *besha'ath hadechak*, i.e. in extremity." In practice the works of the possekim are as the possekim themselves, and they are to be consulted before rendering an halachic decision, Responsa, Shebuth Ya'acob, Pt. 2, No. 64. One who decides without first consulting the works of the possekim, is as if he decided the halachah in the presence of his teacher, Peri Megadim, Introduction to O.H. sect. 3. A practice wholly eschewed by the Talmud, Erub. 63a, and codes Y.D. 242, 4.

30. *Ibid.*, chap. 4.
31. *Loc cit.* Birurim, 7.
32. See *ibid.*, at length.
33. Chajes *ibid.*, p. 377.
34. According to some authorities, Rashba, Responsa, 233; Or Zarua, Succ. 310; Kapoth Temarim to Succ. 34b; this is only so *besha'ath hadechak*. Asheri, to B.B. 1, Siman 50 says, "Since we hold that the law is in accord with the majority, we do not decide for the lone opinion on the basis of our own reasoning." See also Chikrei Lev, Y.D. Pt. 1, Nos. 82–89 at length, on this.
35. See the Introduction to Mishnah Torah—"Since all these things in the Gemmara were agreed upon by all Israel, and the sages who enacted, or decreed or inculcated custom, or judged and taught that such is the law were *all* the sages of Israel, or the majority, and they received the tradition concerning the fundamentals of the entire Torah, generation after generation [back] to Moses our teacher." Also Yad, Sanhedrin, 4, 11. It will be remembered that it was the single opinion of R. Levi b. Chabib that set at nought the attempt to revive ordination in the sixteenth century. As Maimonides *ibid.* rightly foresaw: "But they are spread abroad and it is impossible for them all to agree!" Chazon Ish, Kontress Hashiurim, O.H. 39, also calls the Ba'alei Hagemmara "the Sanhedrin of all Israel."
36. Beth Habechirah, Introduction to Aboth, E. D. Waxman, p. 60. During this time the Talmud, according to Rav Sherira Gaon, underwent two recensions.
37. B.M. 86a. "And we may not turn aside from the Talmud by virtue of a *sevara*, though one fully competent may do so with regards a controversy between Rishonim, Chazon Ish, Y.D. 150, 12." See also, Kontress Hassephekoth, Pt. 5, sect. 9, at length.
38. Chazon Ish, to Mamrim 2,1 (Iggeroth, Pt. 2, No. 24) understands the process of sealing the Mishnah and Talmud differently. According to

Chazon Ish, this is due to two factors: first, appreciation that the former generations enjoyed larger vision and knowledge of Torah; second, the particular Divine guidance that rested on them. He explains the statement of the Talmud, A.Z.9a. "Two thousand years of Torah," to refer to the total revelation of the foundations of Torah which was completed at the end of two thousand years.

The reckoning seems to be from the Patriarch Abraham's fifty-second year, of which it is said, and the souls they acquired for Torah in Haran; see Rashi to Gen. 12, 5, and Talmud ad loc. This would bring us to the hundred and seventy second year after the destruction of the Temple, i.e., 240 of the present era, the period when R. Judah Hanassi, the redactor of the Mishnah flourished. If the difference between Abraham's fifty-second year and the relevation of Sinai is calculated, we find that it comes to four hundred and forty-eight years. Hence, if the two thousand years would be calculated from *mattan Torah*, we would arrive at the year 688. This is the period of the final closing of the Talmud by the Saboraim. Hence both Mishnah and Talmud were redacted during the period of particular heavenly influence and inspiration for Torah. After writing this, I was overjoyed to find that Prof. Assaph, Tekuphath Hageonim Vessiphurtha, (Mossad Harav Kook, 1955), p. 135, shows, on the basis of Iggereth of R. Sherira Gaon, that there are sections of the Talmud that are as late as R. Huna, Gaon Sura, c. 655.

39. Of later generations, Chazon Ish, O.H. 9, 6, says, "It is impossible to say that they act against the *din* since the sages of the generations instructed them and on this basis were the mitzvoth given to Israel."

40. The sages hold that only the actual circumcision is permitted on the Sabbath when this is the eighth day but not the preparations, which can be completed before the Sabbath.

41. Sabb. 130a.

12

Kiblu Alaihu—*They Accepted Upon Themselves*

The notion *Kiblu al atzmam,* or *kiblu alaihu,* they accepted upon themselves, bears several distinct applications and connotations within the corpus of practical halacha and its authority.

The Shulchan Aruch[1] states that a proselyte may not act as a judge in particular cases. R. Jonathan Eibushutz in his famous commentary to *Choshen Mishput,* the Thumim, raises the question of Shemaya and Abtalyon: Who, though proselytes,[2] acted as Nassi and Ab Beth Din, respectively?[3] He quotes Knesseth Hagedolah to the effect that in their case it was permitted since the community accepted them as judges upon themselves. Continues Thumim:

> According to this we must say that if the worthies of the community accepted one, though the majority of the community did not [expressly—see on,] agree, it is as if all accepted him upon themselves and he is allowed to act as a judge. For, in the case of Shemaya and Abtalyon did then the majority of Israel, in all the places in Eretz Yisrael and outside of it, agree? This is impossible![4] But since the Sanhedrin and Chief Sages and High Priest of those days agreed it is as if all Israel had accepted them upon themselves.

Thumim remains, however, doubtful concerning the efficacy of *kiblu alaihu* in capital cases since such acceptance would be tantamount to saying "Put me to death," which one is unable to do.[5]

Acceptance by the Individual

It is clear that according to Thumim, the concept of *kiblu alaihu* means in fact that every individual accepts upon himself but that this acceptance may be formally vested in the Assembly of Sages, or in the public body. The acceptance by the public body does not, however, void the stance of the individual in particular matters with respect to which their acceptance on his behalf is of no avail.[6]

It is, however, possible that Thumim's argument is irrelevant for, since the authority of the Beth Din Hagadol is absolute in halachah, they are able to accept whomsoever they see fit, and the individual has nothing to say in the matter. Once the Beth Din Hagadol has accepted the proselyte as a judge, he becomes a fully fledged judge enjoying the full authority of a judge of the Beth Din Hagadol in all matters.

Community Enactments

The force of community enactments also stems from *kiblu aleihu*, Ribash[7] holding that such enactments are "as if accepted by each individual, who henceforth becomes obliged by the enactment."[8] The area of jurisdiction, regarding enactments but not regarding actual halachic pessak,[9] also depends on acceptance by the communities or areas concerned.[10]

The *Tubei ha'ir*—that is, those appointed to care for the affairs of the community—[11] are free to act in all communal affairs, and their decisions are valid and binding as biblical law[12] since the majority of the community[13] accepted them upon themselves.[14] Neither may the individual demur or opt out;[15] the decision of the majority is binding on all "for otherwise no public matter would ever be capable of solution."[16]

They are not, of course, empowered to enact ought contrary to Torah,[17] and the binding nature of the enactments of the *Tubei ha'ir* is dependent on the presence of all of the *Tubei ha'ir* at the time of the enactment.[18] The *Tubei ha'ir* may not promulgate any enactment unless the appointed sage or dayyan or rav of the community agrees.[19]

While we cannot enter into greater detail here, for our purposes it is essential to note that the *Tubei ha'ir*, the dayyanim as well as the rabbanim are all appointed by the majority vote of the community, so that the entire organization and authority of the kehillah, its religious and secular life, is grounded in the principle *kiblu alaihu,* they, the community accepted upon themselves.[20]

In essence, this acceptance is undertaken by every member of the kahal and is grounded in the principle that one may not appoint any authority over a community without first consulting the community.

> R. Isaac said: we must not appoint a leader[21] over the community without first consulting them;[22] for it is written: See, the Lord hath called by name Bezalel the son of Uri.[23] The Holy One Blessed be He, asked Moses: Is Bezalel suitable in your eyes? He replied: Lord of the Universe, if he is acceptable to Thee, how much more so to me! He said: nevertheless go and tell the people. He went and asked Israel: is Bezalel acceptable to you? They answered: If he is acceptable to the Holy One Blessed be He, how much more so to us![24]

There are further, very important senses to *kiblu alaihu,* and these are intimately connected to everyday pessak halachah. Again, the meaning of *kiblu alaihu* will be seen to be actual acceptance by the individual members of Klal Yisrael, though this acceptance may well be spread over a long period of time. In order to clarify our thesis, it is necessary to quote a paragraph of the Talmud.

In discussing the attitude of the mind of one about to engage in prayer, the Talmud stresses that one should not engage in a difficult subject of study immediately before prayer since then one's thoughts will stray from the prayer to the subject of study; hence:[25]

> One must not stand up to say the Tephillah immediately after being engaged in a lawsuit or the discussion of a halachah; but he may do so after the discussion of a *halachah pessukkah,* a halachah which has been decided. What is meant by a halachah which has been decided? Abbaye said: Like that of R. Zera who stated: The daughters of Israel act strictly with themselves, for if they see even a drop of menstrual flow as small as a mustard seed, they wait seven clear days after it.

The passage seemingly presents a difficulty in that since the waiting period of seven days in this particular instance[26] results from the strictness of the daughters of Israel with themselves, why is this termed a halachah pessukah? The explanation is as follows.

The actual biblical laws of separation between husband and wife during the menses and afterward are quite complicated and can lead to numerous problems.[27] R. Judah Hanassi tried to obviate the majority of these by "streamlining" the different counting periods and thus simplifying the problem of the actual date for *Tevillah*, ritual immersion.[28] However, on the basis of his enactment, the daughters of Israel acted strictly with themselves and in order to eschew all possible doubt adopted the simple solution of waiting seven days after any show of blood.

Now Rabbi Judah Hanassi was unable to enact this general *chumra*[30] since, as explained by Turei Zahav,[31] the Sages cannot forbid anything explicitly permitted by the Torah. Since, however, the daughters of Israel conducted themselves in this fashion of their own accord, in order to avoid complications, over a period of time, R. Zera, a third-generation Amora, was able to declare it a halachah pessukah.[32] *Kiblu alaihu* in this case becomes the basis for the pessak, which thenceforth is independent of the individual.[33]

"Voluntary" Becomes "Duty"

A further example may be noted with respect to the evening prayer. Originally *reshuth* — voluntary,[34] but in the course of time "all Israel, wherever they live are accustomed to recite the evening prayer and they have accepted it upon themselves as *chovah* — duty."[35] In this case also, *kiblu alaihu* leads to a rejection of the more lenient halachah in favor of the more stringent.

Custom and Pessak Halachah

In the first example quoted, the *kiblu alaihu* was essential because of an halachic restraint on outright enactment. However, in numerous instances, the principle acts under a different guise. It appears as *minhag*, custom. In Tractate Sopherim,[36] this process is defined as follows: "And so the people were accustomed to act. For the halachah is not determined until it becomes custom, and it is in this context that they stated: custom revokes halachah, i.e., a custom of the Sages. But a custom which has no proof from Torah is simply a mistake in sober judgement."

Maimonides tells us that custom is inaugurated by the Beth Din Hagadol in Jerusalem.[37] Obviously this is not so of all customs, many of which are, as Rabbenu Tam retorted,[38] simply *Gehhinom* backward.[39] The force of custom as intimated in Tractate Sopherim lies in the realm of a halachah that is subject to disagreement among the possekim and in regard to which no decision has been reached. In the course of time, custom usually prevails in accord with one opinion, and this determines the halachah. The widespread acceptance of the pessak in accordance with one opinion gradually endows that opinion with the force of law. Thus Asheri[40] states:

> If there is a weakness in the halachah, i.e. that it is not clear in accordance with whom the halachah is decided, and you see that they act [in accord with one opinion], follow that custom, since we may verily assert that it appeared to the Gedolim who initiated the custom that so is the halachah. But where there is no doubt as to the halachah, you may not follow that custom which is against the halachah.[41]

This understanding of the *minhag* is the basis for the continual use by Isserles of the word, *vehachi nahug*—and so is the custom—or *vechen nahagu*—and so they have acted. Isserles does not by these words intend to leave the matter open to mere custom. On the contrary, his intention is to declare that this is the law since, during the course of time this opinion has been acted on.

The Individual Rabbi

In this broad field also, then, *kiblu alaihu* is at work though in a very subtle manner, to determine over periods of time, the halachah pessukah.[42] The individual rabbi and possek has very much indeed to do with this gradual inculcation and development. This is in fact the direct continuation of what was taking place during the period of the Tannaim and Amoraim.[43]

According to some authorities,[44] the rule that "we do not decree anything on the community unless the community is able to conform to it"[45] is dependent on the degree to which the *gezera* has spread, taken hold, and been adopted by the community (i.e., the degree of *kiblu alaihu*). If the particular *gezera* has not been accepted, it is automatically revoked.[46]

The Determining Factor

The principle of *kiblu alaihu* is, however, even more fundamental than we have so far shown. It is not too much to say that since the sealing of the Talmud it is the determining factor governing halachic decision in its entirety, and hence it is *the* determining factor in halachic authority. We shall illustrate this assertion by two very potent examples. In both examples, it seems that the crux of the *kiblu alaihu* lies with the scholars, the possekim, and not to any noticeable extent the general public. This, it will be noted is in accord with the basic assumption of the Thumim previously quoted.

Maimonides, Asheri, Caro

Let us first consider Maimonides' Mishnah Torah. With all the veneration that this work enjoyed—"And I can believe the Rav, Maimonides, even that left is right."[47]

> There is none among the possekim who explains himself more than our teacher Moses. And though his proofs are sealed he explained much . . . see my brother see, that R. Moses expounded this whole Torah so that one needs no other explanation. And though in places one may raise questions against him from the *shitath hatalmud,* and in our poverty we weary to find the door, had our teacher been before us he would have opened a door wider than the entrance to the sanctuary. In any case his meaning is clear only we find difficulty because of another source.[48]

—to quote but two of many possible examples, the Yad Hachazzakah never became the ultimate halachic code.

In the areas where the Yad held sway, this was either because Maimonides was considered the *Mara De'athra,* Egypt and Eretz Yisrael[49] or because of *kiblu alaihu.*[50]

The inhabitants of Eretz Yisrael before the advent of the Spanish exiles, the *Mustarbim,* traditionally followed Maimonides in all things,[51] and this tradition was continued until the advent of R. Joseph Ashkenazi in Safed. R. Ashkenazi contested the accepted pessak of the Rambam with respect to the problem of tithing produce grown by a non-Jew. The hegemony of the Rambam within the community was weakened. The rabbis of Safed issued an enactment including a ban on those who refused to act in the matter according to the traditional pessak of Maimonides.[52]

In fact, Rabbenu Asher came to be accepted as the equal of Maimonides,[53] a recognition by R. Joseph Caro of what had already become common practice in Spain since Rabbenu Asher's arrival there.[54] When Caro stated in the introduction to the *Shulchan Aruch* that he would rely on the majority opinion of the three great possekim, Alfasi, Maimonides, and Asheri, a criterion that caused much furor, he was not in reality proposing a new criterion — he was merely perpetuating it formally.[55] In Ashkenaz and France, the home of the Ba'alei Hatosaphoth, Asheri reigned supreme, and with the influx of Ashkenazim into Eretz Yisrael over the course of time, this also became fact in Eretz Yisrael.

Kiblu alaihu, first of Maimonides, then of Asheri in Europe, Spain, and finally Eretz Yisrael, decided the major trend of pessak to our own time.[56]

The Shulchan Aruch

Four hundred years after the appearance of Mishnah Torah, R. Joseph Caro once again attempted the unification of halachic schools of possekim since "the Torah has become as several Toroth."[57] It is important to note that in fact R. Joseph Caro succeeded where Maimonides had failed, for the *Shulchan Aruch* was accepted, after initial opposition,[58] together with the *Mappa,* the tablecloth of Isserles, by Klal Yisrael. Caro's work had to overcome opposition in Eretz Yisrael itself, since Maimonides was still considered the *mara de'athra;* in spite of this he was accepted.

One of the major stumbling blocks to acceptance was the reliance of Caro on the three pillars of *hora'ah,* Alfasi, Maimonides, and Asheri, for after all these are but three of many *rishonim.* Birchei Joseph[59] quotes the tradition that the two hundred rabbis of Safed agreed with Caro's pessakim, hence the title *MaRaN,* acrostically understood as *le Matta'im Rabbanan Nismach,* ordained by two hundred rabbis. The acceptance of the rule "two out of three" by such a quorum lent unparalleled weight to Caro's decisions, and he was not considered as a single possek.[60] Even the Rema, writing of him,[61] says that "one who argues with him is as one arguing against the *Shechinah*."

The second problem lay in overcoming the entrenched custom and habit resulting from adherence to either Maimonides or Asheri alone. Once again *kiblu alaihu* prevailed among both the possekim and the kehilloth. For though there was agreement during the lifetime of Caro to his rule for determining halachah and its consequences, in practice the previous custom still prevailed widely. Only during the period of Mahram Galanti (mid-sixteenth century) did the general agreement become widespread.[62] The later words of the Chatham Sopher[63] "and in actual halachah who may raise his hand against the decision of the Beth Joseph" reflect the actual situation. Klal Yisrael had accepted the *Shulchan Aruch* upon themselves.

This is not to "stifle" halachic development. The *Shulchan Aruch* itself often quotes more than a single opinion,[64] which fact alone ensures the continuation of halachic discussion, certainly so with the incorporation of the Rema.[65] The point is that in view of the *kiblu alaihu* of possekim and populace alike, it is impossible to decide halachah without reference to and justification by the *Shulchan Aruch*. It alone is the authoritative ground on which contemporary halachic decision stands or falls.[66]

Commentaries and Later Compilations

The same standards of *kiblu alaihu* apply to the recognized master commentaries on the *Shulchan Aruch*.[67] Latterly, one might say also to the Mishnah Berurah and Chazon Ish. The intensity of the *kiblu alaihu* varies with the degree of inculcation by the disciples of each, especially in the case of the Chazon Ish or the more popular case of the Mishneh Berurah.

Summary of *Kiblu Alaihu*

In principle, we may sum up as follows. Absolute binding halachic authority upon all Israel, resides in the Talmud alone. Relative halachic authority is dependent upon the principle *kiblu alaihu*. This principle is responsible for the differences in halachic practice evident between entire segments of Jewry, such as Ashkenazi and Sephardi Jewries, and even between communities within particular segments or areas.

Broadly speaking, the meaning of *kiblu alaihu* is that the individual accepts upon himself. The individual is either the possek or the layman. Acceptance results in the initiative of the possek in influencing his adherents to accept an halachah upon themselves; and in accepting the decisions of the possek, dayyan, rav, or lay body of the community upon himself, by the individual. Acceptance by the community may create a halachah or determine halachah when this is undecided. Acceptance by possek and layman alike determines the authority of particular halachic codes.

Thus, side by side with the immutable halachah of the Talmud, *kiblu alaihu* is the determining factor in halachic practice.

When new problems arise, as they do continually, *kiblu alaihu* in its varied forms determines the halachic stance concerning them, so that after an indeterminate period, a definitive halachah emerges that then becomes independent of the process and adopts the guise of halachic precedent.

We have not, of course, exhausted the principle of *kiblu alaihu*, which requires a great deal of more detailed halachic research. Our intention has only been to show how this principle operates in a general sense as the arbiter of halachic authority for both the possek and for Klal Yisrael. As such it is operative today among Torah true Jewry and is largely responsible for many of the halachic divisions evident among observant Jews who follow the possekim of their individual teachers.

The period after the expulsion from Spain and the divisive spirit among the kehilloth required a renewal of centralized halachic authority.[68] On the one hand, the attempt was made to renew the original, traditional *semichah*, ordination, by Mahri b. Rav who writes in his Kontress Hasemichah that the religious anarchy and spiritual despair of the times led him to advocate renewal of ordination. This did not gain acceptance. On the other hand, R. Joseph Caro produced the *Shulchan Aruch*, filling the need. It was accepted. Historically, Jewry has witnessed the emergence of authoritative codes from time to time. These codes, in one way or another, attempted to draw together the strands of halachic development and pessak so to enable authentic, authoritative halachic voice to guide contemporaries and point the way to the future.

It would seem that our age is ripe for such a code, in particular with respect to the laws pertaining to renewed, autonomous *malchuth* and the halachoth dependent on Eretz Yisrael.

Notes to Chapter Twelve

1. Choshen Mishpat 7, 1.
2. Yoma 71b. From these sources it seems that they were descendants of Sennacherib, while Tanhuma, Vayakhel, Siman 8, traces their lineage to Sisera. Maimonides, however, in conformity with Eduyoth 5, 6, writes in his Introduction to Mishnah Torah that they themselves were proselytes.
3. Hag. 15a.
4. Though it does seem to have been the actual case with the acceptance of Purim by Klal Yisrael, see Esther 9, 27–32.
5. See App. 3, infra, end.
6. Thumim concludes that Shemaya and Abtalyon could not have sat on capital cases, for this reason.
7. Responsa, No. 399.
8. Whether the individual is obliged in such manner that even when he moves to another area of jurisdiction to live, he remains so obliged or not, is questionable. See Peri Chadash, Orach Chaim, 496, sect. 13. In regard to whole communities that have moved or been uprooted and have resettled elsewhere, see *ibid.* sect. 19.
9. Responsa, Iggeroth Moshe, Choshen Mishpat No. 2.
10. *Ibid.* Responsa Shoel Umeshiv, Mahdurah Kama, Pt. 2, No. 32, holds that since it is accepted custom for nearby villages to defer to the rabbi of the town, the enactments of the town apply to them also. Where, however, strong reason exists, Mahram Shik, Responsa, Orach Chaim No. 34, enables these to break away and become independent of the "parent" kehillah.
11. These are so called in the Talmud, Meg. 26a.
12. Responsa, Rashba, Pt. 4, No. 185. Cf. also the commentary of Ramban to Leviticus 27, 29.
13. Responsa, Asheri, 6, 5. Chatham Sopher, Responsa, Choshen Mishpat, 116, adds the rider, "provided all the members of the community were invited to participate in their election."
14. Choshen Mishpat 2, 1 and Rema.
15. Rashba, Responsa 769. "One who takes an oath not to be bound by the enactments of the community is as one who swears to abolish a mitzvah, Semag, Prohibition 238 on the authority of [Hai] Gaon."
16. Responsa Asheri, quoted by Mahrashdam, Yoreh De'ah No. 113.
17. Responsa, Ribash 484, etc.
18. Responsa, Mahram Alshech, No. 59.
19. Shach, Choshen Mishpat 321, 45; Pitchei Teshuvah *ibid.*, note 8; Rashba, Responsa, Pt. 1, No. 1206, and the majority of possekim.
20. The *Tubei ha'ir*—Choshen Mishpat, 2, 1; *ibid.*, Meirath Einayim note 9; Netivoth Hamishpat *ibid.*, note 5, etc. *Dayyanim*—Sepher Hashetaroth, R.

Isaac Algerbeloni, pp. 7 and 131; Responsa, Ribash, 207; Rashba, Pt. 3, No. 417, etc. *Rabbanim*—Responsa, Chatham Sopher, Choshen Mishpat No. 19; Nachal Yitzchak Choshen Mishpat, 3, etc. An examination of the *ktav rabbanuth*, usually sent inviting a rav to become rav of the town, shows that this was invariably sent in the name of the *Parnassim*, the *Tubei ha'ir*, the dayyanim, the scholars of the town and often by all who paid taxes to the kehillah.

21. Heb. *Parness*, which also connotes a manager or administrator.
22. Even if the appointee is exceptional in wisdom and he is appointed by the greatest in his generation, as is evident from this text, Tashbatz, Responsa, Pt. 1, No. 161.
23. Ex. 35,30.
24. Berachoth, 55a.
25. Berachoth 31a.
26. See Rashi and Ma'adanei Yom Tov to the passage.
27. See, e.g., the Mishnah, Arachin, 2, 1.
28. See Nid. 66a.
29. See Taharath Yisrael, Be'er Yitzchak to Y.D. 183, note 14, end.
30. Cf. also the remarks of Chazon Ish, Y.D. 125, 3, on stringent rulings that prevent engaging in Derech Eretz unnecessarily.
31. Orach Chaim, 558; Y.D. 117: Choshen Mishpat 2. See also Birchei Joseph, O.H. *ibid.*, sect. 2, at length.
32. Responsa, Mishnath Eliezer, Pt. 1, No. 62. The Talmud in Nid. 66a quotes the words of R. Zera immediately after those of Rabbi Judah Hanassi emphasizing thereby both the time lapse and the process.
33. Mahrshal, Responsa, 7. Peri Chadash *ibid.*, 496. See also Rashi, to R.H. 18b, s.q. Demepharsem.
34. Ber. 27b.
35. Maimonides, Tephillah, 1, 6.
36. Chapter 14, halachah 18.
37. Mamrim, 1, 2–3; *ibid.*, 2, 2.
38. Shiltei Giborim to Mordechai, Gittin, 444.
39. The Hebrew letters of *minhag*, form *gehinnom* in reverse.
40. Responsa, 55, 10.
41. Even in the case of an Issur Miderabbanan, Peri Chadash, *ibid.*, end of sect. 10.
42. This sense of *kiblu alaihu* is not to be confused with the individual who voluntarily accepts upon himself to act stringently in a permitted matter. Such acceptance involves one in *Neder*, a vow, see Y.D. 213, 1. A similar case involving an entire community or even country requires expression of regret by the entire community or country; Responsa, Chavoth Yair 126; Peri Chadash, *ibid.* See also Responsa, Nachlath David, Vilna 1864, No. 31, who analyzes the problems of the individual who wishes to opt out of an enactment entered into for the purpose of heightening the religious condition of the community.
43. See end of previous chapter.
44. See *Encyclopedia Talmudith*, Vol. 1, p. 600.
45. B.B. 60b.

168 Halachic Authority and Its Transmission

46. *Encyclopedia Talmudith, ibid.*, pp. 601–602.

47. Kaphtor Vapherach, ed. Lunz, Pt. 2, p. 65.

48. R. Joseph Colon, Responsa No. 121.

49. Ridbaz, Pt. 4, 1164 etc., Beth Joseph, Y.D. 265; R. Bezalel Ashkenazi, Responsa 1: "And as the great Rav, Maimonides, the father of Israel, the *mara* of Eretz Yisrael, whom they accepted upon themselves as Rav from the end of the land of Yemen to the end of the land of Israel and Shinar [Babylon]."

50. See, e.g., the Takkanoth of Toledo in I. Ber, *The History of the Jews in Christian Spain* (Berlin, 1929), p. 955. In a later Takkana, 1487, the kahal of Castille accepted the authority of Maimonides only when his opinion did not conflict with that of Asheri; see, Ber *ibid.*, pp. 384–385.

51. Once a community or area accepts a possek upon themselves, there is no distinction between acting in accord with his opinion both in lenient as in stringent pessak. Peri Chadash, *ibid.*, sect. 11.

52. See Kesseph Mishnah to Terumoth 1, 11 at length, in particular, the final section where he says, "Afterwards the matter spread until the scholars of the town were forced to repair the harm, and they gathered together and decreed with the ban that henceforth and forever one should not tithe produce purchased from a non-Jew, but only as they were until now accustomed in accord with our master."

53. See Introduction to Beth Joseph.

54. Circa 1300.

55. Responsa, Ridbaz, Pt. 2, 626, and Birchei Joseph to Choshen Mishpat, 25, note 29.

56. A full and detailed treatment of the historic controversy surrounding the determination of the halachah in accordance with Maimonides is found in Cahana, loc cit., pp. 8–88.

57. Introduction to Beth Joseph.

58. Some of which we have mentioned in a previous chapter.

59. To Choshen Mishpat 25, and Shem Hagedolim s.q. Beth Joseph.

60. Birchei Joseph *ibid.*

61. Responsa, 47.

62. J.M. Toledano in R. Joseph Caro, Iyyunim etc. (Mossad Harav Kook, 1969), p. 187.

63. Y.D. 327.

64. In regard to this, see, Yad Malachi, Klallei Hashulchan Aruch, 1–17; Sedei Chemed, Klallei Hapossekim, Shulchan Aruch etc.

65. On the Rema see *ibid.* and numerous methodological works. See also our remarks toward the end of chap. 8. "The inhabitants of Ashkenaz and surrounding countries accepted upon themselves and their descendants the law of Moses, the Rema . . . neither turning from him to be lenient or stringent." R. Akiva Eger, Letter 26, Iggereth Sopherim. "And I am afraid to move a hair's breadth from the Rema," Chatham Sopher, E.H. 151.

66. And one is nonetheless permitted to argue with the Shulchan Aruch; see Obadaiah Joseph, Yalkuth Joseph, Introduction pp. 16–18, Chazon Ish, Kontress Acharon, Pt. 2, 15–"And it is our duty to use our minds as far as we are able and to search out that which is most decisive according to our

sober judgment. And none are allowed to say: accept my opinion, but as for ourselves we are bound by the portion bestowed upon us." See also Y.D. 242, beginning, and commentaries ad loc. in particular Hanhagoth Hora'ath Issur Vehetter, at the end of the siman, No. 8.

67. Chazon Ish, Shebi'ith, 25, 5. "And we are accustomed to decide according to the Gedolei Ha'achronim, even against the Shulchan Aruch, as the Shach, Peri Chadash, Gera, and we also rely in particular cases on Achronim such as the Noda Biyehuda, against the Shulchan Aruch." See also Chazon Ish to Choshen Mishpath, Likkutim, 1.

68. Shem Hagedolim, s.q. Beth Joseph.

Afterword

Modern Halachah and Philosophy

In a previous chapter, we quoted at length the responsum of Rabbenu Asher dealing with the relationship between halachah and philosophy. Rabbenu Asher decries the employment of philosophy in deciding halachah. Despite the fact that this distinction remains sine qua non, the modern period has witnessed a drawing together of the two realms, and this on the part of Gedolim who are accepted as impeccable halachists.

While R. Amiel employed R. Chaim's terminology philosophically and R. Kook erected his exalted vision of the Jewish state on the hard facts of halachah, and R. Soloveitcyk philosophizes on the halachic universe, only the Gaon of Rogachov, Rabbi Joseph Rozin actually fused basic philosophic concepts with pessak.

Neither R. Amiel nor R. Chaim who are basically searching for analytical tools, nor R. Kook nor R. Soloveitcyk who have been variously preceded in approach, can be considered radical innovators in the relationship between halachah and philosophy. R. Chaim, certainly, would have been horrified at the thought of such innovation. Not so the Rogachover. He is an innovator unique in the long annals of halachah.

> The world of the Rogachover's thought is the world of philosophy with which he became familiar through Maimonides' Guide. This thought found its way to the world of halachah. He detected the line of thought that unified Maimonides the halachist with Maimonides the philosopher. Because of this his words seem abstract, finding no expression in practical halachah. Nonetheless, it is interesting to note that despite veering from accepted methods of

study, he arrives at the very same conclusions as the possekim. The only difference between them and between him being of approach. Whilst the possekim arrive at their decision by direct halachic approach to the subject in hand, he perceived the general, abstract principles behind the problem. [R.M. Grossberg, *Zephunoth HaRogachover* (Jerusalem, 1975), pp. 7–8]

These modern giants of halachah collectively stress the unity that pervades and binds Jewish thought and vision together with Jewish life. On the one hand, we visualize the erection of society and its ideals with the building bricks of halachah; on the other, we see the concretization of philosophy and abstract thought within that same halachah. Be it as either starting or terminal point, the halachah is the fulcrum of the Jewish soul. No philosophy of Judaism is true unless it is either grounded in or terminates in halachah. This is the unique and creative stand of Judaism. It is the dynamic challenge and obligation of Torah on the Jew and on his people.

For, though there are two sides to Torah, halachah and aggadah, the spiritual flight and philosophic milieu, these are not divorced from one another. "God spoke one, I heard two" (Ps. 62, 12). A single spirit underlies, inheres, and governs them both. The one is discarded only to the distortion of the other. The power and vision of the prophet, the yearning and insight of the Psalmist, or the musings of the philosopher pale to insignificance on failure to transform their lofty call into life and living.

Fusion or Wedge

Israel has lived and been preserved by the fusion of both. The modern attempt to drive a wedge between ideal and practice has succeeded in creating a wave of assimilation that threatens, in its frightening proportions, the long-range demographic existence of Jewry in the Golah. In Israel, the realization of the prophetic dream of restoration coupled with the setting up of its institutions and instruments on foundations foreign to Judaism is endangering the unity of the state and its internal peace. Unless the rift in the soul of Jewry is healed, there is no telling where present trends will lead.

But Israel is yet abuilding. There is time and there are those with the ability and the will to fashion a Jewish state, and not merely a state where Jews live—to fashion the state in a manner that will reflect the oneness and strivings of the unique Jewish soul.

Israel and Golah

How Jewishly secure will the state be in the long run, without its distinctive halachic culture? The erosion of Jewry in the Golah is writ large in the annals of the erosion of halachah. On what bases other than halachah can the internal erosion of the state be prevented? All that has been attempted during the past two centuries has failed dismally. Even the greatest miracle of Jewish history, the rebirth of the state, has not succeeded in stemming the drift that has become a tidal wave.

Both Israel and the Golah must face the facts of Jewish life and existence. Without halachah, both are in danger of disappearing as specifically Jewish entities. The Jewish people did not come home in order to step, unaided, from the canvas of history.

A secular Jewish state is a negation of Jewish history. We are beginning to learn that no such creation is either tenable or viable. The Golah already enjoys its secular state and so has little need to come to Israel. The more secular Israel becomes, the less its chance of independent, creative, long-term Jewish survival. The Jewish state, as the Jewish people must find itself within the core of the uniquely creative, stimulating and demanding Jewish soul. It must restore the miraculous saga of rebirth to the bosom of halachah.

The "Bogey" of a Theocratic State

Halachah is vital to the people and to the state of Israel. One of the "bogies" in the mind of the Israeli is that too much involvement with halachah would bring about a theocratic state. But halachah is not interested in politics as such. It is not, neither does it aim to be "constitutional law" in the classic sense of a structure of political power translated into legal terms and machinery for enforcement. It is a structure of the word of God. It alone identifies values in the Divine plan for human and social existence and works them into life, concretely. As such it enables the creation of political power, but it defines both the reach and distribution of powers and authority. More than that it leaves for the Messiah.

Certainly in its commitment to the conservation and further-ance of the values of Judaism, it would cleanse both politics as well as politicians from much of the murk that presently adheres to them—but this can hardly be considered negatively!

New Uncertainties, Fresh Problems

That halachah does not change more rapidly is doubtless due in part, as with all institutions, to the persistence of traditional habits of thought and to the instinct of self-preservation within a hostile environment. But these are by no means the sole factors.

An equally stubborn obstacle, common to all systems of law, is the difficulty of devising improvements that will not create new problems of their own, perhaps as difficult as those they purport to eliminate.

It is unreasonable to demand finished, polished, refurbished halachoth when even such elementary basic laws as, for exam-ple, those affecting Zahal and the civilian authority, are still, in spite of the apparatus of statehood, only in the swaddling stage. We have suggested a possible approach to the present problem-atic state of halachah vis-à-vis the state of Israel. But no panaceas are proffered or possible. Codification and commentary, how-ever vital and however skillfully done, carry with them the seeds of new uncertainties of meaning, fresh problems, in a never ending cycle.

The problem is not primarily a question of halachah. It re-solves itself into the single question as to whether Jewry wishes to survive as a Jewish people, a Jewish state, or not!

Appendices

Halachic Methodology, Assumptions, and Concepts

In the following short appendices, we shall endeavor to outline the salient features of the logical rules employed by halachah for interpreting Scripture, some of the logical premises of halachah and finally several basic halachic concepts.

A working knowledge and insight of these must be grasped for an at least initial understanding of the principles governing both theoretical and practical halachah (see Yad Talmud Torah, 1, 11, and Yoreh De'ah, 246, 4).

Appendix 1

Logical Forms—Middoth

The Rules for Interpreting Scripture

The logical rules for interpreting Scripture are formulated in the Baraitha of R. Ishmael that prefaces the Sifra. These are in essence an expanded form of the seven middoth[1] of Hillel, also quoted there.[2]

While the middoth of R. Ishmael by no means exhaust the number of rules by which Torah is expounded,[3] his Baraitha has long been accepted as the authoritative summation of such middoth and has, since as early as the Siddur of R. Amram Gaon, been incorporated in the Daily Prayer Book, forming by its inclusion something of a confession of faith in the unity of the written and oral laws on which Judaism stands.

Only the middah of *kal vachomer*, inference from minor to major or vice versa, is employed explicitly in the Torah. The Midrash[4] lists ten such instances, some from the Torah, others from the remaining books of the Bible. Others have listed more than four times this number of examples.

The middoth are the vehicles by means of which Torah is expounded, and their employment unfolds practical laws that are of the body of the Torah though not stated explicitly.[5] They may not, however, be applied to those laws that are termed halachah leMoshe miSinai.[6]

Authority

Apart from the middah, *gezerah shaveh*[7] the middoth were used by the sages without recourse to received tradition;[8] hence,

Maimonides, though determining on different criteria with respect to decrees, institutions or customs, states:[9]

> If the Great Beth Din expounded the law by means of one of the
> middoth, and so applied it, and there later arose another Beth
> Din that, in virtue of different reasoning [of the middoth] contra-
> dicted them, it [the later Beth Din] may void [the earlier decision]
> and adjudicate according to that which appears correct to it. As it
> is written:[10] "And to the judge who will be in those days" – you
> are only obliged to follow the ruling of the Beth Din in your
> generation.[11]

Failure to observe a ruling of the Beth Din when this is based
on deduction by means of the rules involves one in transgression of the positive mitzvah to "observe and do according to all
that they shall teach thee,"[12] and the prohibition not to "turn
aside from the word which they shall declare unto thee, to the
right hand, nor to the left,"[13] since such laws carry particular[14]
biblical status.[15]

Object

Though the middoth are employed freely by the sages, their
origin is Sinai. They do not represent a logical system invented
by the sages for interpreting Scripture. They were handed down
as such together with the Torah.[16] Their object is to prise the
halachah from the written text. In doing so, they illustrate how
the oral law is in fact embraced within the wisdom of the written
word. We shall examine them briefly.

The Thirteen Rules

Rabbi Ishmael says: The Torah is expounded by thirteen middoth.
   1. *Kal Vachomer*, inference from minor to major or from major
to minor.
   This middah is based on the straightforward use of logic. The
form is well expressed in Moses' argument before God: "Behold,
the Children of Israel have not hearkened unto me; how then
should Pharaoh hear me"[17] or in the argument from major to
minor: "If the Torah teaches with respect to the High Priest,
whose sanctity is not terminable, that he may defile himself for a

meth mitzvah, this must certainly be so of the Nazirite whose sanctity[18] is limited in time."[19]

Apart from the particular limitations with respect to *kal vachomer,* which need not detain us here, two basic principles must be mentioned in its connection.

The rule is that no punishment is inflicted by Scripture unless Scripture specifically warned against the prohibition in a separate verse. The reason for this is to prevent the potential transgressor from considering the prohibition optional. That is, one might think to himself, "I am prepared to transgress and will take the consequences." Scripture, therefore, warns against transgression, separately.[20] Such warning cannot be deduced by means of a *kal vachomer;* it must be stated specifically. Not only may the warning not be so deduced, but no punishment may be inflicted in virtue of a *kul vachomer.*[21]

Several reasons have been advanced for this. Principally, one school of thought holds that since the *middah* may be employed freely by the individual teacher, there is always the possibility that faulty logic has been used.[22] Others hold that when a strict law is deduced from a lighter law, the punishment declared in the Torah for the lighter law may not suffice for the stricter case, and we are unable simply to invent punishments.[23]

2. *Gezerah shavah,* when in two passages words that are similar or have identical connotation[24] are employed, the laws of both passages, however different they may be in themselves, are subject to the same regulations and applications.

The *gezera shavah* may be used either to explain a terminum found in the Torah or to promulgate fresh law. An example of the former is found in the beginning of tractate Kiddushin[25] where the Talmud explains the term *yikach* used by the Torah with respect to betrothal, by means of the same term employed in acquisition. "With regards betrothal the verse says:[26] 'When a man takes— *yikach,* a wife,' while with regards acquisition the verse states:[27] 'I have given the money for the field, take it—*kach,* from me.' Hence *'kichah'* refers to acquisition by means of money."[28]

An example of the latter is to be found in the famous discussion between Hillel and the Benei Bithyra[29] as to whether bringing the pascal lamb is permitted even on the Sabbath. The solution is found by means of a *gezera shavah.* "In connection with the continual daily offering the verse says that this is to be brought 'in its due season—*bemo'ado'*[30]; also with regards the pascal lamb the verse says: 'in its due season.'[31] Just as the continual daily offering sets aside the Sabbath, so also the Passover offering sets it aside."

The incident between Hillel and the Benei Bithyra has given rise to conjecture by scholars on other grounds, for how was it possible to "forget" a continually recurring halachah? Reuben Margolies[32] suggests, plausibly, that though calendrically in every cycle of nineteen years the eve of Passover indeed falls on the Sabbath, this is only so since the calendar was fixed by Hillel the Second. Previous to this, when the calendar was determined by the Sanhedrin, it was possible to obviate the coincidence of dates by the addition or subtraction of a day from the month of Adar. Such manipulation was apparently employed over an extended period so that the eve of Passover did not in fact fall on the Sabbath.

When passages are placed in juxtaposition to one another, or when several subjects are included in the same verse (e.g., "This is the law of the burnt offering, of the meal offering, and of the sin offering, and of the guilt offering, and of the consecration offering and of the sacrifice of peace offerings"[33], these are to be considered analogous,[34] and the one subject clarifies the other.[35]

This rule, not listed under the thirteen but allied to the *gezera shavah*, is called *hekesh*. However, unlike the *gezera shavah*, which can only be employed when received by tradition,[36] the *hekesh* may be employed without such reference.[37]

The reason that *gezera shavah* may not be used without the authority of tradition is as stated by Ramban:[38] "Since the middah of *gezera shavah* is an instrument which could be employed all day by someone to refute all the laws of the Torah. For words are repeated many times in the Torah. It is impossible for a large book never to use the same words again."[39] Hence, "only He who gave the Torah can tell which words were written to teach what."[40]

Logical affinity or analogous content, even when congruous terms are lacking, is sometimes employed in the sense of a *gezera shavah*.[41]

3. *Binyan ab,* a comprehensive principle derived from one text or from two texts.

For example: "The school of R. Ishmael taught: Since the Torah mentions 'garments' in connection with several mitzvoth without specifying their texture, and in one case the Torah specifies 'a woollen garment, or a linen garment'[42]; wherever else 'garment' is mentioned it also refers to a woolen or to a linen garment."[43]

The same is true when the principle is deduced from two texts, such as:

> The class of damages termed *shor* [ox] which move and cause damage are not the same as those classed *hor* [pit], which are stationary. Nor are those termed *bor*, whose owner was the cause of the damage, as those termed *shor*, whose owner is not the cause of the damage. They have, however, a common factor, viz. that they both cause damage and one is responsible for watching them [to prevent it]. So also I may include.[44]

The deduction from two texts operates only when both texts are required in order to complete the teaching in the cases from which the texts are drawn, and one subject could not be deduced from the other. But if the second text merely reiterates what was taught in the first, no general principle could be drawn from them and their teaching remains specific to the context. This is called *"shenei ketuvim haba'im ke'echad,"* the law being reiterated to show that it only applies to the two cases. Hence, in our example, it is necessary to show that had the Torah written either *shor* or *bor* alone, the other class could not have been deduced from it.[45]

4. *Klall uperat,* a general proposition followed by a specifying particular.

For example:

> "Ye shall bring your offering of the cattle, even of the herd or of the flock."[46] "Cattle" is a general term, "herd and flock" are particulars and they are mentioned in order to limit the general term to those specified in detail. Hence we learn that "beast," which would normally have been included in the generic term "cattle" [animal], may not be offered for sacrifice.[47, 48]

5. *Perat ukelall,* a particular term followed by a general proposition. In this case the particular is extended by the general term that follows, to include everything.

For example: With respect to the return of lost articles, the Torah says,[49] "And thou shalt restore it to him. And so shalt thou do with his ass; and so shalt thou do with his garment." Mention of these particulars would limit the mitzvah to restore a lost article to these alone; therefore, the Torah continues, "And so shalt thou do with every lost thing of thy brother's which he hath lost," to cover every lost item.[50]

6. *Kelall uperat ukelall,* a general law limited by a specific application and then again referred to in general terms, must be
interpreted according to the tenor of the specific limitation.[51]

"If a man give his neighbor [anything—an all-embracing term]
money or stuff [particulars] to keep [anything—a further embracing term]."[52] Just as the specified details are moveable goods with
intrinsic value, so the laws of this section apply only to what is
moveable and has intrinsic value. This excludes lands, which are
immoveable . . . and documents, which, though moveable have
no intrinsic value."[53]

R. Shimon of Kinon[54] points out that this middah may be
applied even when the second general term does not immediately juxtapose the previous general term and its specific limitation, provided that the second general term is written in the
same section.[55]

7. *Kelall shehu tzarich liperat,* or, *perat shehu tzarich likelall.* A
general term that requires a particular or specific term to explain
it, or conversely, a particular term requiring a general one to
complement it.

"Sanctify unto Me all the firstborn, whatsoever openeth the
womb."[56] I might think that this is so even if the firstborn is
female? Therefore the Torah says:[57] "All the firstling males that are
born of . . . shalt thou sanctify." This excludes females.[58] Let the
Torah state the verse with the particular only [i.e., the verse in
Deuteronomy] and what need is there for the general rule? If that
verse alone were stated I might have thought that every firstling
male must be sacrificed, whether it opens the womb or not[59];

hence, the particular requires the general rule to limit it.

The difference between this middah and *kelall uperat* (supra) is,
as pointed out by Rashi,[60] that in the case of the former middah
we understand the general rule and the detail is emphasized only
to limit its application, whereas with the present middah, without the detail the general rule remains obscure.

8. *Davar shehayah bikelall veyatza min hakelall lellamed, lo lellamed
al atzmo yatza ella lellamed al hakelall kullo yatza.* When a subject
included in a general proposition is afterward particularly excepted to give information, the exception is not made for that instance
alone but to apply to the generality of the proposition as a whole.

Ra'abad explains this rule as follows. There are two points involved. First, why was that which was included within the general rule excepted? Obviously to teach something special. Second, it cannot have been excepted to teach only with respect to its own context since in this regard it teaches nothing new, all being in any event included within the general proposition. Hence, it must be meant for application to the generality embraced by the proposition as a whole.

For example:

"Whosoever he be of the Children of Israel, or of the strangers that sojourn in Israel, that giveth of his seed to *Moloch*; he shall surely be put to death; the people of the land shall stone him with stones."[61] *Moloch* is but one of the abominations, and why is its punishment mentioned more than the others? But this does not come to teach the law only in the case of *Moloch*, but to teach that stoning is the punishment for all the abominations.[62]

9. *Davar shehayah bikelall veyatza lit'on to'an echad shehu ke'inyano, yatza lehakel velo lehachmir.* Whenever anything is first included in a general proposition and is then excepted to prove another similar proposition, this specifying alleviates but does not aggravate the law's restriction. For example: "As when a man goeth into a forest with his neighbor to hew wood, and his hand fetches a stroke with the axe to cut down the tree, and the head slippeth from the helve, and lighteth upon his neighbor that he die; he shall flee unto one of the cities and live."[63]

One who kills another in error is also a murderer, since the verse declares,[64] "And he that killeth a man shall be put to death," no difference being made as to how the killing was done. In Deuteronomy, the murderer in error is excepted from the general rule of murder to alleviate his punishment from death to exile but not to aggravate it.

10. *Davar shehayah bikelall veyatza lit'on to'an acher shelo ke'inyano, yatza lehakel ulehachmir.* When anything is first included in a general proposition and is then excepted to state a case that is not a similar proposition, such specifying alleviates in some respects and aggravates in others the law's restriction.

"And when a man or woman hath a plague upon the head or upon the beard."[65] Now the head or the beard are actually included in the already mentioned plague that affected the skin or flesh.[66] They are now excepted in order to state a different condition of defilement, namely, yellow hair,[67] whereas the general sign for defilement is white hair.[68] We do not say that both white *and* yellow hair render him unclean. But, his situation is in one respect alleviated, that is, that white hair is not for him a sign of defilement; in another aggravated, that is, that yellow hair defiles him, though this is not a defiling symptom with respect to skin or flesh.

11. *Davar shehayah bikelall veyatza lidon bedavar chadash, iy attah yachol lechachziro likellalo ad shehecheziro hakatuv likelallo beferush.* Anything included in a general propositon and afterward excepted to determine a new matter cannot be applied to the general proposition unless this be expressly done in the text.

With respect to the sacrifice of the Nazirite, the verse says,[69] "And he shall present his offering unto the Lord, one he-lamb of the first year . . . and one ewe lamb of the first year . . . and one ram . . . , and their meal offering and their drink offerings." The question arises as to why it is necessary to state "and their meal offering and their drink offerings" that these are normal procedure for a burnt offering or peace offering?[70]

Answers the Sifri. Since these offerings of the Nazirite have a special requirement, namely, the loaves, we would think that the normal laws of the sacrifice may not apply to them, and no meal or drink offering is required. Hence the need by the verse to restore them explicitly to the general requirements of sacrifices.

12. *Davar halamed me'inyano, vedavar halamed misopho.* Interpretation deduced from the context, or from the subsequent terms of the text.

" 'Thou shalt not murder, thou shalt not commit adultery, thou shalt not steal.'[71] Since the first two cases are capital crimes, so also must the third be. Hence the 'theft' referred to here must be that mentioned in Ex. 21, 16."[72]

"None of you shall approach to any that is near of kin to him"[73] forbids all relatives. But the subsequent list of forbidden consanguinious relationships teaches also those that are in fact permitted.

13. *Shnei ketuvim hamakkchishim zeh eth zeh ad sheyavo hakatuva hashlishi veyachria beyneihem.* When two texts contradict each other, the meaning can be determined only when a third text is found that harmonizes them.

Ra'abad comments that when one discovers two contradictory texts, one is not allowed to push them aside and consider them erroneous. One must endeavor to harmonize them as far as possible until the third text that truly harmonizes them is discovered.[74] Then one must act in accord with the harmonization.

"Ye yourselves have seen that I have talked with you from heaven"[75] is contradicted by "The Lord spoke with you face to face in the mount out of the midst of the fire"[76] and harmonized by "Out of heaven He made thee to hear His voice, that He might instruct thee; and upon earth He made thee to see His great fire; and thou didst hear His words out of the midst of the fire."[77]

We see then that the middoth employ both deductive and inductive processes based on *a fortiori*, syllogism, analogy, and analysis, as well as inference dependent on juxtaposition and context. In these capacities, the forms of logic predicated by the middoth are common, independently of scriptural text, throughout Talmudic literature.

Notes to Appendix One

1. Middah—dimension, measure, proportion, principle, standard, hence logical argument, rule of interpretation.
2. Commentaries on Sifra and all authorities on the Middoth.
3. Rabad, Sifra loc cit. etc. R. Ishmael himself uses additional middoth, Sot. 3b; Mechilta 20, 25; Sifri, Bamidbar 15, 2; but these are more in the form of general exegetical principles rather than logical deductions. Thus in the three examples I have mentioned we find him saying: (a) A section that is stated and then repeated is repeated only because of that which is newly stated therein. (b) Wherever the word "In your dwelling places" is used, it refers to Eretz Yisrael. (c) "If" in the Torah signifies the voluntary nature of the obligation except for three places. The same is true of his rule "The Torah speaks in human language, Ker. 11a, etc." and "The Torah teaches the way of the world, Ber. 35b"; and there are others of similar character. Likewise, other Tannaim employ general exegetical principles, e.g., "The Torah uses synonyms, Sifri to Num. 6.3," etc.
4. Bereshith Rabbah 92, 7.
5. For this reason, the final middah mentioned in the Baraitha "When two texts contradict each other the meaning is determined only when a third text is found which harmonizes them" is not included in the thirteen by some authorities, Rashbatz, Yabin Shemuah, Shelah, since this third text shows that the explanation is stated explicitly in the Torah. These authorities list the thirteen differently.
6. Shelah, Pt. 4, Torah Shebaal Peh, p. 2. On Halachah *leMoshe miSinai* see supra, chap. 5.
7. The second of the thirteen middoth; see infra.

8. Yad Malachi 144, 2. One is, however, only prevented from using the *gezerah shavah* for the promulgation of new law. It may be adduced in support of a known halachah, Jer. Pess. 6, 1.

9. Yad, Mamrim 2, 1.

10. Deut. 17, 9.

11. With respect to argument against the Talmud, see Kesseph Mishnah ad loc. Rambam le'am no. 3. Chazon Ish ad loc. Kellalei Alfasi by Yad Malachi, printed after the Alfass in the Rom, Wilna Talmud, Berachoth, No. 2; Azulai, Yair Ozen, Ma'arecheth Heh, 51; Responsa, Hith'oreruth Teshuvah (Budapest, 5683), Pt. 2, No. 44, sect. 7; Noda Biyehudah, Tinyana, Eben Haezer, no. 79, etc. And our remarks supra chap. 11 of the present study.

12. Deut. 17, 10.

13. *Ibid.*, 11.

14. For the exact status of laws deduced by the rules and their difference from laws stated specifically in the Torah, see TaRYag. See also chap. 11 supra in this study.

15. See Chajes, Mishpat Hahora'ah, chap. 2; also TaRYag.

16. Maimonides, Introduction to Mishnah, ed. Rambam Le'am, p. 10.

17. Ex. 6, 12.

18. Num. 6, 8.

19. Sifri to Nos. 6, 7.

20. Chinuch, Precept 69. This reasoning of the Chinuch with respect to "warning" may be compared with the words of the Sifri to Shelach, Malbim's ed. no. 74, with respect to all mitzvoth—"Why does the Torah again say: 'I am the Lord thy God'? So that Israel should not say: 'Why did God command us, so that we shall do the mitzvoth and take reward; we are prepared not to do them and not to receive the reward . . .' "

21. San. 73a, etc. In this respect *kal vachomer* differs from *gezerah shavah* and *hekesh*. Since laws deduced by *kal vachomer* carry no punishment, opinion varies as to their exact status. While all hold that they are biblical, some authorities hold that laws so deduced carry preceptive or prohibitive force, while others hold that such laws enjoy the status of *issura be'alma*—mere injunction, with neither positive nor prohibitive preceptive status. See Porath Joseph on Yeb. and Ket. (Warsaw, 1898), Introductory Rules, Rule 5, and the sources quoted there. In fiscal matters, see Kehillath Ya'acob, Tos. Aleph, Siman 30; and Responsa Imrei Esh, chap. 17, No. 31.

22. Middoth Aharon; Ginath Veradim, rule 1.

23. Mahrsha to Sanhedrin 64b.

24. See Shelah on this middah.

25. Kidd. 2a.

26. Deut. 22, 13.

27. Gen. 23, 13.

28. "There is no intention to compare a woman with a field. It is only that from the common term "*kichah*" we learn that money is a mode of effecting *kinyan* in betrothal, Ramban." Colloquially we indeed say that one acquires property and one acquires a wife, but we must bear in mind that the underlying ideas are entirely different. In the one case one acquires ownership, in the second it is an act of marriage and the act of marriage gives the husband [the

acquirer] no rights whatsoever in the person of his wife, it succeeds only in creating status, i.e., the status of a married woman. See also infra, Status, App. 3.

29. Jer. Pess. 6, 1.
30. Num. 38, 2.
31. *Ibid.* 9, 2.
32. Yesud Hamishna Ve'arichtatah, pp. 47–49. Though he does not mention the fact, Margolies is probably basing himself on Responsa, Chut Hameshulash, R. Eliezer Yitzchak, Pt. 3, pp. 134 ff.
33. Lev. 7, 37.
34. Zeb. 97b and Rashi ad loc.
35. Hence Sifri to Nasso, no. 133 in Malbim's ed., explains: "Which is waved, and which is heaved up, Ex. 29, 27," the verse compares 'heaving up' to 'waving.' Just as the act of waving requires thrusting forward and drawing back, so heaving up requires thrusting forward and drawing back; and just as heaving up requires elevation and descent, so waving requires elevation and descent."
36. Pes. 66a. Kin'ath Sopherim, to Sepher Hamitzvoth, Root Two, holds that the power to employ *gezera shavah*, rested with the B.D. Hagadol, whilst the tradition of its use must be traceable to that body alone.
37. Tos. to Succ. 31a; Rashi to R.H. 34a, etc.
38. Sepher Hamitzvoth, Root 2.
39. Similarly, Ramban, Sepher Hageulah, ed. Chavell, p. 262, explains the possibility of *reductio ad absurdum* when employing *gematria'oth* – the numerical value of letters – or *notarikon* – the interpretation of words stenographically or acrostically – in instances not mentioned by Chazal.
40. Middoth Aharon to Baraitha of R. Ishmael.
41. See Mishnah, Betz. 1, 6; cf. also the remarks of Darchei Hamishnah, p. 19.
42. Levit. 13, 47.
43. Yeb. 4b.
44. B.K. 6a.
45. Ra'abad and commentaries.
46. Levit. 1, 2.
47. Zeb. 34a.
48. On the relation of this middah to the rule of extension and limitation, employed by R. Akiba and R. Elazar, see Rashi to Sheb. 4b. The differences apply to this and to the following two middoth. Briefly they are (a) While in the case of *Kelall uperat* the particular restricts the general completely to its own content, in the case of extension (*ribui*) and limitation (*miut*) the limitation merely limits the preceding extension in some way. (b) In the case of the particular preceding the general rule (the following middah), the general includes everything akin to the general, whereas an extension following a limitation includes only that which is similar to the limitation. (c) In the case of the *kelall uperat ukelall* (middah no. 6), only that which resembles the particular is included, but in the case of extension, limitation, and extension, even that which is not akin to the limitation is included, the limitation excluding only that which is manifestly unlike to it.
49. Deut. 22, 2–3.

50. See Nazir 35b. Cf. Responsa, Chavoth Yair, no. 66 end. The question arises in regard to this and the previous middah as to why the general rule is mentioned at all in the former middah, and why the detail is mentioned by the Torah in the latter? In the former middah, we ignore the general rule; in the present middah, we ignore the particular? The answer is that these are mentioned in order to obviate deduction of exceptions from the general rule. The mention of the details, being redundant, prevents any such attempt, since when such attempt is made we immediately argue that though the exception may indeed be excepted logically, the Torah added statement of the detail in order to reinclude the exception within the framework of the general rule. In the preceding middah, the kelall is mentioned in order to convey that everything was in fact embraced by it but that all is limited by the perat.

51. A further middah, similar to this one, *perat ukelall uperat*, is mentioned in Nazir 34b. It is not mentioned by R. Ishmael since it follows the rules pertaining to *kelall uperat ukelall*, Ra'abad. But see his subsequent comments.

52. Ex. 22, 6.

53. Sheb. 43a.

54. Sepher Hakerituth, Pt. 1, sect. 7.

55. Cf. Rashba to Gittin 77a and the discussion of Rabad in his commentary to our Baraitha.

56. Ex. 13, 2. Rabad is of the opinion that in the example quoted, the deduction is made entirely from the verse in Deuteronomy, and he rewords the Mechilta accordingly.

57. Deut. 15, 19.

58. So that here the general term required the particular to explain and qualify it.

59. Mechilta.

60. To Bechoroth 19a.

61. Levit. 20, 2.

62. Avudraham.

63. Deut. 19, 5.

64. Levit. 24, 21.

65. Levit. 13, 29.

66. *Ibid.*, 13, 1–3 ff.

67. *Ibid.*, v. 30.

68. *Ibid.*, v. 3.

69. No. 6, 14–15.

70. No. 15, 1–16.

71. Ex. 20, 13.

72. Mechilta.

73. Lev. 18, 6.

74. See the interesting responsum of Duran, Pt. 1, No. 172, in regard to harmonization of verses from the later books of the Bible.

75. Ex. 20, 19.

76. Deut. 5, 4.

77. *Ibid.*, 4, 36.

Appendix 2

Premises, Legal Principles, and Notions

Torts

Besides the logical forms outlined in the previous appendix, halachic jurisprudence employs legal, logical premises, assumptions, and principles. These principles affect all branches of halachah, but they are especially evident in the realm of torts of which the Mishnah[1] says, "He that would become wise let him occupy himself with cases concerning property, for there is no branch of the law greater than they; for they are like a welling fountain." To this, Tiffereth Yisrael[2] comments:

> For there is no subject among the laws of the Torah in which the Torah gave as much permission to soar in accord with one's capacity, to dig, to search out and to decide as seems good in one's eyes, as in the realm of fiscal matters. Here, the Torah opened for one an unlimited realm to weigh, judge and analyze intellectually. In fact most of the laws relating to claims, of which so much is said, as a wagon filled with ears of corn as it were, are all embraced by the few words in the Torah: "Thou shalt judge thy fellow with righteousness."
>
> But, since man's intellect is liable to err in this delicate weave, our early sages gathered together in their multitudes and laid down foundations and roots for them all. Withall, there yet remains place for the judge to break loose to the right or to the left, to compare matters or to distinguish between them, sometimes with as fine a distinction as a hairsbreadth. Hence busying oneself with fiscal matters sharpens the human mind to become exact in determining the basis of truth, this in addition to the obligation to act truly.

In all other branches of Torah, when in doubt one can always decide stringently, not so in fiscal matters. One cannot avoid doubt by taking the stricter course, for what is strict for the one party to the dispute, is lenient for the other. So one must toil to discover the exact truth.

Two of the major premises of halachic principle are the *chazzakkah*—presumption or assumption, and the *miggo*—literally, since, because, or while.

Chazzakkah—Presumption or Assumption

Though we cannot go into great detail regarding these,[3] it will suffice to say that apart from *chazzakkah* in the capacity of an act of acquisition, the legal presumptions of halachah are based primarily on the nature of men, things, and circumstances. They are adduced as proof in determining status or law, on grounds of both previous state and that pertaining presently, while several are grounded in common reasoning, usage, or natural fact and serve in these capacities as bases for laws and enactments. We shall treat a few examples briefly.

1. It is assumed that a thing that is in one's possession is the property of the possessor. In the words of the Talmud,[4] leave the money in the possession of its master. Hence the general principle that the onus of proof is on the plaintiff.

This rule is carried further. Even when neither party is now in possession of the article in dispute, but it is proved that there was a time when one of them was its owner, he is accorded the same advantage vis-à-vis the other claimant in that the latter bears the onus of proof.

Some authorities[5] base the *chazzakkah* in this case on the general concept pertaining to status in ritual law. When a doubt arises as to whether an object is *kasher* or *trefah*, ritually fit or unfit, we refer to its previously known status and say, "As it was before the doubt arose, *kasher* or *terefah*, so it is now." Others[6] reject the derivation from ritual law and turn to jurisprudence for their explanation of the *chazzakkah* in this instance.

2. No man will pay his debt before it falls due;[7] hence, a plea that a debt has been repaid before it fell due is not accepted. As the Talmud exclaims,[8] "Would that a man pay his debt when it falls due!"

Some authorities[9] hold that the reason for this assumption is that since the debtor determined a date for repayment he knew that he would be unable to repay sooner. Others[10] opine that it is simply not usual to pay debts before they are due.

The effect of the presumption is that, on the one hand, it enables the claimant to recover his debt even from heirs when the father died before due date,[11] and, on the other, though ordinarily when one produces a bond of indebtedness against another and the latter says, "Swear to me that I have not paid you," he has to swear;[12] if the claim is made prior to due date, the creditor need take no oath.[13]

The assumption is only effective when a repayment date was stipulated, but not regarding the rule[14] that the usual period for repayment of a loan without terms is thirty days.[15]

The *chazzakkah* operates regarding both money payment and delivery of goods[16] and in fact regarding everything where delay is to the advantage of one failing to deliver on time. Knesseth Hagedolah is of the opinion that this *chazzakkah* holds only of the time of payment, but a person may indeed send payment prior to due date with the object of such payment reaching the creditor on due date.

3. No woman will make a false assertion in front of her husband[17] when he is aware that she is lying.[18] Hence if she said to him, "You divorced me," she is believed.[19] Similarly, if she accused him of impotency.[20]

Some authorities maintain that nowadays, "with so much shamelessness about," she is believed only in a restrictive sense, namely, that if she accepts *kiddushim* from another it is valid, but we do not believe her to the extent of permitting her to marry another or demand the marriage settlement[21] unless circumstances support her (e.g., she is still childless after ten years of marriage and she pleads that he is impotent).[22]

This *chazzakkah* is only operative when she herself makes the declaration, but not if another makes it on her behalf.[23]

4. No one is by nature so brazen-faced as to deny a debt in the presence of his creditor. Some authorities[24] hold that this is so only in regard to a benefactor but not with respect to a bailee; others[25] hold it to be true irrespective of whether the claimant is his benefactor or not. One simply cannot lie in the face of one who knows that one is lying.

On the basis of this presumption, the Talmud[26] explains the requirement for one who admits part of a claim to take an oath—

even though he could have been believed by reason of the fact that he could have denied all, which would have legally exempted him from an oath.[27] For, in view of the presumption that no man would be so impertinent in the face of his creditor, an entire denial cannot be considered as probable, so no better plea was available to him.

5. An agent will carry out his commission.[28] This is, however, assumed only with respect to adopting a stringent result of the circumstances, but not in order to take the lenient one.[29] However, if the agent volunteered to undertake the commission, we do assume that he carries it out.[30]

It is in any event only applicable when the agent is free to act on his own, but not when he is dependent on others.[31]

6. The guest[32] arrives in time. It is assumed that the body functions normally; hence, if a woman failed to examine herself in time, she is deemed ritually unclean (niddah). According to some authorities, this assumption is the basis for the requirement to abstain from marital relations shortly before her period is due.

7. We assume that one who was known to be alive is still alive.[33] Hence, an agent who brought a divorce from distant parts, though he left the husband aged or sick, may deliver it to the woman on the assumption that he is still alive and able to divorce her. The same is also true of one who was known to have had issue and has now died. His wife is free from levirate marriage (yibbum) because we assume that the issue is still alive.[34] Also one does not enter upon mourning out of doubt,[35] for this reason.

The principle operates also in stricter vein, for example, in the case of aguna, where the presumption is to the detriment of her freedom.

Miggo — Literally, Since, Because, or While

Let us now turn to the second mentioned principle, the miggo. Basically, the miggo is a line of reasoning that leads the court to accept the assertion of a litigant and consider it trustworthy since, had he wished to lie, he could have put forward a better case. The detailed principles of miggo are numerous, and they are dealt with at length by the commentaries to Choshen Mishpat.[36] Here, we shall confine ourselves to listing some of the major exceptions to the rule.

For the most part, *miggo* is insufficient to force another to pay money or part with property. According to Shach,[37] when the *miggo* is supported by a *chazzakkah*, it is strong enough for this purpose also.

A *miggo* is not accepted against witnesses or against established custom; neither is it accepted if based on rare happenings.

If the defense that could have been presented would not have definitely been accepted by the court, no *miggo* exists, nor is a *miggo* that is based on conjectural as opposed to actual grounds accepted. Doubt exists as to the validity of a *miggo* where such a plea would be self-incriminatory.[38]

Zechiyah—Acquiring on Behalf of Another When This Is to the Latter's Benefit

Of the many legal notions of halachah, *zechiyah* is one that affects a broad spectrum of practical affairs. The rule is that when it is of advantage to a recipient, one may acquire on his behalf even without the recipient's knowledge. This is in contrast to instances of disadvantage to him, in which cases one can only act as his agent upon specific appointment.[39]

Umdena—Legal Assumption and Application, Discretion

We shall conclude our remarks in this section with a few words on but one more major topic, the uses of *umdena,* legal assumption and application.

Umdena arises in the absence of sufficient factual evidence in a case that is the subject of legal investigation. It may be employed either to determine the intention of the one who did the act in question or to determine whether the act was done at all. It is then a forceful, flexible instrument in the hands of a competent court for the prosecution of justice and right, and, while *umdena* may not be employed in cases of murder,[40] it is employed in regard to fiscal matters,[41] in certain instances of divorce,[42] with respect to vows and oaths,[43] the sanctification of objects or of property[44] and charitable gifts,[45] etc.

R. Eliahu Klatzkin[46] explains that *umdena* is forbidden only to witnesses[47] who must relate exactly what they know without any surmise on their part, but the interdict does not apply to the court. His opinion conforms with that of Chatham Sopher,[48] who writes:

> The Torah required witnesses only with regards those matters which the court could not become aware of without them. But that which is clear to the court without recourse to witnesses is as if the members of the court had seen it for themselves. In the same way as when they see for themselves they require no other testimony, so they may adjudicate whatever is clear to them without recourse to the trustworthiness of witnesses or without witnesses.

The gedolei ha'achronim employ the principle of *umdena* and the discretion it affords as a powerful instrument, when collated with other factors, in alleviating the problem of *aguna*.[49] As such, *umdena* is employed to establish a factual state of affairs.[50]

Notes to Appendix Two

1. B.B. 10, 8.
2. Commentary *ibid.*, note 84.
3. The discussion of *chazzakkah* alone takes up over seven hundred pages in the *Encylopedia Talmudith*, in Vols. 13–14.
4. B.K. 35a; B.M. 100a; Ket. 20a; etc.
5. Penei Yehoshua.
6. Kontress Hasephekoth, sect. 2.
7. B.B. 5b.
8. *Ibid.*
9. Asheri, Responsa, Klal 66, 3.
10. Ketzoth Hachoshen, 78, 8.
11. B.B. 5b.
12. Sheb. 41a.
13. Tosaphoth to B.B. *ibid.*
14. Makk. 3b.
15. Nimmukkei Joseph to B.B. *ibid.*
16. Yad Malachi, 218.
17. Yeb. 116a; Gitt. 89b.
18. Ned. 91a.
19. Ket. 22b.
20. Tosaphoth to Yeb. 65b.
21. Beth Joseph, Eben Ha'ezer, 17.
22. Mahrik, Shoresh 72.
23. Beth Shemuel, Eben Ha'ezer 141, 81. Hence the problem of representation of a party before the Beth Din. The lawyer has fewer scruples in the matter.
24. Rashi to B.K. 107a.
25. Tosaphoth *ibid.*
26. B.M. 3a.

27. Such reasoning is an example of *Miggo,* infra.
28. Erub. 31b; Gitt. 64a.
29. Tosaphoth to Gitt. ibid.; Resp. Noda Biyehuda, E.H. no. 2.
30. Magen Avraham, 409, 16.
31. Mishnah Lemelech.
32. A euphemism for menstruation; Nidd. 16a.
33. Gitt. 28a, and Rashi s.q. nothnu.
34. Responsa, Mahri weil, 88.
35. Yoreh De'ah, 397, 2.
36. Siman, 82.
37. Rules of *miggo, ibid.,* 15.
38. See, Aruch Hashulchan, Choshen Mishpat, 82, 15.
39. See Chatham Sopher, Pt. 1, pp. 69–71, at length on Zechiyah.
40. Sheb. 34a.
41. Kidd. 49b.
42. Gitt. 65b. But not with respect to *kiddushin,* Rema, Ebcn Ha'ezer, 62, 4. However, see the lengthy discourse in Chelkath Yoab, E.H., Nos. 7 and 8.
43. Yad. Nedarim 8, 8.
44. Shach to Yoreh De'ah, 251, 9.
45. Rema, Yoreh De'ah, 251, 5; 253, 7.
46. Responsa, Devar Eliahu, 68.
47. San. 37.
48. Res. E.H. no. 94.
49. See, e.g., the remarks of Aruch Hashulchan, E.H. 17, 172, who merely sums up the practical trend of all those who have engaged in this difficult problem.
50. Responsa, Massa'ath Binyamin, quoted by Beth Shemuel, E.H. 17, note 49; Kontress Ha'agunoth, in E.H. after Siman 17, No. 226; Beth Yitzchak, Res. 84; Mabit, Resp. 138, quoted and discussed at length in Sheb Shemaatza, 7, 17; Eyn Yitzchak E.H.; Hechal Yitzchak, Pts. 1 and 2, etc.

Appendix 3

Some Basic Concepts

We shall confine our remarks to three such concepts, obligation, status, and self-incrimination. These will be treated just sufficiently for an insight to be gained into the essential nature of the concepts concerned. They have been chosen as examples because of their broad scope within the spectrum of practical halachah.

Obligation

Obligation may arise as a result of the consent of the parties (e.g., in lieu of a loan or contract), or as the result of injury caused to another and his consequent right to damages, or as the result of the voluntary obligation of self though no actual obligation exists in law.

An example of this latter is to be found in the obligation undertaken by a bailee to be responsible for that which the law does not hold him liable. Thus, an unpaid guardian, free from payment in law, may accept upon himself the responsibilities and liabilities of the borrower.[1]

The effect of accepting obligation, whether by means of *kinyan*, or witnesses, or verbally,[2] is in the first instance to bind the person. His estate *(nechassim)* then becomes surety for him. Thus, while one's estate is his surety, and even when a responsibility clause is omitted, such omission is regarded as a scribal error that in no way affects the lien on property as security;[3] the creditor must always first sue the debtor and, only if he fails him, may he seize the surety (i.e., the property).[4]

Normally, the acceptance of obligation renders one legally bound because either a form of *kinyan* is involved[5] or, in consideration of a certain mental satisfaction, the promissor resolves to bind himself.[6] Hence, in the example quoted here, where the gratuitous bailee accepted the obligations of a borrower, the Talmud states[7] that he does so because of the satisfaction he enjoys in the public eye as a trustworthy person.

Obligation is not legally binding on the basis of "words alone;" some consideration of definite obligatory form must be present. There is, however, an exception to this. It is the form of obligation assumed under the title *oditha*, fictitious admission.[8]

Though A admits in the presence of witnesses that his property belongs to B, and it is known that B has in reality no rights whatsoever in the property, the admission itself is considered a statement of fact that enables the one in whose favor it was made to recover the property, at court.[9] Or, as others understand it, *oditha* is a form of *kinyan* that on initiation transfers the property there and then to the one in whose favor it was made.[10]

The difference between *oditha* and *hoda'ah* — admission — lies in the fact that *hoda'ah* is the result of another's claim and constitutes genuine admission. As such, it comes under the law of evidence in fiscal matters to the effect that "the admission of a party in a suit is equivalent to the testimony of a hundred witnesses."[11]

Status

In order to appreciate something of the concept and importance of "status" in halachah, we shall return for a few moments to the section of the Talmud quoted earlier from Tractate Kiddushin.[12] There the Talmud asked, "Whence do we know that a woman is freed for remarriage by her husband's death?"

The immediate answer of the Talmud is on the basis of logic: "He [the husband] bound her, hence he [by his demise] frees her." The Talmud is not satisfied with this and eventually proves the matter from the Torah itself.

Now if it had been the rights of the husband in his wife that rendered her forbidden to others, obviously since his rights bound her, removal of his rights or their cessation should suffice to free her, but the Talmud refuses to accept this. The reason for the refusal lies in the fact that it is not the husband's rights that forbid her to others but her status as a married woman. She is regarded as an *erva* — a forbidden relationship — and the rule is that once in the status of *ervah*, one remains so. Hence the need for biblical proof that the status ceases to exist upon the husband's death.

We have already referred[13] to the similar language used by the Torah for both acquisition and marriage. It is true that the act of marriage (i.e., the *kinyan* that renders it valid,) is performed by the man. But it is essential for the willing consent of the woman in order to render the *kinyan* binding. The Talmud,[14] quoting R. Huna, explains that a sale made under duress is valid. This is not so with respect to marriage. Though the formal requirements of *kinyan* be fulfilled, if agreement was obtained under duress, there is no marriage. The difference lies in the essential nature of the two acts.

Normal acquisition can be accomplished under conditions of even passive consent. If marriage were merely acquisition, the same would be true of it. But marriage is the creation of status, and this requires the positive willingness of the woman.[15]

The analogy in the Talmud[16] between the institution of marriage and the sanctified animal is now also clarified. The analogy is based on the fact that both enjoy status—the woman that of marriage, the animal that of *hekdesh*, a consecrated article. Hence, the gemmara seeks illumination for problems involving status from other realms where status is involved.

It is because *kiddushin* involves the creation of status that civil marriage, based merely on contract or consent, or marriage without witnesses, or with one witness alone, is invalid.[17] The Torah admits the creation of the married status in a particular manner only. Any other method of coming together remains in the realm of mere acquisition, and this is irrelevant by itself to the creation of marriage. In the eyes of the Torah, such forms of marriage relegate a lofty institution to barter.

Self-Incrimination

One cannot incriminate oneself in Jewish law. This concept is closely allied to the principle that one is considered a relative of oneself and hence disqualified to be a witness against oneself.[18]

If, therefore, a man testified that he, together with another person had committed an offense, his testimony is accepted as far as the other person is concerned but not in regard to himself.[19] This, however, is the opinion of Rabbah in the gemmara.[20] R. Joseph considers his testimony invalid also in regard to the accused since, having admitted to a felony, his testimony, though not self-incriminating, succeeds nonetheless in disqualifying him as a witness.[21]

The point at issue is whether a statement of evidence must be accepted or rejected in its entirety or whether we may simply disregard that part of the evidence that is self-incriminating, and the remainder of the evidence is valid.[22] Rabbah holds the latter alternative; R. Joseph, the former.[23]

The principle applies only insofar as not disqualifying him as a witness or to subject him to bodily penalty; he can, however, render himself liable on his own admission, for money payments, since one's admission may be construed as the present acceptance of obligation[24] and has nothing to do with testimony.

Maimonides offers[25] a psychological explanation[26] for the inadmissibility of self-incriminating statements with respect to capital crimes or corporal punishment. He says:

> The Torah decrees that the court may neither put to death nor inflict corporal punishment on a person as a result of his own admission. This may only be done by [the evidence of] two witnesses. . . . [P]erchance his mind is deranged. Perchance he is one of those suffering or bitter souls longing for death, who thrust swords into their bellies or throw themselves off rooftops. Perchance for some such reason this one came and confessed to something that he had not done, so that he might be put to death. Withall, it is a decree of the King.

Notes to Appendix Three

1. B.M. 94a.
2. See the discussion in *Encyclopedia Talmudith*, Vol. 11, pp. 245–252.
3. B.M. 13b.
4. B.B. 174a.
5. The *kinyan* binds both the person and the estate in such fashion that by the assumption of a personal obligation, the estate becomes automatically charged. Isaac Herzog, *The Main Institutions of Jewish Law*, Vol. 2, p. 9.
6. *Ibid.*
7. B.M. 94a.
8. A fully detailed explanation of *oditha* is to be found in Chatham Sopher, Pt. 1, pp. 52–54.
9. Ritva to B.B. 149a.
10. Ketzoth Hachoshen, 40, 1, etc.
11. B.M. 3b.
12. Supra, beginning of chap. 8.

13. See note on *Gezerah shavah*, supra.
14. B.B. 47b.
15. See Birkath Shemuel, Kiddushin 1, sect. 2, and sect. 25, where three kinds of intention of the part of the woman are differentiated and explained. Also Massa'ath Moshe, Kidd. 1 and 4, on the special *ratzon* required by the Torah in kiddushin.
16. Kiddushin *ibid.*; see the text quoted supra, chap. 8.
17. This is not to say that because no *kiddushin* exists, the woman is entirely free to remarry without a divorce. Opinions differ, and, for a variety of reasons, some authorities, notably R. Joseph Rozin (the Rogotzover), Resp. E.H., hold that a divorce is required, since an intermediate status "not single yet not married" is held to be present.
18. Such disqualification is deduced from Deut. 24, 16. See San. 27b.
19. Choshen Mishpat 34, 25–26. Birchei Joseph, ad loc. sects. 30 and 34, discusses various basic problems in connection with self-incrimination at length.
20. San. 25a.
21. "Put not your hand with the wicked to be an unrighteous witness, Ex. 23,1" means you may not accept a wicked person as a witness; B.K. 72b.
22. Tosaphoth to Yeb. 25b. s.q. Leima. This is called *palginan dibure*—splitting his words. On this subject, see Noda Biyehuda, Kama, Eben Ha'ezer, No. 72, at length; Responsa Sho'el Umeshiv Chamisha'ah, No. 40; Shev Shematza 7, Section 5; Thumim, 46, note 42, etc.
23. See the remarks in Jacob Ginsberg, *Mishpatim LeIsrael* (Jerusalem, 1956), p. 361, note 78.
24. Ketzoth Hachoshen 40, 1. Such obligation is termed *oditha*, vide supra, under Obligation; it is valid even though we know that no obligation exists in fact.
25. Yad. Sanhedrin 18, 6.
26. There are other psychological explanations of halachoth to be found in the Talmud, in the commentaries and in the possekim. E.G. *yetzer albeshah*, Yeb. 51b; A man is anxious for his property, Sabb. 117b; or for his dead, *ibid.* 43b. See also Meiri to Sanh, ed. Sopher, p. 44, on the measuring by members of the Sanhedrin required in the case of *eglah arufah*. Most of the particular laws governing the suicide, Yoreh De'ah, 345, are rendered innocuous by the assumption that the suicide became deranged before committing the act and was therefore technically not a suicide at all; see Pitchei Teshuvah *ibid.*, no. 2; since one of unsound mind is never halachically considered a suicide, Birchei Joseph *ad loc*. See also Responsa, Rav Pa'alim, Pt. 3, Yoreh De'ah, Nos. 29 and 30, where the exact conditions rendering one halachically a suicide are detailed. Rav Pa'alim further concludes that even in the event of a proper suicide, one is obliged to recite the *kaddish* for him, and one may dedicate *Tashmishei Kedushah* in his name. On the suicide, see also Yalkut Hagershuni, Pt. 2, Kontress Acharon, s.q. *Me'abed*, as to whether he is a *ben olam haba*.

Index

About the Author

Rabbi Abraham Hirsch Rabinowitz was a well-known author and scholar. An alumnus of Gateshead Yeshiva and Hebron Yeshiva, he received rabbinical ordination from Chief Rabbi Hertzog, Rabbi Meltzer, and Rabbi Sarna. He attained academic degrees from Leeds University and the University of Witwatersrand. He served as rabbi to distinguished communities in England and South Africa. In 1961, he returned to Israel with his family, and in 1968 he was appointed chief rabbi of the Israeli air force. Rabbi Rabinowitz contributed widely to periodicals and encyclopedias on various Jewish and general topics. His books include *The Jewish Mind, Israel: The Christian Dilemma, Science Today—Religion Tomorrow* (unpublished), *Hamitzvah Vehamikra, TaRYaG: A study of the Tradition that the Written Torah Contains 613 Mitzvot*, and the award-winning *Olam Ehad*. He prepared and edited the momentous *Ali Tamar*, a seven-volume commentary on the Jerusalem Talmud, written by his father-in-law, Rabbi Yisachar Tamar. Rabbi Rabinowitz died in 1987.